HELLS & HOLY
GHOSTS

HELLS & HOLY GHOSTS

A Theopoetics of Christian Belief

David L. Miller

SPRING JOURNAL BOOKS
NEW ORLEANS, LOUISANA

Hells and Holy Ghosts:
A Theopoetics of Christian Belief

Published by
Spring Journal, Inc.;
627 Ursulines Street;
New Orleans, Louisiana 70116

Printed in Canada
Text printed on acidfree paper.

Cover image, *Descent into Limbo*, Zoan Andrea engraving on laid paper, ca. 1475-1480, after Andrea Mantegna, Italian, 1431-1506. Published by permission of the University of Michigan Museum of Art, Museum Purchase made possible by the Friends of the Museum of Art 1979/1.159.

Cover design by Northern Cartographic, 4050 Williston Road, South Burlington, VT 05403.

Library in Congress Catalog in Publication Data Pending

Grateful acknowledgment is made to the following persons and publishers for permission to quote from published material:

Earlier versions of the materials in this book were given as lectures at the Eranos Conferences of 1981 and 1983, and are published in the *Eranos Jahrbuch* 50-1981 (Frankfurt: Insel-Verlag, 1982) and *Eranos Jahrbuch* 52-1983) (Frankfurt: Insel-Verlag, 1984). They are used here by permission of the Eranos Foundation, Ascona, Switzerland.

Scripture quotations, other than brief paraphrases or unless otherwise noted, are from the Revised Standard Version of the Bible, copyright 1946, 1952, 1971 by the Division of Christian Education of the National Council of Churches of Christ in the U. S. A. Used by permission.

"The Lagoon" (7 lines) and "The Wife" (3 lines). By Denise Levertov, from COLLECTED EARLIER POEMS 1940-1960, COPYRIGHT © 1957, 1958, 1959, 1960, 1961, 1979 by Denise Levertov. Reprinted by permission of New Directions Publishing Corp. and by permission of Pollinger Limited and the proprietor.

"In Cold Hell, In Thicket" (13 lines). By Charles Olson, from SELECTED WRITINGS OF CHARLES OLSON, Copyright © 1966 by Charles Olson. Reprinted by permission of New Directions Publishing Corp.

"Concerning the Synthetic Unity of Apperception" (3 lines). By Delmore Schwartz, from SELECTED POEMS; SUMMER KNOWLEDGE, copyright © 1959 by Delmore Schwartz. Reprinted by permission of New Directions Publishing Corp. and by permission of Pollinger Limited and the proprietor.

"The World is a Wedding" (2 lines). By Delmore Schwartz, from THE WORLD IS A WEDDING, copyright © 1948 by Delmore Schwartz. Reprinted by permission of New Directions Publishing Corp.

"The Mythology of Dark and Light" (7 lines) by Hayden Carruth (Syracuse, NY: Tamarack Editions, 1982). Copyright © 1982 by Hayden Carruth. Reprinted with permission of the author.

"I Lie" (8 lines) from *Striking the Dark Air for Music* by William Pitt Root. Copyright © 1973 William Pitt Root. Reprinted with permission of the author.

"Halloween," "Prelude to Memnon" (36 lines), pp. 141-2, "Time in the Rock" from SELECTED POEMS by Conrad Aiken, copyright © 1961, 2003 by Conrad Aiken. Used by permission of Oxford University Press, Inc.

"The Philosophy of No" (7 lines) from *Why Persimmons and Other Poems: Transformations of Theology in Poetry* (Atlanta: Scholars Press, Studies in the Humanities Series, 1987) by Stanley Romaine Hopper. Reprinted by permission of author.

"Antrim," by Robinson Jeffers from *The Collected Poetry of Robinson Jeffers*, edited by Tim Hunt, Volume 2, 1928-1938. Copyright ©1938 and renewed 1996 by Donnan and Barth Jeffers.

Excerpts from THE COLLECTED POEMS OF WALLACE STEVENS, by Wallace Stevens, copyright © 1954 by Wallace Stevens and renewed 1982 by Holly

The author wishes to express deep gratitude to Mr. Art Mielke for his help in preparing the manuscript for publication.

CONTENTS

PART FOUR: RESURRECTIONS OF THE DEAD

Introduction

On Not Giving Up the Ghost

The great historian of religion, Mircea Eliade, made the following entry in his diary during one midwinter period of intense research and writing:

> The meaning of my "learning": I grasp the true meaning only after having gone through all the material (enormous, inert, somber documentation); I would compare my immersion in the documents to a fusion with the material—to the limit of my physical resistance: when I feel that I'm suffocating, that I am being asphyxiated, I come back to the surface. A descent to the center of dead matter, comparable to a *descensus ad inferos* [a "descent into hell"]. Indirectly, the experience of death. Drowned in the documents, what is personal, original, living in me disappears, dies. When I find myself again, when I return to life—I see things differently, I *understand* them.[1]

Writing a book on the Christian beliefs concerning "Christ's descent into hell" and "the resurrection of the dead" is an experience not unlike that which Eliade describes. That is, writing about the *descensus ad inferos* in these postmodern times involves the author in an experience of the very thing about which he or she is writing.

HELLS AND HOLY GHOSTS

There are certainly no two beliefs in all of the Christian faith which are more dubious to believer and unbeliever alike. The twin notions that Jesus, after his execution and before he left his historical ministry, made a journey to the interior of the earth to a place called Hell and that the dead have an active life in ghostly form are not easy to sustain at the end of the twentieth century. These beliefs are dead and gone, and to probe them for their present meaning is like a descent into some underworld and is like a resurrection of ghosts of former signification.

Perhaps—as Eliade's journal entry indeed suggests—all academic work is descensional and is a work with ghosts. Lucian once wrote a satire set in the underworld in which Socrates founded, not a Platonic academy, but an "academy of the dead."[2] Socrates had himself mused: "What would not a person give if he [or she] might converse with Orpheus and Musaeus and Hesiod and Homer? Nay, if this be true, let me die again and again."[3] And Steven Simmer has, only a few years ago, written an important set of reflections on these texts of Lucian and Socrates in which a compelling case is made for the "academy of the dead" as the dominant trope of contemporary education.[4] On Simmer's view, words and phrases like "writer's block," "deadlines," and "buried in a footnote" become obvious clues to the postmodern educational imagination.

If Simmer and Eliade are typical (and indeed we shall see already in this Introduction that they are), then "the descent into hell" and "the resurrection of the dead," however dubious as literal beliefs, are alive and well as important postmodern metaphors.

Following the descensional figure in his essay, Simmer writes about the writing of books and about their authors. "The author of a book," argues Simmer, "is not this meek person. For his book, too, was written through his own internal dialogue, his own imaginal faculty meeting [with the academy of the dead]. Any author writes fiction when he places his name on the cover. The real authors are under cover—the invisible daimones [ghosts] refuse to be forgotten."[5] What Simmer says is as true of *this* book as is the prefiguring of the present

2

work by Eliade's use of the metaphor of the descent into hell concerning his writing. By way of beginning the "descent" into the under-the-cover world of this book, I (the author?) should like to acknowledge the work's "ghosts," resurrecting "the dead" (not dead authors, but works that have gone on before this one), in an introductory attempt to situate my essay in a continuing, if "dead" and somewhat "ghostly," theological conversation.

There are three sorts of texts ancestral to this one. These ghostly pretexts serving as present context have to do with (1) lineage, (2) content, and (3) function.

Lineage. Two of my earlier books haunt the argument of this one. The prolegomenon for those past works—*Christs* (1981)[6] and *Three Faces of God* (1986)[7]—was outlined in an even earlier book, *The New Polytheism* (1974).[8]

The argument of *The New Polytheism* was, contrary to the maxim of Tertullian that Athens has, or should have, little or nothing to do with Jerusalem, that in fact ancient Greek mythic themes have had a powerful formative function in regard to Christian theological categories. Further, it was argued that behind Christian dogmatic structures, which are monotheistic in content, there lurks a manifold of mythic themes which are polytheistic in form. So, any given Christian doctrine may have as many archetypal motifs as there have been theological perspectives. In the forms of Christian hermeneutics reside the "shades" of Greek gods and goddesses (e.g., Christ as Hermes or Odysseus, and so forth).

The two books which followed upon the program outlined in *The New Polytheism* were attempts to demonstrate that the program could be followed, usefully, especially in terms of insights for the present relevance of Christian beliefs in a post-Christian world. So in *Christs*, three christological motifs were examined ("The Good Shepherd," "The Holy Fool," and "The Intoxicated Teacher"), and were placed in relation to their Greek mythological prototypes and also in connection with their residues in modern literature. Similarly, in *Three Faces of God,* the thematic of the Trinity was treated in relation to

3

ancient and modern mythopoetic expression, demonstrating the universal power of the trinitarian archetypal motif and the variety of its manifestations in everyday life and meaning.

A part of the purpose of these earlier works was to demonstrate the importance and perduring power of Christian archetypal structures, apart from belief or unbelief: the lifelikeness of theology's forms of thought and feeling. Especially it was my intention to attempt to show the importance for Christian theology of the American secular study of religion, two of whose unique contributions have been the disciplines of "Religion and Literature" and "History of Religions." Like Tertullian's Athens and Jerusalem, the academic study of religion and traditional theology have been imagined to be antithetical. The latter has drawn its resources in the first half of the twentieth century largely from German theology and philosophy and in the latter half of the same century largely from French philosophy and literary theory. These are rich mines, but there is ore aplenty in America, too; and there is a suspicion that the hermeneutics of German and French philosophical modes may harbor a cryptic theologism that is long since anachronistic. American theology does not need always to be the poor stepchild of Northern European Protestant and Mediterranean Catholic theology in hermeneutic or deconstructive disguise. We have some important insights of our own to offer out of the movements of "Religion and Literature" and "History of Religions."

The same purpose motivates the present work. But here a new set and sort of belief-structures, theological thought-forms, provides the content. Whereas the creedal basis of the first two works was christology and trinitarianism, the beliefs in question here are the *descensus ad inferos Christi,* "the descent of Christ into Hell," and "the resurrection of the dead," especially in the form of uses of the term "ghost" to refer both to divinity (Holy Ghost) and to the motif of "life after death." Again, the strategy is to locate the form of the Christian content in comparative mythological antecedents and in modern literary likenesses. The idea is to try to discover some of the functions of the *images* that have been promulgated by Christian *ideas.*

4

INTRODUCTION: ON NOT GIVING UP THE GHOST

Content. Others in these latter days of the twentieth century have been impressed that the problematic Christian form of the *idea* of the "descent into hell" provides postmodernity with a powerful *image* apart from belief or unbelief. The books of these persons represent a second set of "ghosts" haunting and provoking the present work. The books fall into four areas. Besides theology, the areas are the history of ideas, literary theory, and depth psychology.

In theology, the "dead" to which this book is most grateful (though the authors, like this one, are very much alive) are: *The Descent into Hell: A Study of the Radical Reversal of the Christian Consciousness,* by Thomas J. J. Altizer,[9] and *Epiphanies of Darkness: Deconstruction in Theology,* by Charles E. Winquist.[10]

In the history of ideas, three books and one important essay work "under cover" throughout the pages that follow: *The Decline of Hell: Seventeenth-Century Discussions of Eternal Torment,* by D. P. Walker;[11] *Powers of Horror: An Essay on Abjection,* by Julia Kristeva;[12] *The Life Below the Ground: A Study of the Subterranean in Literature and History,* by Wendy Lesser;[13] and "Descensional Reflection," by David Farrell Krell (a chapter in the book *Philosophy and Archaic Experience,* edited by John Sallis).[14]

In literary theory, the "underground" conversation of the present work has been with the following: *The Artist's Journey into the Interior,* by Erich Heller,[15] and *Descent and Return: The Orphic Theme in Modern Literature,* by Walter A. Strauss.[16]

And in depth psychology, the work that has most "shadowed" this one is *The Dream and the Underworld,* by James Hillman.[17]

To be sure, other relevant conversational partners in this modern and postmodern academy of the dead could be named—in theology, Ralph Harper's *Path of Darkness*; in the history of ideas, Jacques LeGoff's *Birth of Purgatory* and Martha Himmelfarb's *Tours of Hell*; and in literary theory, Elizabeth Sewell's *Orphic Voice* and Gwendolyn Bays' *Orphic Descent*. These simply confirm the cruciality of the crypto-theological images of "descent" and "ghost" in a time when these same ideas are stumbling blocks to religious belief. But it is the

5

books first mentioned whose ghostly presence is pervasive on nearly every page that follows, doubtless even when I am unaware of it and so have not acknowledged it in the notes.

Yet this book means to be authentically an additional voice from theology's underside. In the works by earlier theologians and historians of ideas, depth-psychological and poetic dimensions have sometimes been lacking. In the works by psychologists and literary theorists, theological connections have not always been explicitly drawn. This book, then, hopes to situate itself, not so much in league with any of its ancestors, but in the midst of them, introducing them to one another in a sort of general resurrection, lest some of the "dead" receive improper burial by being forgotten or avoided.

Function. There is one last "spirit" whose presence moves powerfully in and out of this work (or at least in and out of its author), and this ghostly presence is nowhere acknowledged in the text or notes of the work. This predecessor is a work written by Rudolph Binion, a work entitled *After Christianity: Christian Survivals in a Post-Christian Culture.*[18] The passion of Binion's book is presaged in a poem by Théophile Gautier, which is cited in the work:

> The self I was confronts me: silhouette
> That lost its likeness once its form was set;
>   Portrait of no sitter here today;
> Ghost with a living corpse; dead image cast
> Into a present ravished by the past;
> Shadow of a substance flown away.[19]

The "silhouette" is that of Christendom in the West. To Binion, this "shadow of a substance" has "flown away" and is, in a postmodern time, not the "portrait" of any living meaning. Yet, precisely because Christianity's "forms were set" in Western structures of meaning by twenty centuries of the institutional church, these "dead images" are "living corpses," "ghosts" that are "cast into our present." The result, in Binion's view, is that our "present is ravished by the past," if unconsciously so. Binion believes that we are now in the position of the Germans in the time of Theodor Mundt, who described the condition as "grappling to the death in the grip of a ghost."[20] Christian meanings are, so to say, more potent dead than alive.

Specifically, Binion identifies three unconscious Christianisms in postmodern literature and life: (1) the view that the past is decisively determinative of the future, a view that Binion traces from the particular Christian belief in afterlife to post-Christian literary texts, and a view he calls "the present past"; (2) the notion that things are ineluctably not the way they ought to be, a sense which Binion links to a dominant ideology in Christendom, having to do with the fantasy of being "born guilty," originally a sinner; and (3) the idea that worldly reality is in absolute contradistinction to ultimate reality, an idea not unconnected with platonic forms of Christian theology and one Binion refers to as "true seeming."

Binion's case is well made and compellingly so. He—like Freud, Frazer, Marx, and Nietzsche before him—wants us to "get over Christianity." My own view is not quite the same, but is surely haunted by his, as it is also by the other "hermeneuts of suspicion" just named. What I am haunted by is precisely the "shadow"-side of religious structures of meaning, which, if they at some time and for some persons seem to have been salvific and therapeutic, have also in some times and in some places had a demonic underside. Precisely in the interest of religious meaning—yes, Christian meaning—I am concerned, with Binion, to expose the "ghosts," though, as opposed to him, I am a bit cynical about the possibilities of their ultimate exorcism.

This book's project is a therapy of ideas—Christian ideas. It is a quest for the images lurking in those ideas like specters, unconscious images, which, if religiously positive, are also, and at the same time, humanly negative. There is here a presupposition that images of deep human signification are "fundamentally ambivalent" (Freud) and are in their natures a *complexio oppositorum*, a "complex of opposites" (Jung). Therapy would consist in facing the negative capabilities of positive religious ideas, making conscious the "ghosts," "descending" into the underworld of Christendom's creedal beliefs, and observing the modern "resurrections of the dead" in literature and life.

In a recent book, *Shadow Dancing in the USA,* Michael Ventura has spoken powerfully about the task:

> What has marked you is still marking you. There is a place in us where wounds never heal, and where loves never end. Nobody knows much about this place except that it exists, feeding our dreams and reinforcing and/or haunting our days. ... Bloody, half-flayed, partly dead, naked, tortured, my mother really does hang on a hook in my closet, because she hangs on a hook in me. ... My closet is full of hooks, full of horrors, and I *also* love them, my horrors, and I know they love me, and they will always hang there for me, because they are also good for me, they are also on my side, they gave so much to *be* my horrors, they made me strong to survive. There is much in our new 'enlightened' lexicon to suggest that one may move into a house that doesn't have such a closet. You move into such a house and think everything is fine until after a while you start to hear a distant screaming, and start to smell something funny, and realize slowly that the closet is there, alright, but its been walled over, and just when you need desperately to open it you find yourself faced with bricks instead of a door.[21]

So it is with our so-called Christian culture. There are ghastly, ghostly horrors lurking in its closets carefully walled up by sacred and secular conventions. Like Ventura, I *love* these ghosts; but like both Ventura and Binion, I feel deeply that it is crucial to bury them properly,which is to say, to remember them, honor them, and make them visible. This book means to be a theological version of theirs—an exploration of the closets of our Christianly haunted house of meaning.

8

HELLS & HOLY GHOSTS

PART ONE

Descents

CHAPTER ONE

History is Hell

"**M**y life is hell!" Uttered in anguish or felt so deeply as to be unutterable, these words involve the woman or man experiencing them, unwittingly to be sure, in ancient theological controversy. Indeed, it may well be that an unconscious residue of Christian thinking informs the person's feeling in this moment, a *theological* habit of mind (rather than one's psychological reality) leading the individual to believe that history can be hell.

Early Christian groups argued about this matter of whether history can be hell. For example, in the "Trimorphic Protennoia," a so-called Gnostic document from the Nag Hammadi library, a document likely dating from 200 C.E. or shortly thereafter, one can read of three descents of a figure named Barbelo, who is the First Thought of the Father. The following passage is typical:

> Now I have come down and reached down to Chaos ... I am the Father and I shall tell you an ineffable and indivulgeable mystery from my Forethought: Every bond I loosed from you and the chains of the Demons of the underworld I broke, ... I am the first one who descended ... For I went down below their language and I spoke my mysteries to my own—a hidden mystery—and the bonds and eternal oblivion were nullified.[1]

13

In this text it seems clear that the descent is from the heavenly realm and into the earthly one. Yet this latter place, human history, is spoken of as "chaos" and as "the underworld." History here is pictured as hell—a descent into life's history being precisely a descent into the underworld—similar to the image felt so deeply by the woman or man in anguish.

But some early Christian thinkers wanted to deny this view, if not also the feeling and experience which accompanies it. At least by the time of Irenaeus (second century C.E.) and Hippolytus (third century C.E.), so-called Orthodox Christian interpretation encouraged the discrimination of the descent into history and the descent into hell, as if to say that life is not (or cannot be) hell. Life, rather, is history. Hell—or so the faith went—has been conquered by Christ.

To be sure, this theological debate is usually reported from the "orthodox," rather than from the "gnostic" side (let alone from the side of the suffering individual!). This means that the "gnostic" view that this world is dark and evil is itself an "orthodox" view. Indeed, the perspectives of Irenaeus and Hippolytus have predominated, so that, for example, Bousset draws upon Hippolytus to interpret the "gnostic" group called Naasenes as holding to the notion that the descent into the underworld refers not to a descent into Hades but rather a descent of primal man into the terrestrial world.[2] Similarly, Huidekoper, referring to Irenaeus' work *Against the Heresies,* says: "By the Underworld they [Gnostics] understood, according to the passage quoted from Irenaeus, 'this world of ours.'"[3] Kroll and MacCulloch concur with this "orthodox" perspective. The former writes: "The whole world was seen as Underworld."[4] And the latter tells us that for Gnostics there can be no *descensus ad inferos* because their eschatology has no underground.[5]

It may come as something of a surprise for a person who is suffering the feeling that his or her life is hell to learn that precisely in this feeling there is a heretical religious perspective, an unorthodox stance! Indeed, to such a one the "descent into hell" may be more real than for many of today's orthodox Christians, not a few of whom would rather forget that portion of their creed which speaks about a descent into hell. The oddity is that those today who may be closest to this underworldly aspect of traditional Christian belief are those whose profound expression most resembles heretical belief, while those who most adhere to conventional Christian belief may well be most out of touch with the reality of depth to which that belief attests. Such is the awkwardness to which the theological idea of a "descent into hell" has led.

The awkwardness of this belief in postmodern times is the subject of the first half of this book. Concerning this awkwardness, another early Christian thinker, one quite different from either Irenaeus or Hippolytus, has provided an image which may stand as a parable of this book's aim.

Origen of Alexandria is writing a commentary on the Gospel of John when he introduces an image for the relation of actual history to hell and for the possible awkwardness involved. In particular, Origen is wondering about the saying of John the Baptist in John 1:26-27: "Among you stands one whom you do not know, even he who comes after me, the thong of whose sandal I am not worthy to untie." The Alexandrian theologian asks rhetorically, "What are Jesus' sandals?" And he answers, "I think that the incarnation, when the Son of God took flesh and bone, constitutes one of the sandals, and the descent into Hades and the voyage in spirit unto the prison is the other."[6]

Origen was likely familiar with the Greek mythological notion of *monosandalos*. Indeed, he may have been appropriating a mythological notion for his own Christian theological purposes. But, if so, he was surely transforming its meaning in the process.

Karl Kerényi tells the traditional meaning of *monosandalos* when commenting on the artistic portrayal of a man with one sandal off in the frescoes of the Villa of Mysteries in Pompeii. He cites the tradition about heroes who maintain the resource of communication with the underworld when going into battle by having one shoe off.[7] But this instance is by no means unique in the classical Greco-Roman world.

15

James Frazer has collected numerous other examples.[8] According to Apollodorus, an oracle warned Pelias, king of Iolcus, to beware of the man with one sandal. So, when Jason arrived with one foot bare, the king knew his fate.[9] Thucydides reports about the hopeless plight of two hundred prisoners who, in bad weather, stole out of Plataea and successfully broke through the lines of the attacking Spartans. The historian thinks that they succeeded because having only one sandal made better going in the stormy conditions, but Frazer has another notion about the reason.[10] The Scholiast on Pindar claims that all Aetolians wore only one sandal "because they were so warlike."[11] Virgil mentions that the rustic militia of Latium went to war with boots of rawhide on the right feet and nothing on the left feet.[12] According to Artemidorus, Perseus wore only one sandal when he set forth to the heroic task of cutting off the Gorgon's head.[13] When Dido has been deserted by Aeneas and has resolved to die, she invokes the gods with one foot bare.[14] And so on. But why?

Frazer thinks it has to do with the knots in the shoelaces. "The magical action of a knot," Frazer holds,

> is supposed to be to bind and restrain not merely the body but the soul, and this action is beneficial or harmful according as the thing which is bound and restrained is evil or good. It is a necessary corollary of this doctrine that to be without knots is to be free and untrammelled . . . . Hence we may suppose that the intention of going with one shoe on and one shoe off is both to restrain and to set at liberty, to bind and to unbind .... to bind his enemy by a spell while he himself goes free.[15]

Edward Edinger has recently offered a less magical and more psychological interpretation than Frazer's. A person does not need to read Jung to know that experiencing the deepest aspects of the self's emotion and thought is a shocking and wounding event for the ego and its conscious and volitional interests. Discovering shadowy portions of one's own personality is often traumatic, like a descent into hell. Thus, Jung's sayings—cited by Edinger—that "the experience of the Self is always a defeat for the ego"[16] and that "the integration of contents that were unconscious and projected involves a serious lesion of the ego"[17] can hardly be heard as controversial. Edinger draws upon this common, if deep, human sense to interpret instances in mythology where the hero is lame (like Oedipus), has an amputated extremity (like the Sun King), or has only one sandal (like Jason). The one bare foot indicates, according to Edinger, that this figure has experienced something deep, has integrated resources of the personality that others may repress, and has, therefore, a diminished ego-perspective (lesion of ego), which has given rise to a vision that is more powerful and more realistic by virtue of its being more holistic.[18]

Somewhere between Frazer's magical anthropology and Edinger's Jungian psychology lies Origen's theological interpretation of Jesus' sandals, and if Origen was drawing upon the mythological background, he was surely parodying it. Christ—Origen's divine hero in the battles of history, in the hell of life—had *two* sandals, not one! The Christian example, Jesus, had descended into history *and* into hell. He had two ways of walking about in this life, two ways of being grounded. It is as if Origen were suggesting that awkwardness would ensue if one were to spend one's life hobbling about on one leg, being one-sidedly in the depths or one-sidedly too attached to life, too much into that which undergirds life deeply, or too much into ego and its concerns. History is not hell (in this Origen is with the "orthodox" tradition); but history and hell are both here and now (in this he is with the "Gnostics").

To be lacking a notion of life as a descent into hell is as laming to the human psyche as would be a denial of life as a realistic descent into history—or so seems to be the moral of Origen's parable about the shoelaces of Christ's sandals. If there is a tendency to want to deny the hell of life, what Wallace Stevens called "the step to the bleaker depths of his descents,"[19] then perhaps it is "time to turn back," as Eliot put it, "and descend the stair,"[20] lest we stumble lamely into a feeling that "life is hell" and that only. Not that the retrieval of hell in relation to our history will be simple. Kafka wrote: "Then I descended the stairs. The descent was more tiring than the ascent had been, and not even that had been easy."[21]

CHAPTER TWO

A Descent into History:
The Story of the Descent Motif

U ndoubtedly, a descent into hell is a fundamental part of a
Christian's belief, even if the belief is sometimes repressed or
forgotten. If it were not always and already obvious from
those moments in one's personal history when life seems to be hell,
then the less immediate and existential insistence of one of the
statements of anathema by the Council of Constantinople (381 C.E.)
should make matters clear in the extreme. The Council declared that
those persons who deny that Christ had descended in soul (*in anima*)
into Hades shall be condemned, presumably to the Hades in which
they do not believe.[1] One might say that the history of the so-called
good news of salvation includes a descent into hell, at least
Christianly speaking, and, as we shall soon see, not from that
religious perspective alone.

In the face of the dogmatic insistence of the Council of
Constantinople there is a curious and puzzling fact. Roman Catholic,
Protestant, and secular historians all seem agreed that a formal belief
in Christ's descent into hell did not appear in creedal statements until
some three centuries after he was supposed to have made that descent.
The belief is first affirmed when Rufinus says that *descendit ad
inferna* was used in the creed at Aquileia by 359, which is the same
year the words *katachthonia* and *hades* are named as the place of
Christ's underworld journey in Sirmium and Nicean creeds. Christ's

descent was also mentioned explicitly in the creed of Constantinople in the following year of 360.[2] Why—one might wonder—was formal recognition of this belief so slow in coming, especially in the light of a later literal belief which promised damnation if denied?

The Beginning of the Theological Story

Formal belief was surely not slow in coming because Christ's descent into the underworld had not been mentioned in Christendom prior to the fourth century. To the contrary, especially when one reads history backward, seeing it creedally and doctrinally from the perspective of the later formulae, it is possible to find much testimony to the *descensus* motif, not only in the works of the church fathers and in apocryphal scriptures, but even in biblical texts, particularly if one reads the Bible a bit imaginatively.

For example, among apocryphal writings one finds elaborately mythologized versions of Christ's descent in the Odes of Solomon, dating from the end of the first century, as well as in the Gospel of Peter, the Epistles of the Apostles, the Ascent of Isaiah, the Testament of the Twelve Patriarchs, the Sybilline Graces, the Acts of Thaddeus, and the Acts of Thomas, not to mention the later Anaphora of Pilate and Questions of Saint Bartholomew, in which Christ's descent is made in stages of five hundred stairsteps each. There is also in the Gospel of Nicodemus an elaborate conversation between Satan, Hades (the Lord of the underworld which bears his name), and Christ, in which Christ and Hades end by being on the same side against Satan.[3]

Perhaps even more impressive than this list of fanciful apocryphal reports of Christ's descent is the array of church fathers who spoke of this matter, which was later to become a creedal formula. They include: Ignatius,[4] Polycarp,[5] Justin Martyr,[6] Irenaeus,[7] Tertullian,[8] Clement of Alexandria,[9] Origen,[10] Cyprian,[11] Hippolytus,[12] as well as the later fathers, Augustine[13] and Ambrose, who declared that the "substance of Christ is present even in the underworld."[14] There were also comments on the descent by Hilary of Poitiers, Cyril of Jerusalem, Cyril of Alexandria, and so on and on.[15]

The point of this recital of burgeoning lists is not merely to provide an enumeration of texts and theologians. Rather, it intends to give a sense, a real historical sense, that though the *descensus ad inferos* had only quite late been made into a matter of literal belief, the fantasy was nonetheless already in the minds and hearts of Christian men and women. It is as if in one sense or another a *descensus* was simply self-understood as a part of fundamental religious meaning and experience. Being "down" is a part of life.

These early Christians also found evidence for their fantasy already in Scripture, though there are some serious problems in the Bible in this regard. For example, Matthew 12:40 says: "As Jonah was three days and three nights in the belly of the whale, so will the Son of man be three days and three nights in the heart of the earth." If this is to be taken literally as referring to a historical descent of Christ to an actual geographical place, then the question arises as to what one can make of Jesus' supposed saying from the cross while addressing the penitent thief: "Truly, I say to you, today you will be with me in Paradise" (Luke 23:43). Where was Jesus going to be on that day—Hell or Paradise?

Augustine troubled over this, saying first one thing and then another.[16] But Irenaeus and Tertullian, using a bit of theological sleight-of-tongue, solved the problem. Like the Bosom of Abraham in Jewish belief of that period, Paradise, they said, was the name of one of the regions of Hades, there being, as Dante later was to make vivid, better and worse ways to be located in the underworld. So, one modern interpreter reports, concerning this problem of Scripture, "According to the beliefs of the ... Fathers regarding paradise, all that Christ could accomplish on the occasion of His *descensus* was—to put it somewhat crudely—to place the ... saints in a better region of Hades."[17]

Using such subtleties of interpretation, early Christians found ample testimony to the *descensus* in their Bible. Not only is there the passage in Matthew saying that the Son of Man, like Jonah, will be in the depths for three days and nights, but also there is the promise

21

in Acts 2:24-31 that David will not have been abandoned in Hades, and the witness in Romans 14:9 that Christ died to be Lord of the Dead as well as of the living, and the belief stated in Ephesians 4:8-10 that if Christ is said to have ascended it is also implied that he descended, and Christ's own words in Revelation 1:18 that he has the keys of Death and Hades, and so on. Some eighteen passages may be cited by stretching the imagination.[18] None is more direct or explicit than the ones here mentioned, unless it be the problematic text of I Peter 3:18-19 (cf. I Pet. 4:6), which reads:

> For Christ also died for sins once for all, the righteous for the unrighteous, that he might bring us to God, being put to death in the flesh but made alive in the spirit; in which he went and preached to the spirits in prison [*en phylakē*]

For this passage to refer to a *descensus ad inferos,* the term for "prison," *phylakē,* must be read metaphorically as referring to hell, as seems to be the ancient Jewish convention (see Isa. 24:22; 42:7, etc.).

Most especially did the early Christians like to see in Hebrew Scriptures prophecies and prototypes of the *descensus ad inferos,* which they thought they saw in their own New Testament. Jonah was, as has been pointed out, a favorite prototype. Prophecies were seen in the following:

> Shall I ransom them from the power of Sheol?
> Shall I redeem them from Death?
>
> > (Hos. 13:14; cf. 6:2)

> From the depths of the earth
> thou wilt bring me up again.
>
> > (Ps. 71:20; cf. 68:18; 115:17)

> [God] saying to the prisoners, "Come forth,"
> to those who are in darkness, "Appear."
>
> > (Isa. 49:9)

> Who is this that darkens counsel by words without knowledge? .... Have the gates of death been revealed to you, or have you seen the gates of deep darkness?
>
> > (Job 38:2, 17)[19]

Enoch, however, was one of the most notable instances by which the fathers saw in Christ a fulfillment of Jewish prototypes. In the book of Enoch, there are remarkable accounts of Enoch's descent into Sheol to preach to the condemned angels.[20] Christ's perfection of Enoch's activity, or so the Christians thought, was that where Enoch preached condemnation to the captives, Christ preached salvation in the underworld.[21]

However farfetched the Christian interpretations may have been, the point remains, and must have been strongly felt, that a *descensus ad inferos* is a part of the faith concerning life and its history, part and parcel of a proper belief about how things really are from a religious perspective, that is, from a perspective beyond the merely personal.

Before the Beginning:
Christan Backgrounds in Pagan Mythology

Although this mythico-religious fantasy has in fact a certain uniqueness in its Christian version,[22] it is by no means without counterpart in other traditions and among other peoples. Myths of descent into the underworld are associated with Osiris and with the war between Horus and Seth in Egypt; with Tammuz, Attis, Adonis, Ereshkigal, Gilgamesh, and Marduk in Babylonian myths; with Ashura Prajapati, Indra, and Vishnu in India; with Manda d'Haije and Hibil-Ziwa in Mandaean stories; with Izanagi, Izanami, and the Sun Goddess, Amaterasu, in Japan. There are so many accounts of the *descensus* in Greek mythology alone that one may suppose that each myth imagines one of the many ways of being "down," one of many ways of viewing the descent. One thinks immediately of Helios in the Hole (Hell) of Aion, of Trophonius and Herakles, of Orpheus, Dionysos and Psyche, of Hyacinth and Persephone, not to mention Odysseus.

The myths in their variety not only differentiate ways of descent, but also they give a clue, as MacCulloch has elaborately shown, of reasons why a person finds herself or himself "down" or "under." (1) There are, for example, tales which suggest that judging the soul or self to be either good or evil goes with the descent. An Egyptian

23

papyrus of the first century C.E. tells of the descent of the high priest of Memphis, Setne Khamuas (c. 1250 B.C.E.), who witnessed the judgment of souls in the halls of Amenti (i.e., Hades). (2) A second reason for descent is for visiting the realm of vision and dream, as for example in the myths of the Maori, Japanese, Native Americans, Inuit, Melanesians, Borneans, and Norse. One may say of this motive that the deep dreams of self have a way of bringing ego and ego's perspective "down" and "in." (3) There is also the descent made when one tries to get in contact with something or someone who seems dead, when one attempts to discover what haunts one, or when one sees what haunts one as bringing with it a feeling of descent. Stories like this are told by the Wyandot Indians, by Polynesians, Japanese, and African Wachaga, by Babylonian and Greek, by Navajo and Tibetan, Scandinavian and Hindu. (4) Sometimes one thinks that one may obtain a boon (say, immortal life) by descending, or perhaps that the descent is itself a boon, as for example among Inuit, Yoruba, Ainu, Estonian, Finnish, Chinese, Japanese, Egyptian, Hindu, Greek, and Mandaean. (5) Hindu, Buddhist, Jewish, and Egyptian myths, not to mention Christian, tell that a reason for the descent is to free the damned. Or is that when we think we would like to be free of damnation, from life experienced as hell, that we find ourselves down? (6) And finally, there is the motive of curiosity. Apparently, curiosity not only killed the cat, as folk wisdom says, but curiosity also brings the human animal "down," as if there may be some insight to be gained, something to be curious about, in the *descensus ad inferos*.[23]

Again, this mere listing of myths and peoples has as its purpose to show the pervasive power of the fantasy. It is indeed an archetypal motif, as many have noted.[24] Perhaps the universal and collective nature of the fantasy of a *descensus ad inferos* may help to account for its early persistence among Christian men and women, in spite of the fact that creedal insistence came to official Christianity so late. It is as if the church finally came to affirm what is sensed deeply in every person's soul. Acknowledging what the people somehow already knew, the church, however, turned matters a bit. What is interior in every

24

person's experience came to be required as an article of literal belief attached to the person of one historical figure—Christ. And the requirement of believing this deeply archetypal matter literally, as the anathema says forthrightly, comes with the price of one's soul.

The End of the Theological Story

The Christian story has still another strange twist.[25] Not only was the church reticent about a matter of soul, slow to connect the fantasy to Christ's life and meaning, but, odd to say, it also could not sustain *literal* belief in what men and women everywhere seem to assume as self-understood. The Reformation is the beginning of the end. Luther is already wavering, preaching one thing to the people and reserving another view for his theology. In the exordium of his Torgau discourse, his back and forth are clear. Luther says:

> And it pleases me well that, for the simple, it [the descent into hell] should be painted, sung, or spoken in the manner represented by artists, but I shall be quite content if people do not vex themselves greatly with high and subtle thoughts as to how it was carried out; for it did not take place in the body at all, as He remained in the grave for three days.[26]

The reformer Zwingli took the matter even farther. At first he had adhered closely to official Catholic literalism, but he was later to say, in the *Fidei expositio,* that the descent of Christ into hell as spoken in the creed signifies only that Christ really died ("inferis enim connumerari ex humanis abiisse est").[27] John Calvin, however, finished matters entirely, speaking in the *Institutes* (7.27; 2.16) of this belief as *fabula* ("fable") and saying of it that the idea that the souls of the dead are confined in a prison is simply "childish."[28] The Heidelberg Catechism speaks decisively on behalf of Reformed Christianity, saying that the *descensus* refers *metaphorically* to the fact of the "unspeakable distress, agony, and horror, which He suffered in His soul, and previously."[29] Christian literalism—at least in the case of the descent of Christ into hell—simply does not hold up.

25

Nor has it held up in Roman Catholic tradition. Herbert Vorgrimler, writing in the journal *Concilium* in 1966, spoke of the *descensus Christi ad inferos* as a "forgotten truth" in Catholicism. He observed that "the systematic theology of this descent has failed," and he noted that "during the last twenty years the question of Christ's descent into hell has been dealt with in a variety of ways by various theologians such as Aloys Grillmeier, Hans Urs von Balthasar, and Karl Rahner. All the same," continues Vorgrimler, "even today there exists no proper treatment of this question in a way which would incorporate the relevant results of the study of patrology and put the whole question in the context of modern theology."[30]

Vorgrimler's opinion is far and away the majority view.[31] Many churches in America today no longer speak the phrase "he descended into hell" when the creed is recited in holy worship, and in the latest edition of the Episcopal *Book of Common Prayer,* one version of the service of Morning Prayer omits the phrase from the printed creed.

Why—if this fantasy of the *descensus* is so universally crucial to the soul's self-understanding—does it wane after the Reformation and in modernity tend to die out altogether in religious belief and in theological literature?

The answer to this question may be obvious. Insisting that Christ literally descended into the underworld, that a historical person journeyed through the lower reaches of the planet Earth on a particular Friday, following his crucifixion, until Sunday morning, at which time he was raised up into some place in outer space—a belief that indeed *was* insisted on in the Christian anathema—is a belief, in postmodern times, absurd and untenable.

An American Unitarian writing at the end of the last century had the following to say, before Jacques Cousteau dove into the aquatic bowels of the Earth, and before astronauts explored the outer skies:

> That a considerable portion of men should be subject to an error that cramps their own independence, ought not to be a matter of indifference. ... If we have evidence that the Catholics of the second and third centuries believed

26

any proposition unanimously, we have evidence they believed the following: "Jesus Christ at his death went on a mission to the subterranean world." But the earth is now known to be a solid globe revolving in space. Their belief, therefore, of a subterranean world and the mission to it was incorrect. ... It is a tenet which every intelligible Christian, who does not wish to make a mockery of Christianity or to trifle with his own candor, ought to recoil from subscribing or uttering.[32]

Similarly, Friedrich Loofs, who spoke on the theme of Christ's descent at the Third International Congress for the History of Religion in Oxford (1907), would conclude:

The modern mind cannot bring to it [the belief in Christ's descent] more than interest; we cannot now accept it as a part of our faith [because it] ... belongs to a cosmology which even the most determined *lauditor temporis acti* cannot now accept. The conception, moreover, is really inseparable from these underlying (cosmological and scientific) beliefs, and, when the latter crumble away, nothing of the former remains. ... It were fitting, therefore, that the Churches ... should omit the Article "descendit ad inferos" from their programmes of instruction in Christian doctrine and worships.[33]

Strong language! It is probably too strong, for something does indeed remain, and strongly so, as we shall see next. Nonetheless, the conclusion seems clear: At least in the case of the *descensus Christi ad inferos,* literalism makes belief impossible. Faith, or so it would seem, possible only on the grounds of some other way of seeing and thinking, as the German scholar Josef Kroll implied in his work *Gott und Hölle* (1932), when he wrote: *"Descensus bedeutet Mythos"* (The descent implies myth.)[34] The descent of Christ into hell leads theology toward a descent into mythology, a mythological way of seeing and thinking, a way that is nonliteral.

27

HELLS AND HOLY GHOSTS

After the End:
Religious Residues in Secular Literature

Perhaps—since the motif of the descent into hell is archetypal in nature, fundamental to the human soul, universal in scope, yet dead in the wake of ecclesiastical literalism and theological rationalism—it will come as no surprise to discover that what begins in myth, and then turns into doctrinal belief in institutional religion, re-appears in a new form long after the literal belief dies away. Indeed, there occurs a virtual flowering of images and metaphors of the *descensus ad inferos* in secular poetry, and this happens precisely at that moment after the Reformation and Enlightenment when the notion was dying out in sacred theology and in church practice.

To be sure, the *descensus* had always been present in literature. It was already explicit in the classical poetry of Homer and Aristophanes, and in that of Virgil and Dante. But it is particularly in the poetry of the nineteenth and twentieth centuries that this "journey to the interior," as Erich Heller has named it,[35] has burgeoned with Orphic enthusiasm. When archetypal *mythos* fails as literalism in theology, it is reborn as metaphor in poetry. The Spirit is never without witness, as the scripture promises (Acts 14:17), even if it may surface in some surprising places.

The literary critic Northrop Frye once observed, "In the twentieth century ... images of descent are ... in the ascendant."[36] There is Charles Williams' novel, *Descent into Hell,* and Dostoevski's *Notes from Underground.* And Samuel Beckett's dramas often resonate out of infernal regions, in the play called *Play,* for example, where three characters are buried in the earth with only the top parts of their bodies showing from the funeral urns in which they are stuck. However, though the *descensus* is to be found in modern novel and drama, it mainly appears in poetry. If one takes a step back into the past century, the list is truly impressive.

There is Novalis' *Hymns to the Night* and Rilke's *Elegies,* which were written in a period of the latter's life about which he said: "Work of sight is achieved, / now for some heart-work / on all those images, those prisoned creatures within you."[37] But if the *Elegies* represents the climax of what Heller calls "the progressive colonization of inwardness," there are already indications of the motif of the descent in Rilke's earlier poems. In *Das Stundenbuch* ("Book for the Hours of Prayer"), written from 1899 to 1903, we read this, in Robert Bly's felicitous translation:

> Yet no matter how deeply I go down into myself
> my God is dark, and like a webbing made
> of a hundred roots, that drink in silence.[38]

That this deepening sentiment is not accidental is confirmed two poems later in these lines:

> I love the dark hours of my being
> in which my senses drop into the deep.
> I have found in them, as in old letters,
> my private life, that is already lived through,
> and become wide and powerful now,
>   like legends.[39]

That Rilke and other German poets are not alone in the use of the motif of the descent is noted by Geoffrey Hartman. Hartman writes that Rilke "is aware that in submitting to sense experience he follows a long line of literary precursors who sought a modern descent into hell. The myth of this descent," notes Hartman, "may be said to start with Novalis, reaching its climax in French symbolism—Nerval, Baudelaire, Rimbaud—and its conclusion in Rilke, although Thomas Mann will still concern himself with it." Hartman's judgment is that "the descent into hell is the total acceptance within art of everyday reality."[40] If Hartman, like Heller, notes the prominence of the descent in modern poetry, he may underestimate its scope.

To be sure, in France it is expressed in Baudelaire's *Flowers of Evil* and in Rimbaud's *Season in Hell,* in the latter of which we read about the author's request for the reader to allow him to "tear out these few, hideous pages from my notebook of one of the damned."[41] But Walter Strauss, in his magnificent study on the Orphic theme in literature, adds to Hartman's list the following: Valéry, Supervielle,

Eluard, Cocteau, Pierre-Jean Jouve, Pierre Emmanuel, Mallarmé, and Saint-Jean Perse.[42] Nor is Europe the only site of hell in our time.

American letters, also, has its descent, and in a widely pluralistic display of styles. There is *Kora in Hell,* an early poetic-prose improvisation by William Carlos Williams, and the well-known lines of e. e. cummings: "gee i like to think of dead it means nearer because deeper firmer / since darker."[43] Wallace Stevens' "The Rock" and Theodore Roethke's "In a Dark Time," give similar testimony to the motif, as does the latter's poem "The Abyss," which says:

> Is the stair here?
> Where's the stair?
> "The stair's right there,
> But it goes nowhere."
>
> And the abyss? the abyss?
> "The abyss you can't miss:
> It's right where you are—
> A step down the stair."[44]

This is reminiscent of the poem by Charles Olson, "In Cold Hell, in Thicket":

> ya, selva oscura, but hell now
> is not exterior, is not to be got out of, is
> the coat of your own self, the beasts
> emblazoned on you
>
>   ... Who
> can endure it where it is, where the beasts are met
> where yourself is, your beloved is, where she
> who is separate from you is not separate, is not
> goddess, is, as your core is,
> the making of one hell.[45]

And there is Robinson Jeffers' poem "Descent to the Dead":
> I have lain and been humbled in all these graves,
>   and mixed
> new flesh with the old and filled the hollow of
>   my mouth
> with maggots and rotten dusts and ages of
>   repose. I lie here
>   and plot the agony of the
>   resurrection.[46]

30

A DESCENT INTO HISTORY

More recently Jack Gilbert wrote these lines:

> From the beginning,
> it had gone badly.
> From the beginning.
> From the first laughter
> It was Hell.[47]

And in another poem from the same collection:

> What if Orpheus,
> confident in the hard-
> found mastery,
> should go down into Hell?
> Out of the clean light down?
> And then, surrounded
> by the closing beasts
> and readying his lyre,
> should notice, suddenly,
> they had no ears?[48]

This ironic twist on the descent motif is confirmed soberly by Stanley Kunitz, demonstrating the postmodern durability of the motif of the descent. Kunitz wrote retrospectively about his poetic life in the *New York Times Book Review* of February 1987: "One of the first poems of my youth, a tortuous elegy written in my 23d year, opened with the apostrophe, 'O ruined father dead,' and concluded with the lines, 'Let sons learn from their lipless fathers how / Man enters hell without a golden bough.' Aeneas," Kunitz explains, "did not dare to descend into the underworld to consult the shade of his father until, on the advice of the sibyl, he had gone to the sacred grove and plucked 'the pliant shoot of gold' that would guard him from the terrors awaiting him below. The force of the allusion, as I [Kunitz] read it now, is that modern man must make his descent, braving the worst, without the sanction of the sacred or the hope of salvation."[49] This would surely be the impulse of others who also work the lower regions of the psyche and of the society in their poetries: Yeats, Trakl, Hermann Broch, Hans Erich Nossack, or—perhaps most important—that major work bringing the descent into twentieth-century ascendancy, the *Cantos* of Ezra Pound.[50] In sum, the testimony from literature is overwhelming!

31

HELLS AND HOLY GHOSTS

Against Literalism

As if it were not surprising enough, in this brief history of the motif of the descent in myth, religion, and literature, to discover that the theme burgeons in secular poetry at the very moment it is in descendancy in religion, there is yet another astonishing matter. The secular poets are alerting us to the nonliteral dimension of a belief in descents into the depths, saying, for example, "Hell now is not exterior, but is the coat of your own self," and, "The abyss? it's right there where you are." What is astonishing is that this very figural and poetic interpretation of *descensus ad inferos* may be found in the ancient theological tradition from the beginning. But it has been widely ignored. Two instances will suffice to make the point plain that there has all the while been a poetry of the deep self in theology. The examples are those of a third-century theologian, Origen of Alexandria, and a fifth-century Christian writer, Macarius Magnus.

Origen is writing a commentary on Matthew 8:12, which speaks of the "sons of the kingdom" being cast into the "outer darkness" (*to skotos to exouteron*). Origen asks what one is to make of such phrases as "outer darkness," "eternal fire," "prison," "furnace," and others connected with the place where men and women "will weep and gnash their teeth" after death. He says, first, that such matters are "hidden from us" and are known "only to physicians of souls." Then he adds: "The 'outer darkness' is in my opinion not to be understood as a place with a murky atmosphere and no light at all, but rather as a description of those who through their immersion in the darkness of deep ignorance become separated from every gleam of reason and intelligence."[51] This is to say that at least one early theologian reads the *descensus ad inferos* as psychologically as do ancient myth and modern poetry.

Indeed, there was good intuition in the church's decision finally to settle on the word *inferos,* rather than *infernum,* as the proper term for the Creed, though there was indeed some vacillation on this matter.

The formula *descensus ad inferos* was not in the version of the Apostles' Creed used at Rome and elsewhere, nor was it in the creeds of 359 and 360 from Sirmium, Nicea, and Constantinople, although Rufinus indicates in his book on creeds that the words *descendit ad inferna* were already inserted in the version used at Aquileia. This phrase, using *inferna* or *infernum*, is the Vulgate rendering of phrases from the Septuagint (e.g., I Sam. 2:6; Ps. 113:17; Isa. 14:11; Ezek. 31:15). It is not clear whether the so-called Athanasian Creed, the *Quicunque Vult,* which may have been composed by Honoratus of Lerins between 420 and 430, contained *inferos* or *inferna*. But when the Council of Toledo quotes this creed and that of Pope Damasus, it uses the formula *descendit ad inferos*. Nonetheless, at the beginning of the seventh century, *inferna* is still in use, for example, by the hand of Venantius Fortunatus, the hymn-writer who was bishop of Poitiers; though at the same time the creed in the Bangor antiphonary of the Irish church used *descendit ad inferos*. Not only was this latter form used by the fourth Council of Toledo in 633, but also it finally became universally accepted in the eighth century. An eighth-century manuscript contains a copy of a Gallican creed made in Gaul in the fourth century. The words there are *descendit ad inferos,* and this is the formula that has stuck.[52]

This is no mere quibble with terminology. *Infero* means "to carry inward," "to gather in." Therefore, as Origen observed, when *inferos* is used, the *descensus* may be read as referring, not to some actual physical place, but rather to a "journey to the interior." The *descensus* is *ad inferos*. It is a "carrying inward." Hell is a *descensus,* and encountering it is a "deepening." So it is that the homily of Macarius Magnus vindicates modern poetry's metaphor when it says clearly:

> The grave is in your heart;
> hell is in your soul.[53]

Fifteen centuries later, Delmore Schwartz echoes this mythopoetic theology in his postmodern short story "The World Is a Wedding," saying:

> This Kingdom of Heaven is within you;
> but also the Kingdom of Hell.[54]

And Charles Williams, in the same vein, can end his novel, *Descent into Hell,* with these lines:

> He was very near the bottom of his rope. ... He knew he
> was lost ... now he was there at the bottom, and there was
> nothing but noises and visions which meant nothing. The
> rope was not there. ... If he only had hold of the rope still,
> he could perhaps climb out of this meaningless horror;
> at least he could find some meaning and relation in it all.
> ... He shrank into himself ... and he was drawn steadily,
> everlastingly, inward and down through the bottomless
> circles of the void.[55]

Inward and downward, indeed!—*inferos* and *descensus.*

CHAPTER THREE

A Descent into Imagination:
Images of the Descent in the Ideas of Theology

If hell be the human heart and soul and mind, and especially if that heart be, as Conrad said, a "heart of darkness," then some words of the poet Rilke may become a guide for mining the meaning of psychotheological depths. In the poetic act—Rilke said in the *Duino Elegies*—there can be an "erweckten sie uns ... ein Gleichnis" (a "waking of likeness within us").[1] The methodological clue implied in this saying urges an examination of theological ideas, such as *descensus Christi ad inferos,* for their images, and particularly for lifelikenesses, images residing within ideas which serve as a resource for imagining deeply and reflectively the human situation, a perspective on history from the theological imagination of hell.

Following this mythopoetic clue—a clue that is as old as Origen and Macarius—one might now ask: What is the descent into hell? When does it happen?

Whether one means these questions theologically or psychologically, traditional theology offers helpful images of hell and descent. Indeed, images and dreams, circles of metaphors and nightmarish visions, commonly accompany our various historical descents into whatever hells. When we are "down," we discover that images come feelingly to mind. We see faces, and have matters to face; we hear a throng of accusing voices and angry resentments, and feel emotions and moods otherwise uncommon to daily experience.

Much of what we feel is personal, and we take it personally in our periods of descent. The collective and archetypal images of the theological tradition may help us in such moments, help us discover, not what is individual to our persons, but rather what is persistent through history and geography, those universal and objective fantasies which may lead to a deeper understanding of the human heart. The aim is to take theology's images really seriously for life here and now. In short: religious images of descent as lifelikenesses.

Anima

The first image traditional Christian theology has given us to aid in understanding our various descents may well be the most important one. In 1215, when the Fourth Council of the Lateran was interpreting how Christ could be in the grave for three days and yet at the same time be sojourning in the depths, that is, how a person could be at once dead in history and alive in spirit or in the spirit-world, the Council's formulation was succinct and definitive. "Descendit in anima et resurrexit in carne" (He descended in soul and he raised up in body).[2]

This was an old teaching made explicit. It was already implied in I Peter 3:19, where the descent is spoken of as being in *pneuma* ("in spirit"), and it was what Orthodoxy insisted on when the anathema of Constantinople affirmed that the Logos (Christ) had descended into Hades "in soul." It was also the standard view of the Fathers, implied for example by Origen, who wrote in his argument against Celsus that Christ descended in *psyche*.[3]

The implication of this language of the church (*descendit in anima*) is that when the body is in the grave, dead and buried, or when there is a death of ego and its perspectives during one's lifetime, then a deeper spirit or soul can come to be. A deepening of historical being occurs by way of an under-the-worldly point of view. The descent into the underworld of souls (*psychai, animae*) is a descent into a soul-perspective or depth-perspective concerning history. One might say that the descent into hell is actually the ascent of soul. It brings a sense

36

of soul into ascendancy in life, and it gives the human ego a perspective from a soulful point of view. The descent is itself a resurrection. Such is the mystery of the life of faith.

Thus, a primary theological image of what happens in life's descents is that soul (*anima*) is activated and animated. Hell is not history. It is a soul-perspective on history. *Ad inferos* is *in anima*. To discover the depth-dimension of soul—the Christian formulation implies—one might take note of things when one is "down."

Implied in this also is that one might read other mythico-theological images of the descent into hell, those lurking in Christian theological ideas, as a guide to a sense of "soul" and to a transpersonal perspective on ego's history. So, if the tradition imagines the descent into hell as a descent into "darkness," or into a "hole," or into a "pit," or into "invisibility" (Hades' name means "invisible"), then no matter how a person may feel about such experiences of being in the "dark," in a "hole," in the "pits," or "invisible" to others, that person is encouraged to search such deep moments for their disclosures and expressions of profound "soul" (*anima*) in life.[4]

Prison

B esides images of "soul," "darkness," "hole," "pit," and "invisibility," there are numerous other images traditionally associated with the *descensus ad inferos*. A favorite and persistent one is that of "prison," as if when we feel down, one way of expressing the experience to ourselves is by saying that we feel "trapped," like being in "prison." The converse is also implied, namely, that when we feel as if we are "trapped" or "imprisoned" by a situation, we may imagine that there is a deepening of life's meanings, a journey into the interior (*ad inferos*). The deepening comes about as a result of the reflectiveness produced by the emotion of feelings of entrapment. The passage from I Peter 3:19, about the "spirits in prison," has already been cited. Similarly, the *Acts of Callistratus* (c. 300-350) speaks of Christ going down into the prison, as does Venantius Fortunatus in these terms:

Set free the chained shades of the infernal prison;
Recall whatever sinks to the depths.[5]

It is as if to say that when we recall the moments we feel as if we are in prison, in those moments we will also discover a shading or a nuancing of our customary understanding, a newly discovered set of reflections about our life.

Animals

The ancient theological writers also depict the *anima*-depths with imagery of animals, as if the descent into hell, into interiority, were a descent into a fundamental animality. So the Psalmist writes (Ps. 22:1, 12-13, 20-21):

My God, my God, why hast thou forsaken me? ...
Many bulls encompass me,
    strong bulls of Bashan surround me;
they open wide their mouths at me,
    like a ravening and roaring lion ...
Deliver ...
    my life from the power of the dog!
Save me from the mouth of the lion,
    my afflicted soul from the horns of the wild oxen!

Christian writers carry on this sort of imagery. Prudentius spoke of Christ's descent as taking the poison and hissing from the serpent.[6] Synesius wrote that in the christic descent the dog is pushed back from the gate of the underworld.[7] In the Odes of Solomon the infernal confrontation is with a seven-headed dragon.[8] Procla, who was Pilate's wife, had a vision of the risen Lord, who told her, "I have loosed the pangs of Death and wounded the many-headed dragon."[9] And in the Greek Apocalypse of Baruch, Hades is itself depicted as a monstrous dragon.[10] It is as if to say that when one is "down," an animal-sense is added to life, and different sorts of animality, depending upon the way one is "down."[11]

A DESCENT INTO IMAGINATION

Stomach

Sometimes the ancients were more specific and spoke of particular aspects of the animal, for example, the belly. The Son of Man, said the Gospel of Matthew, will descend as did Jonah into the belly of the animal. Proverbs 1:12 says that Sheol (Hades) will "swallow them alive and whole, like those who go down to the Pit." So also in the Gospel of Nicodemus, Satan addresses Hades as the "insatiable devourer," and Hades answers Satan by admitting, "I have a pain in the stomach."[12] Similarly, in the Gospel of Bartholomew, Hades says, "My belly is torn to pieces, and my entrails rumble,"[13] as if to express that a person's descents may be experienced as a literal or figurative pain in the belly, a bellyache, an acute rumbling in the very center of a person's being, there being a sense of soulful feeling in such psychic and somatic knots in the stomach. "The monster in terror," Venantius writes, "vomits the multitude [of souls] whom he had swallowed, and the Lamb withdraws the flock from the jaws of the wolf."[14] This suggests that for the sake of soul a person may wish to note carefully what she or he swallows too easily, for it may turn out to be difficult to digest in life, and, therefore, be vomited back to ego's history in the form of projection and acting out.

Swinging Doors, Gates of Brass, and Clashing Rocks

Other parts of the body also became metaphors for hell in antiquity. Most notably, besides the belly and the mouth, the heart was mentioned, and the heart is where, as every person knows all too well, descents are frequently experienced.[15] The fact that images of the body are so commonly associated with the motif of the descent suggests that a descent not only gives "soul" to life, but that it also brings "body" into life ("body" here used in the sense of "body of hair" or "body of wine"). But yet another carnal metaphor, namely that of jaws, is what seems to have opened the door of the ancient imagination to an entirely different range of images of *descensus ad inferos*—jaws being imagined as the gateway to the interior depths.

39

The jaws are not quiet. They are gnashing, furiously opening and closing, whether they be the jaws of the dog guarding the gate of the underworld or the jaws of the seven-headed dragon identified as hell itself. Often a person does not manage to get through such jaws without leaving something behind, as in the folk version of the descent in which a rabbit wrests the herb of immortality from the dog guarding the depths, but then leaves his little white cottontail behind in the grip of the jaws of the animal.[16] Similarly, the folklore of the church likened Christ's passage through hell to the crossing of the Red Sea, because in the "harrowing of hell" the jaws of the dragon yawn wide to let those who are with Christ pass through, but close again on Lucifer, as the Red Sea did on the Egyptians and the dog's teeth did on the hare's tail.

This particular image of the descent is often mentioned in relation to the Symplegades or Clashing Rocks. This indicates that "timing" and "rhythm" are crucial in a *descensus ad inferos*.[17] And since the jaws and the clashing rocks are something of a gateway into the realm of the Other, into the kingdom of souls and "soul," the image of an active door is also invoked, a sort of swinging door, like the ones in the saloons of old Western cowboy movies. These doors open and shut with such speed that one must move just in the nick of time, or risk being struck down as they come together or as they fly apart.[18] It is such a door to the depths about which Pseudo-Epiphanius speaks when in a homily he writes that "Christ who is the Door breaks the woodless door (*axulous thuras*) of Hades with the wood (*xulon*) of the Cross," presumably using the Cross as a sort of battering ram.[19]

That the swinging doors of the underworld are not wood is also depicted commonly in antiquity. Psalm 107:16 says of the Lord that "he shatters the doors of bronze, / and cuts in two the bars of iron." Tertullian connects this psalm with the descent of Christ, saying, "He has broken the adamantine gates of death, and the brazen bars of Hades."[20]

The images of the experience of being "down" are strong. They are themselves adamantine. Where there is a gnashing of teeth (jaws), a clashing of rocky oppositions in life, and a smashing headlong into that which is impossible to subdue—one may discover a door and a gateway to a perspective of depth, which is, to be sure, not to say that such a journey *ad inferos* will be easy, as the next images indicate dramatically.

Earthquake and War

Two New Testament passages are often cited to indicate the veritable shaking of the foundations a soul's descent involves. The first puts the experience in the imagery of earthquake; the second, in terms of warfare in the depths. Matthew 27:51-52 reads, "And behold ... the earth shook, and the rocks were split; the tombs also were opened, and many bodies of the saints who had fallen asleep were raised." Colossians 2:15 tells why the earth shook, namely, because a fight was going on *ad inferos* ("inside"): "he disarmed the principalities and powers," says the text. In fact, the fourth-century writer Firmicus Maternus attributes the earthquake on Good Friday to the cosmic shock resulting from the battle between Christ and Antichrist.[21] Yet even such tremor, such trembling and shock, such shaking of the foundations and polemic, are imagined by the Christian tradition as an initiation into an experience which is not *merely* negative, or at least not that alone.

Treasury

Perhaps the Christians gave expression to the deepening experience with mythopoetic imagery they learned from the ancient Greeks, for whom Hades, as Lord of the underworld, was the god of the treasury. Hades was rich. Ploutos, the god of wealth, was one of his other names. He was resourceful for two reasons: (1) the Greeks stored the silver from their silver mines underground; and (2) Hades was thought to be ultimately the possessor of every person in the world, since it was believed *everyone* went there when, inevitably, he or she died. Hades was truly a god of substance, or means. The *descensus ad inferos,* then, is potentially a rich experience. As the

41

prophet Isaiah put it, "I will give you the treasures of darkness and the hoards in secret places."[22]

Womb

The descent is also imagined to be an experience of birth, a second birth, perhaps, in which a deeper life is delivered out of the deeps. We have already observed that Christian theology located the Bosom of Abraham and Paradise in the realm of Hades, in the underworld. The "Paraphrase of Shem," a work from the Nag Hammadi library which seems to have had an important influence on early Christology, adds to the Bosom of Abraham and to Paradise the notion that the underworld is a sort of vagina through which everything may be born.[23] Not only does a descent into hell produce substance for life and its significance; it can also bring to life, which is often "dead" or deadly, new life and liveliness.

.

Moisture

There is a natural association between the imagery of "birth" and another early Christian image of the descent, namely, that of baptism. The key is the connection in the imagination between the amniotic fluid of birthing and the baptismal water. A primary source for this linking of baptism with *descensus ad inferos* is Romans 6:3-4, which says:

> Do you not know that all of us who have been baptized into Christ Jesus were baptized into his death? We were buried therefore with him by baptism into death, so that as Christ was raised from the dead ... we too might walk in newness of life.

Based on this, John Chrysostom can write, "The action of descending into the water [in Christian baptism] ... symbolizes the descent into hell."[24] The Syriac Office of the Rite of Baptism has this very interesting set of images given by St. Ephraem:

42

A DESCENT INTO IMAGINATION

Like a diver, Thou didst go down into Sheol,
To seek Thine image which had been swallowed.
Thou didst go down like one that is poor and wretched;
Thou didst penetrate to the abyss of the dead.[25]

We will return later to the notion of the function of the descent as a recovery of an image of self, or of having an image of self. Suffice it for now to observe concerning the association of the descent and baptism that such a connection seems to imply that, however difficult being "down" may be from the standpoint of ego and its history of sufferings, not only can a descent bring new life and a second birth, delivering one into a deeper perspective, into a perspective of soul rather than of ego alone (of historical perspective only), but that also such descents may moisten a dried-out life, making the juices of mind and emotion flow a bit more *in anima.*[26]

The Keys to the Depths and Magic

Early Christians believed that baptism was a key to a new religious life. It was a Christian form of initiation. In John's vision of the Son of Man (Rev. 1:18), the association between "key" and descent is made direct and explicit. The scripture says that the Son of Man says: "I died, and behold I am alive for evermore, and I have the keys of Death and Hades." Morton Smith has completed this notion by showing that Jesus as the keeper of the keys was like ancient magicians, not only of the Near Eastern world, but also of the world around.[27] Indeed, Mircea Eliade—citing instances from Avam Samoyed shamans, Smith Sound Inuit, the Goldi of Siberia, the Telumni Yokuts, and many others—has pointed out that just "any ecstatic cannot be considered a shaman [or magician]; the shaman specializes in a trance during which the soul is believed to leave his body and ... descend into the underworld."[28] This is how the shaman heals; and it is the way she or he learned the healing art at the time of initiation. So it is perhaps not so surprising that MacCulloch and Kroll, as well as others, have linked Christ's descent into hell with magical practices

43

and beliefs. It would seem that the fact that the church insisted on a belief in Christ's descent in the creedal formulae of the fourth century is continuing testimony added on to the evidences Morton Smith has already adduced, showing that Jesus was, and was viewed by the faithful to be, a magician.[29]

For the purposes of the present argument, however, whatever other significance this evidence holds, it also tells what every soul knows all too well, namely, that significant descents in the course of a life may hold a "key" to a sense of magic in life, and that the magical aspects of a person's history give a depth to that life which would otherwise be unknown. Thus, the descent of Christ as being a key to the magic in life may well contain, not only historical significance concerning Jesus of Nazareth, but also psychological meaning about the soul of every person.

Bars and Chains and Bolts of Iron

Every man and woman has indeed known the imprisoning images of hell, the feeling of being in chains, being behind bars, and being locked into situations that seem bolted shut. The descent is, among other things, a descent into sensing what we sense in history *as* being behind bars, within chains, and locked with iron bolts. But somehow, and at the same time, early Christians witnessed to the descent as a bursting of the bars, a breaking of the chains, and a smashing of the iron bolts. The images were borrowed from Hebrew scriptures. The Psalmist writes (Ps. 107:16):

> For he shatters the doors of bronze,
> and cuts in two the bars of iron.

And in Isaiah's prophecy (Isa. 45:2*b*-3) we read:

> I will ... cut asunder the bars of iron,
> I will give you the treasures of darkness
> and the hoards in secret places.

Coptic and Ethiopic versions of the creed, which were used after baptism, continue this Hebrew motif. They describe the descent as a freeing of those who were in chains (*liberavit vinctos*).[30] In the treatise *De virginitate,* which is attributed to Athanasius, Hades says:

> Who is this breaking the brazen gates of Hades and shattering the adamantine bolts? ... Who is this loosing the bonds of those conquered by me?[31]

And in the early Christian wisdom text, "The Teachings of Silvanus," there is this description:

> This one, being God, became man for your sake. It is this one who broke the iron bars of the Underworld and the bronze bolts. ... It is he who loosened from himself the chains of which he had taken hold.[32]

So, the descent is an enchainment and a breaking of chains, a being put behind bars and a breaking of bars, a being bolted-in and a shattering of locks and bolts. How can this be?

How can there be an experience which is both at once? How can a person's descents be sensed as being in the hole, in the pits, in darkness, in prison, in the midst of a gnashing of teeth, deep in the belly, among clashing rocks, earthquakes and war, *and,* at the same time, as an experience of the treasures of soul, a second birth, a moistening of a dried-out life, the initiation which is a key to the magic of life, a doorway to a deeper perspective?

Conclusion

Origen, whose third-century perspective on these matters we have been following all along, provides a clue to this conundrum when he speaks precisely about the Scripture having to do with "breaking the iron bars." This Alexandrian Father implies that the descent may be seen as referring to the reading and interpreting of the texts of Scripture. One goes down—as it were—into a text of the Bible, descending into its historical imagery. But sometimes the nature of the passage is such that we simply cannot take it literally without its becoming absurd. That is, we cannot take the historical imagery in a historical way as referring to some actual event in the literal and physical past. The descent of Christ into the center of the planet Earth and his breaking iron bars Superman-style is one such text. If one is to take such texts seriously, rather than casting them aside as out of date, he or she must, given the nature of such Scriptures, understand them figuratively as referring *ad inferos,* "interiorly," to soul, *in anima.* As Macarius put it, "Hell is in your soul."

Origen calls this metaphoric reading of Scripture a "bursting of iron bars."[33] Such a reading reveals "hidden treasures of wisdom and knowledge," he says.[34] That is, the reading of lifelikenesses or analogies from the images of sacred texts is a "deep" reading, which discloses, as Origen believes, "the depths of wisdom of God."[35] Such interpretation implies that religious texts refer, not to past history, not to future eschatological happenings, or at least not to these alone, but to the self and its sense of itself here and now, in every and any time and place. To descend into the bars and chains and bonds of such texts is to allow one's ordinary historical understanding to burst wide open. One mode of understanding (the historicist, the personalistic) is in bondage precisely so that it may at the same time be balanced by a deeper vision, which is freed from temporal and individual constraints.

So, according to Origen, the testimony of the breaking of iron bars has to do with prophetic iconoclasm, with smashing literal attitudes toward religion, enabling a person to see the literalisms of history with imagination, rather than seeing imagination's images merely historically, which would be like trying to hobble along on one foot.

Thus, the *descensus ad inferos* is a perspective. It is a perspective on any event in life, rather than being itself a single event. It is that deep perspective on worldly things, a transpersonal way of understanding things personal. Hell is a way of viewing history. It is history's other foot.

The other foot (the descent into hell) functions in life as imagination. It gives image to life-event, and in so doing it smashes the literalism of a person's history. Bars are burst. Chains break. Bolts are smashed. Now things may be sensed differently.

If Christ's descent *ad inferos* is a bursting of literalism's bonds, then those who take Christ's person and work literally are not taking Christ at all. Indeed, that there is a Christian tradition which attempts to take the *descensus* with historical literalism has been noted appropriately, and for psychological (rather than theological) reasons attacked by James Hillman.[36] This tradition assumes that since Christ descended on behalf of Christian men and women, they do not themselves ever have to make a descent. This, of course, has the psychological effect of making the pious person feel that she or he *should* not and *ought* not to feel "down," that it is one's own fault (sin) if reality seems depressed and if life seems like hell. One imagines that if one were good enough (Christian enough), one would not feel as one indeed feels. In such a situation, the psychological depression has its source, not in a personal cause, but in an unconscious theological understanding, and one whose literalism has not been able to be maintained even by Christianity itself.

Indeed, though such literalism exists in popular Christianity, it is by no means the only way of interpreting the *descensus ad inferos*. Many church fathers asserted outright that Christ's descent does not exempt mortals from making the descent themselves. For example, Tertullian and Irenaeus expressly opposed the notion that Christians are saved by Christ from going to hell.[37] And it would certainly be my hope that this book has amassed enough data from the side of a mythopoetic reading of the *descensus* (from Origen, Macarius, et al.) to demonstrate that a more psychologically wholesome interpretation of the descent of Christ into the underworld has been present in the tradition from the very beginning.

The point is that literalistic religion is religion whose descent into history lacks a corresponding descent into hell. Hobbling along on its human leg, it lacks depth and soul. It is worldly by trying to be literally otherworldly. It tries to live without being able to imagine living. It is dead.

The descent into hell has precisely the purpose of restoring the imagination. So St. Ephraem said:

> Thou didst go down into Sheol,
> To seek Thine image.[38]

And again he wrote concerning Christ:

> I sought and found Adam.
> I descended
> and carried forth our image.[39]

Similarly, the homily of Easter Eve by Epiphanius pictures Christ entering the underworld and saying:

> Arise from the dead, for I am the life of the dead.
> Arise my image [*plasma*].[40]

And in the Gospel of Nicodemus, Christ says:

> Come unto me all my saints who have
> my image and likeness [41]

Having Christ's image and seeing it as a likeness for life means that we may expect descents in our life, and it means that they may well be descents into hell (*ad inferos*), which means into the interiority of our own transpersonal selves.

A part of being Christian is taking note of the descent. But in the descent we may expect to recover the image of selfhood. If nothing else, the descents of life provide images upon which to reflect.

Sensing the deep images lurking in life's history, and then understanding the history with imagination, is the function of the descent. It gives us a second leg to walk on, which is what we need. History takes on a perspective of depth in the lifelikenesses. It is not that "my life is hell," but rather that "hell (hell's imaginal function) is my life." Indeed, in order that we may have a way to imagine the unimaginable sufferings experienceable in a lifetime, in order to be brought "down" a bit, we may need to make our prayer, "Thy will be done on earth, *as* it is in hell."

CHAPTER FOUR

A Descent into the Middle:
Between Death and Resurrection

S o we have two testimonies. The first comes from Ephraem Syrus, Epiphanius, and the Gospel of Nicodemus. In these sources we are told that one of the effects of a descent into hell is that we may gain an image of self, be it a recovery of Adam's image before the so-called Fall or an attainment of the image of the Christ-in-us, a second Adam. But another and not unrelated testimony comes from Origen, who suggests that there may come a new perspective from our descents. This would be an imaginal perspective, achieved when the "bars" and "chains" and "bolts" are burst asunder, when we find ourselves descending into the impossibility of meaning, an impossibility which results from our locked-in literalistic ways of understanding. Both testimonies—the recovery of a sense of self and the achievement of an imaginative perspective—are confirmed by what may at first appear to be a somewhat obvious aspect of the Christian theme of Christ's descent.

A Theological "Middle"

T he Roman Catholic theologian Hans Urs von Balthasar put the obvious matter forthrightly. Speaking of Christ's descent into hell, he said that it happened in the "Mitte zwischen Kreuz und Auferstehung," in the "middle between the crucifixion and resurrection."[1] The *descensus* is in the "middle." It has to do with the realm of the "between" (*das Zwischen*). Bousset, in his well-known study, *Kyrios Christos,* amplifies the matter further: "The acceptance of the three-day interval between death and resurrection now opened a new door to Christian imagination. People did not stop with the simple idea of rest in the tomb or of the tarrying of the soul with the corpse. There developed the fantasy of the descent of Jesus into Hades."[2] One German theologian goes so far as to imagine that the article on Christ's descent in the creed came about, as he puts it, "through the need to answer the question about where Christ's soul could be in the time between death and resurrection."[3] A French Catholic scholar seems to agree, saying that "perhaps the article was inserted into the creed precisely to fill the hiatus."[4]

The point is clear. The *descensus Christi* followed death and burial and preceded resurrection and ascension according to the Christian imagination. Its place in the liturgy was on Holy Saturday, the day named after the Greek god Saturn who is known for melancholia and depression.[5] This association may suggest that a person's descents put that person "down," in the "middle" between a death and a new birth.

But how is one to understand the "middleness" of this theological idea? How shall one understand the image of this "between"? How is it that a descent into the "middle" can become, as was noted in chapter 2, the source of images of self and of an imaginal perspective on history and life?[6]

A Philosophical "Middle"

That the source of imagination is a "middle realm" is not an unusual idea in Platonic and Neoplatonic philosophical understanding, nor is it odd, according to Henry Corbin, in the mystical philosophy of Persian Sufism.

What Plato referred to as the *metaxy* is called *'âlam al-mithâl* by Islamic philosophers. Corbin translates both terms by the Latin designation *mundus imaginalis,* "world of the imaginal," and intends the phrase to refer to a notion of a "realm" between human sense-experience and the ideas we have about such experiences. It is a "middle" position between empiricism (inducing ideas from experiences) and rationalism (deducing specific conclusions from general ideas), between feeling and thought, between the so-called real and the so-called ideal.

The "third region" between sensation and ideation is, to be sure, not a "place" in the ordinary sense of the term. Some Persian philosophers, according to Corbin, call it the *Ná-Kojá-Abád,* which literally means "the country of nowhere." Rather than a "somewhere," it is a perspective, a perspective of what the Greeks called *phantasiai,* "images" or "ways of imagining."

So, for example, a person has the consciousness or perspective of *mundus imaginalis* when she or he embodies an idea or an experience with an image. When one imagines (gives image to) an idea, already that idea can be felt by way of the concrete example or likeness. Similarly, when one imagines (gives image to) an experience, already that experience begins to be thought and ideated. Ideas imaged are felt, as every teacher knows who has resorted to an example when attempting to explain a difficult idea to a class. Similarly, things felt, when given image, can be known, as every parent has experienced when attempting to communicate an important emotion to a child. In the *mundus imaginalis*—a mode of consciousness radically different from historical literalism (empiricism) or pious religiosity (idealism)— heart and mind, subject and object, experience and idea are together in image and imagination.[7]

The "middle" perspective is a way of thinking about thinking, and it is a way of thinking about experiencing, too. In its purview, literalism about both experiences and ideas is refused. Ideas are fantasies one has about something, whether they be true or false. Experiences are images noted, whether they be real or unreal. Questions of truth or falsity and reality or illusion are not denied; rather, they are bracketed, "put on the back burner," honored as one more way of imagining things.

The descent into the "middle," into the "between," then, implies a perspective of both-and. It is not the "place" of death only, or of life (resurrection) only. It is "between" death and resurrection, and it brings with it a perspective that is dialectical (moving back and forth), fundamentally ambivalent, seeing all things historical under the double sign of a *coincidentia oppositorum,* a "coincidence of oppositions," in the richness of imagination.

A Psychological "Middle"

If the philosophical theology of the "between" is put in psychological terms, it may seem more immediate and more immediately obvious, as if it were something we knew deeply all along, but somehow did not know quite how to express to ourselves.

The creedal witness is that the descent comes between death and resurrection. It comes after the agonizing death of a historical person, and it comes before whatever life is next to be. Or, one may put it this way: The descent comes after the death of the historical and the literal perspectives on life, after we have been deprived of our cherished personal opinions, our favorite idols, and it comes before we have fully gained whatever life-giving perspective will sustain us in the future. The *descensus ad inferos,* the "descent into the interior" (which we sometimes feel as hell), is the "place" in which we find ourselves after the perspective of ego, of "I," "me," and "mine," has failed. And the descent itself is the harbinger announcing a deeper perspective of self to come.

It happens to everyone. William Blake once signed a friend's autograph album, "William Blake, born 28 November 1757, in London, and has died several times since."[8] We all know the feeling! Paul was even more emphatic, saying, "Why am I in peril every hour? ... I die every day."[9] Is this not tantamount to saying that there is a *descensus ad inferos* every time there is a defeat for the ego or for ego's perspective, and that every time there is a defeat for the ego or for ego's perspective there is a possibility for a deeper perspective?[10]

A DESCENT INTO THE MIDDLE

The descent into hell is not a descent into history and its various troubles (which is probably what we intend when we say "my life is hell"). Rather, the descent into hell is a descent out of history, a deepening of history and historical perspective that may well be prompted by the pains and wounds of a suffering life history. It is that deepening which balances historical and personal points of view, giving us another foot to stand on. It occasions the discovery of the images by which history's troubles make themselves known to us. Being between dying and being born, being both at once, we, through the discovery of deep images in our various descents, are enabled to see history imaginatively, enabled to imagine a way of going on deeply.

Eugene O'Neill put the experience into dialogue in a play called *The Hairy Ape.* One of O'Neill's characters says:

> I ain't on earth and I ain't in heaven, get me? I'm in the middle tryin' to separate 'em. Maybe dat's what dey call hell, huh?[11]

Indeed! And to the human ego such experiences seem, not a middle, but only an unimaginable muddle. They seem hardly the beginning of a way of going on imaginatively, but more like the end of it all. So, the question of the prophet Isaiah (6:11) persists always and seemingly forever with men and women in their many daily descents: "How long, O Lord?" How long must we egos be in the middle, between heaven and earth, between life and death, always between? How long? It is to this question we will turn in part 2.

PART TWO

Hells

CHAPTER FIVE

A Descent into Laughter:
The Abominable Fancy

S o, ego asks: "How long, O Lord?" How long must I be in the middle of it all, in the middle of the impermanence and flux of images, where nothing seems real and everything, even when charmingly mythopoetic and imaginative, is so transitory that I am caught between the disappearance of this and the next appearance of that, between a death of one way of understanding and the birth of some new way, dying daily, always and forever descending *ad inferos.* "How long, O Lord?"

The ego and its perspective wants an answer, and it has received many. The theological tradition has had a chronic capacity for chronological literalism. Some have said, "If you will only repent and believe, then the promise will be fulfilled at once." "Today, thou shalt be with me in Paradise." Others have said, "After three days there will be a resurrection of saints." Still others have declared, "Not until forty days and forty nights have passed—or is it fifty?—will the Holy Spirit come upon one pentecostally." Even less optimistic, yet still with historical and temporal literalism, a chiliastic response to ego's cry has been, "Not until the Second Coming, not until the Rapture."

But there has been another sort of answer to the question of "how long?" It is a bolder response, and it has stubbornly persisted through the centuries. "How long shall one be in hell?" The testimony is radical and forthright: *Forever!*

HELLS AND HOLY GHOSTS

The Abominable Fancy

Even though this clear-cut "forever" may be offensive to some, its radical witness resounds already in the words of the New Testament. Matthew 25 and Revelation 14 and 20 speak simply of *to pūr to aiōnion* and *kolasis aiōnios,* "everlasting fire" and "everlasting punishment." However else the term *aiōnios* may be read, it is certainly plain that the fathers of the church, with the possible exceptions of Origen and Gregory of Nyssa, read the term in one way, the way which came to straightforward articulation in the ninth anathema of the Council of Constantinople in 543: "Whoever says or thinks that the punishment of demons and the wicked will not be eternal, that it will have an end and that there will then be an *apokatastasis* of demons and the wicked, let such a one be anathema."[1]

A thousand years later the notion of eternal damnation was still in place. Luther used the words *ewige Strafe* and *ewige Pein,* "eternal strife" and "eternal pain," and Melanchthon unambiguously wrote the Latin words for "without end." So, Article 17 of the Augsburg Confession (1530) reads: "Christ ... will condemn impious men and devils to torture without end [*"ut sine fine crucienture"*]."[2] Once one has made the journey *ad inferos* (unless one is the Christ), one will always be descendant—or so goes the intuition of the church.

The church was coolly rational about the matter, even if the reasoning offends modern ears. The reason given for the torments of hell lasting forever is that such suffering is, in a strange way, blissful, at least for the saints in heaven! Not only did this seem "strange" reasoning to the Reverend F. W. Farrar, a dean of Westminster Abbey in the nineteenth century, it was to him even more than merely strange. According to D. P. Walker, Dean Farrar called the belief "an abominable fancy."[3] Nonetheless, abominable or not, it is firmly a part of the Christian tradition. Now what is the nature of the traditional Christian imagination which insists on being in the deeps forever?

The reasoning and its attendant imagery depend on a notion about the nature of the bliss which accompanies the lives of the eternally blessed. The abominable fancy is that bliss consists in watching the eternal suffering and torment of the damned in hell.

There is actual authority in the Bible for this fantasy. Revelation 14:9-11 tells that the wicked shall be tormented with fire and brimstone while the angels watch. If, in Luke 16, the rich man could see Lazarus, there is every reason to suppose that Lazarus could watch the rich man suffer his fate in Hades. And Isaiah 66:22-24 prophesies that the people of the Lord will go and look upon the carcasses of those who are suffering the fire of God's wrath.

None other than Augustine and Thomas Aquinas confirm this fancy as theological fact.[4] It also appears in Tertullian and St. Cyprian. The modern scholar D. P. Walker has amassed evidence to show that this view is basic to the Christian tradition throughout its history,[5] even though to men and women of today, and to those with a secular and literal imagination, the view is unthinkably cruel and immoral, not to mention psychopathologically sadistic. Pierre Bayle, for example, wrote that "there is even something ('je ne sais quoi') which shocks our reason in the hypothesis that the Saints of Paradise gain part of their happiness from knowing that other persons are being tormented and will be eternally."[6] And the eighteenth-century British Platonist, Thomas Burnet, wrote the following with considerable anger showing through the sarcasm:

> Consider a little, if you please, unmerciful Doctor [Tertullian],[7] what a theatre of providence that is: by far the greatest part of the human race burning in the flames for ever and ever. Oh what a spectacle on the stage, worthy of an audience of God and angels! And then to delight the ear, while this unhappy crowd fills heaven and earth with ailing and howling, you have a truly divine harmony![8]

It is unimaginable to Burnet that one moral mortal could derive pleasure from seeing another suffer.

Yet the tradition has been consistent about its being a pleasure and a bliss. In fact, a particular pleasure and a specific bliss, namely, *laughter*, is often mentioned when one takes note of the descent into hell. In Proverbs 1:26, Wisdom says: "I ... will laugh at your calamity." Laughter at suffering is witnessed to also, and often, in the Psalms. For example, concerning the heathen it is said: "He that sitteth in the heavens shall laugh: the Lord shall have them in derision" (Ps. 2:4 KJV). Or: "The Lord shall laugh at him [i.e., the wicked]: for he seeth that his day is coming" (Ps. 37:13 KJV). Again, in Psalm 59:8 (KJV), we read: "But thou, O Lord, shall laugh at them; thou shalt have all the heathen in derision," and the Psalmist here is speaking about those who "belch out with their mouth [with] swords ... in their lips."

But it is not only God who laughs, as Psalm 52:6 (KJV) testifies: "The righteous also shall ... laugh at him" (referring to the person who trusted in wealth). And in the book of Job, we see that it is not only the wicked who find themselves "down" and being laughed at. Job says (9:23), "When disaster brings sudden death / he mocks at the calamity of the innocent." Surely the saying corresponds with experience. How often do we sense, when we are feeling down, having descended *ad inferos,* that we are making fools of ourselves and that everyone is laughing at us?

One scholar, writing in *The Theological Dictionary of the New Testament,* has confirmed philologically what we all sense psychologically in such moments. Rengstorf observes that the words *gelaō* in Greek and *sahaq* in Hebrew, when used in Scripture, are used, in his words, "exclusively for the true or supposed superiority towards another expressed in scorn or laughter."[9] These terms for "laughter" in the Bible refer purely and simply to the ridicule of those who are "down."

Robert Grant has argued for a possible connection between the Hebrew tradition of laughing in derision at those who suffer, and a Gnostic tradition concerning Christ at the moment when he was supposed to have been descending into hell. The Gnostic tale is told by Irenaeus, who attributes it to Basilides:

> He [Christ] did not suffer, but a certain Simon of Cyrene
> was compelled to carry his cross for him; and this [Simon]
> was transformed by him [Jesus] so that he was thought to

be Jesus himself, and was crucified through ignorance and error. Jesus, however, took on the form of Simon, and stood by laughing at them.[10]

Similarly, in the Nag Hammadi library (in "The Second Treatise of the Great Seth") we may read:

> It was not I whom they struck with the reed. It was another who lifted the cross onto his shoulders—Simon. ... But I was up above, rejoicing over all the wealth of the archons and the offspring of the error of their empty glory. And I was laughing at their ignorance.[11]

And, in the "Apocalypse of Peter," we are told about a vision Peter had. A crowd seizes the Lord, and Peter, in this vision, asks: "What do I see, O Lord? Who is this above the tree [the cross], who is happy and who laughs? Is it another whose feet and hands they are striking?" The Savior replies: "He whom you see above the tree, glad and laughing, is the living Jesus."[12] In the case of these texts, the blessed One is not laughing directly at Simon's suffering, but he is laughing at the victory that occurs at the moment of a victimization.

Again, we may have no taste for this sort of testimony, but the fact remains that the tradition retains a fantasy in which God (according to Hebrew scriptures), Christ (according to Gnostic Christianity), and the "blessed" (according to the orthodox tradition of the church) laugh and take delight at those who suffer *ad inferos*. If it be an abominable fancy, as Dean Farrar indeed thought, it nonetheless exists. So the question remains: What can be made of it? How can we understand it? Perhaps, as the Bible suggests, *laughter* is the key.

Divina Comoedia

Laughter may be the key for understanding this odd and obnoxious fantasy of Western religion because there has existed since Aristotle, which is to say, since well before the time of Christian thinking, a curious correspondence between theories of laughter and

61

comedy, on the one hand, and the notion that the bliss of the blessed consists in taking delight at the eternal suffering of the damned, on the other hand. Classical theories of comedy agree so widely concerning this matter that they serve to force a serious look at what may otherwise be an intolerable and unimaginable idea.

The literary history of the idea begins, as far as historians of ideas know, with Aristotle. This philosopher corrects a misconception about the term "comedy" by pointing out, in book 3 of *The Poetics,* that the word is not taken from the term *kōmadzein,* meaning "to revel," as was popularly thought in his time, but is taken rather from the Dorian term *kōmai,* meaning "village." The idea is that "comedians" are persons who wander, like later minstrels, from "village to village" *(kata kōmas),* likely for the reason that they were excluded contemptuously from the cities for engaging in a base form of drama, that is, one not as sophisticated as high tragedy. Comedy—Aristotle reasoned from this philological clue—is "low" matter and is therefore for the "lower" classes, that is, for those who are "down." So, the philosopher says forthrightly in book 5 of *The Poetics*: "Comedy is ... an imitation of characters of a lower type. ... The ludicrous consists in some defect or ugliness which is not painful or destructive."[13] This is to say that when one laughs at comedy or at a comedian, one is taking delight in something one takes to be beneath one or lower than one.

In his work, *On the Character of the Orator* (55 B.C.E.), Cicero advances the Aristotelian notion in Latin concepts. He writes: "The seat and as it were province of what is laughed at ... lies in a certain baseness and deformity [*turpitudine et deformitate*]; for those sayings are laughed at solely or chiefly which point out and designate something offensive in an inoffensive manner. ... [B]lemishes if nicely managed create laughter."[14]

In the fourth century, Donatus repeats Aristotle and Cicero, and then he adds a concrete detail. He reports that because of the "low" nature of the argument of comedy and because of the baseness of the comedians, Roman comedy was called "low-footed," and the actors, rather than wearing platform heels as did actors in tragedies, used a low shoe or sock.[15] Francesco Robortello, in a sixteenth-century essay, points out that some Latin comedy was called *planipedes* because it was so "low" that it was acted without any shoes at all.[16]

A countryman of Robortello's, Vincenzo Maggi, writing in the same century, connected the notion of laughing at *turpitudo et deformitas* ("baseness and deformity") with the Christian idea of sin and sinner. Maggi wrote that when a person laughs at a comedy on the stage, she or he is laughing at what this Italian thinker called *peccatum,* that is, at a "sin" or a "fault," but one which, through the artistry of the dramatist, is, as he puts it, an "ugliness and ... deformity that yet is without pain." The pleasure one receives from viewing this *turpitudo* Maggi calls by the name *admiratio,* as if "woe," viewed from the perspective of the comic art, is "wondrous." Wonder (*admiratio*) is the key to proper comedic function for Maggi.[17]

This view, in spite of whatever offense or oddness there may be in it, perdures through the centuries. Antonio Sebastiano Minturno, in 1563, wrote that "the way to make comedy [is] by noticing other people's defects,"[18] just like the laughter of the angels and the blessed watching the torments of the sinful, the angels being witness to a "divine comedy." Lodovico Castelvetro, seven years after Minturno, adds that

> it must be borne in mind, however, that these defects would not be comical if they did not appear to us in some disguise so that we could pretend that we were laughing at something else; for we do not wish to give the appearance of being pleased with the wickedness or deformity of others ... though in point of fact we laugh at the ugliness.[19]

It would seem that there is a moral squeamishness, an ethical reservation, creeping into Castelvetro's version of the old idea about the joy of laughter being prompted by suffering; nonetheless, the tradition is still alive and well in the sixteenth century, as it was also in the century that followed.

In seventeenth-century England, Shakespeare, in *King Lear,* used precisely the words "woe" and "wonder" (which are English surrogates for the earlier terms of literary theory, *turpitudo* and *admiratio*). When Lear dies with his beloved daughter Cordelia in his arms, the Duke of Albany says, "Our present business is general woe." But the Duke of Kent comments, "The wonder is he hath endur'd so long." One critic (Cunningham) has followed these two terms through all of Shakespeare's plays, finding them to be central to his notion of tragic and comic drama.[20]

The idea endured in Italy and in France, too. Carlo Goldoni, in 1749, told his readers that comedy was invented to ridicule bad customs.[21] Jean Francois Cailhava d'Estendoux, in 1772, showed that when Tartuffe, in Molière's play, used the words "beatitude" and "blessedness" in a hypocritical way, it caused laughter at a moment "when the wickedness of the person who speaks them would normally cause horror."[22]

But this is just the question, is it not? How can one be moved to delight and to bliss, to laughter, by what should by all rights produce horror, by something like the eternal torment of suffering? The mystery of the comic art and the mystery of the abominable fancy in theology seem oddly to be connected. And the ending of the story about the literary theory of comedy may provide a clue to the theological meaning of the offensive doctrine of such as Augustine and Aquinas, not to mention the Bible.

Dryden and Congreve in the seventeenth century, Dennis and Goldsmith in the eighteenth, and Hazlitt in the nineteenth—all carry on the notion that the proper response when one looks upon *turpitudo* or *peccatum,* comically speaking, is laughter.[23] But just at this point in Western literary theory, the idea, which is by now well over two thousand years old, is divided. Thomas Hobbes may stand for one side; Meredith, Baudelaire, and Bergson may be viewed as representing the other.

For Hobbes the idea we have been tracing has a social, political, and external meaning. "Laughter," he says in the essay *Human*

Nature, "is a sudden glory arising from some sudden conception of some eminency in ourselves by comparison with the infirmity of others."[24] Taken in this sociological manner, the idea is clearly egotistic and cruel. Hence, when one finds the so-called abominable fancy obnoxious or immoral, it could be because one is then viewing it in Hobbesian fashion. If one looks through ego's eye, it is simply not understandable how God or Wisdom, Christ or the Angels, can sit in the heavens and laugh derisively at the suffering of the wicked and the innocent. It is not understandable, however, because the perspective with which one is viewing the fantasy is itself egoic and, as it were, "wicked"; that is, it imagines itself "above" such behavior. The Hobbesian perspective is behavioral and historical, social and political. It represents a descent into history taken as hell, but not a deeper descent into hell taken as an imaginative perspective on history and its behavior.

George Meredith, Charles Baudelaire, and Henri Bergson have a different notion from that of Thomas Hobbes. Their descent into the dominant idea in the long comedic tradition takes a deeper turn, a turn *ad inferos* ("inward").

Baudelaire, in his essay "The Essence of Laughter," sets the terms of the problem, telling his reader in advance that this will not be a "popular subject." Then he says:

> That beauty ... should find a place in works designed to display to human beings their own moral and physical ugliness is something curious and worthy of study. Nor is it less curious that the lamentable spectacle thus offered to mortals should excite in them the deathless and incorrigible spirit of mirth.[25]

Baudelaire, taking the cue from Pascal, supposes that this curiosity is somehow related to laughing, not (as in Hobbes) at another person outside oneself, but at something "profoundly human,"[26] namely, the "perpetual shock" (*admiratio*?) produced by the two infinites: "the infinite grandeur and at once the infinite wretchedness of human beings."[27] It is as if the laughter results from the joy of relief in recognizing that an unreconcilable opposition can be contained within a single self.[28] It is as if the blessed and the wretched are images of what is within the person, and that what is abominable and immoral in the social and political world is nonetheless laughable, blissful, if seen as a projection of split values (either-or rather than both-and). *Ad inferos* ("inside") this two-sidedness is an image of the way things are in the Pascalian nature of human beings.

Like Baudelaire, Meredith asks rhetorically, "How could wickedness have been admired?"[29] It could only have been admired, he thinks, if one were to have a capacity for comic (or religious?) perspective. And, Meredith says, "You may estimate your capacity for comic perception by being able to detect the ridicule of them you love without loving them less," which so far sounds sociological, something like Hobbes. But then Meredith adds, "And more by being able to see yourself somewhat ridiculous in loving eyes."[30] To be sure, this is not so easy for the ego-side of the self. If there is anything the ego does not love, it is its own ugliness, its woe, its *turpitudo,* its *peccatum.* All these are occasions for embarrassment, for being brought "down." They produce shame, guilt, and anxiety. The suffering ego would like to think that these qualities belong outside the self, in some other, and so ego projects the qualities onto the other unconsciously. As a result, when I look upon what I imagine to be *turpitudo,* I see myself in some aspect. The wonder (*admiratio*) would be in the miracle of being able to love and embrace, not ugliness and evil "out there" (which has always to be fought against), but being able to love that which is felt to be a defect in oneself, the "infinite wretchedness." Such loving of one's whole self, both sides, all the sides, is what Meredith thinks is a capacious sense of humor, a capacity for comic perception.

Bergson is even clearer. He writes, "Deformity [ugliness] is comic to the extent that one can imagine imitating it,"[31] that is, to the extent that one can see oneself in it.

None of this should be surprising to the religious imagination, yet it is continually obscured by a reticence to see the depth-psychological truth in theological ideas. Did not Luther say that a human individual, under the aegis of religious perspective, is *"simul iustus et peccator"* ("at once saved and sinful")? And is this not like saying that the self is simultaneously in its very nature in "eternal torment," in "hell," "descending," as well as "ascendant," in "heaven," "laughing"?

If the so-called abominable fancy is viewed from within the history of the literary theory about comedy, laughing at what is low-down is hardly egotistic or sadistic, hardly obnoxious or unethical. Rather, the *image* of laughing at what is low-down is an affirmation that every person is "victim and victor,"[32] laughed at and laughing, dead and alive, descended and by virtue of the descent in soulful ascendancy precisely while being "down."

Traditional literary theory about comic laughter may offer a clue for the reading of the *descensus ad inferos* and especially for its everlasting quality. It is doubtless not for nothing that when, in medieval times, humankind wished to name the "harlequin," a word related to the word "hell" was used. Enid Welsford gives the following account of the first use:

> On New Year's Night, 1091, a certain priest called Gauchelin was terrified by a procession of women, warriors, [and] monks ... who swept past him, dressed in black, half-hidden by flames, and wailing aloud. Astonished and dismayed, the priest said to himself: "Doubtless this is the Herlechin family. I have heard that it has formerly been seen by many people, but I have mocked at such tales. Now, indeed, I myself have truly seen the ghosts of the dead."[33]

The term "herlechin," like "harlequin," is a variation of the word "hellequin," and it designated the leader of a ghostly, ghastly, ghoulish troupe of clowns and comic actors. These actors often employed a trapdoor on the medieval stage, a door through which they dropped out of sight and into the "underworld." The trapdoor was called *la chappe d'Hellequin,* "the mouth of the comedian" or "the jaws of hell."[34] Presumably, we laugh at the poor clown who drops into these "jaws," not because we are relieved that it did not happen to us, but because it has and we are relieved that the "clown" survived!

CHAPTER SIX

A Descent into Psychopathology:
Archetypal Sadomasochism

We began part 2 by asking how long one has to endure the torturous jaws of hells. The religious tradition responded by asserting that once one is "down," it is for ever. We then asked why, imagining from ego's point of view that such an answer could seem ungracious and overly vengeful. But again a response came from the tradition, namely, that the knowledge of being down produces bliss, at least from the perspective of faith. But isn't this absurd? Yes, if one takes the "abominable fancy" literally. And isn't it immoral? Of course, if it is taken sociologically and historically as referring to the behavior of selves in a social world. So, how then is the notion to be understood?

Augustine's answer to this question accords with what we discovered in the last chapter by way of the history of comic theory. Augustine asks:

> But how is it that the good will "go out" to see the punishment of the wicked? Are we to imagine that they are to leave their blessed abodes by a bodily movement and to proceed to the region of punishment, so that they may view the torments of the wicked in bodily presence?

And Augustine answers: "Certainly not. ... It is," he says, "by their knowledge that they will 'go out.'"[1] Then Augustine speaks of the perspective of those for whom "viewing" the torments is a bliss. He uses the word "inside," as if to say that the drama is an interior one (just as Baudelaire, Meredith, and Bergson noted), and that to view it moralistically or sociologically (as did, for example, Thomas Hobbes) places one in "the outer darkness" with no way of sensing the bliss. The *descensus ad inferos* and the witness concerning torment as being eternal is a *divina comoedia* of the *self*. Its proper referent is the human psyche (*in anima, ad inferos*), and to speak of the poetic mythology of the descent is to call to mind an archetypal dimension of psychology from the precincts of theology.

The particular archetypal configuration is difficult to miss. It has to do with the sense of the self which comes when ego feels tormented or when the psyche gains pleasure from viewing the torments of others. Christianity's fantasy of the bliss of the blessed resulting from viewing the torture of the wicked takes one into the realm of sadomasochism, and it takes one there theologically, which is to say, transpersonally or archetypally.

Sadomasochism—that curious complex in which one feels pleasure in being tormented by another or in which one feels pleasure in tormenting another—is a complex which itself has tormented psychologists. Not only did Freud and Jung argue tortuously over this experience of the self in a series of letters during the month of December 1909,[2] but Freud worried over the matter, changing his views radically between the years 1915 ("Instincts and Their Vicissitudes") and 1920 (*Beyond the Pleasure Principle*).

Already in 1915, Freud saw that the feeling of being tormented is somehow intimately connected in the self with the wish to torment others. Masochism is unconscious sadism, and sadism is unconscious masochism. Freud expressed this by showing that certain instinctual senses seem to reverse themselves (*Verkehrung*) in such a way that one aspect of the feeling turns into its opposite (*Wendung*). In the case of sadism and masochism, which belong together in the self, it is a matter of an aggressive feeling toward others being connected with a passive wish. And when one feels passive toward others (resigned), it has to do with an aggressive wish (anger). Even under "normal" circumstances, how often will the expression of anger, say, by a parent toward a child, turn to tears of sadness, the outward directed libido turning against the self in shame or guilt. Similarly, little introspection is required to discover that often a nagging sadness about the nature of one's life as one feels it to be can turn into an anger, as justified as Job's, against whatever gods there may be. Freud's point about psychopathology is easily confirmed by ordinary everyday life.

Yet even at this point in his work (1915), Freud noted a third experience beyond simple sadism and simple masochism. In the flowing back and forth of the active-passive energies of the self, he observed that sometimes "the active voice is changed, not into the passive, but into the reflexive middle voice,"[3] as if a person could sometimes find himself or herself "between," between a sense of ego hurting another and a sense of ego being hurt by another.

It was this third position of the self which came to radical expression in 1920. In *Beyond the Pleasure Principle,* there emerged the view of a total self which experiences itself as instinctually double and simultaneously so. Sadism and masochism, like the instincts for life and death (*eros* and *thanatos*), belong dialectically together, not like a pendulum swinging in alternating moments from one extremity to the other, from anger to sadness, from sadism to masochism, but rather, both poles functioning at once, though a person may be conscious of only one at a time.[4] The anger is already in the sadness; the suffering is already in the rage. Here Freud is confirming and being confirmed by the theological insight that the seemingly sadistic bliss of blessedness is intimately connected with the apparently masochistic stubbornness of the eternally damned.

This idea of the two sides of a complex belonging together fundamentally is quite close to Jung's way of sensing the self, though Jung's terminology is different (*enantiadromia, coincidentia oppositorum*). Yet Jung and Freud did not agree on how to speak about the psychodynamics of sadomasochism. James Hillman has ventured an explanation of the differences between the two theorists. He has first noted that the terms "sadism" and "masochism" do not appear, even once, in the general index to the *Collected Works* of Jung, and yet the tormenting and tormented sense of self, an apparently universal human experience, is dealt with by Jung in other terms. It is as if for Jung the very terminology of "sadism" and "masochism" (two -isms) already suggests an attempt at medically scientific judgment, implying that there is something abominable, wicked, neurotic, and pornographic about this complex of feelings. Jung—Hillman argues— acknowledged the human experience, but wanted to refer to it in language closer to the psyche's experience of the complex, language that would be subjectively more authentic to the self and its situation.

Thus, Jung called the complex by imaginatively concrete terms taken from alchemy, such as "flaying," "torture," *mortificatio* ("mortification"), and *nigredo* ("darkening"). These, according to Jung, were at once faithful to the self's experience of itself in the complex, and, at the same time, reflective of the fact that the situation was archetypal and transpersonal, not idiosyncratically subjective. This latter distancing is achieved by the fact that Jung's terms, taken from the mythopoetic imagination of alchemy, can never be mistaken for abstract, literal descriptions and evaluations.[5] For Jung the so-called sadomasochistic complex was archetypal, collective, and universal in nature (something confirmed by the history of theology's *descensus*), and so it deserved archetypal imagining, whereas for Freud the complex was individually instinctual and so needed terminology and theory that would lend objective diagnosis and evaluation, insofar as that is at all possible.

Jung's point can be made with the example of *mortificatio,* an alchemical image. When a person says, "I'm mortified," he or she means to indicate some sort of feeling of humiliation. Ego is humbled, brought "down." In the experiences that prompt such expression, there is, from the point of view of the person having the experience, no "I" left to torment or to feel tormented. In such moments the sense of "I" has died. So it is also when Psyche is tortured by Love (Eros, Amor, or Cupid) in the old folktale of *Eros and Psyche,*[6] or in Elizabethan love poetry where, as Hillman notes, the impossible tortures of love can only be rivaled by the tortures of impossible love.

If such mortification, such death of ego, such torturings of love are images of what Freud calls sadomasochism, which is somehow psychopathologically pleasurable in the suffering *(Schadenfreude =* "the joy of suffering"), then wherein is the pleasure?

Hillman's psychologically sensitive explanation goes this way. "Suppose," he says, "masochism to be related to dying, imagined as an ecstatic release, as something the soul wants and needs and which it receives through the discovery of an intense, overwhelming value of the flesh and its exquisite enjoyment, which is also our worst pain."[7] Imagined this way, "sadomasochism" can be spoken of by Hillman in terms that bear directly on theology's "abominable fancy."

> "Distortion," "tortured," "torment" are words that refer to the twisted nature of the psyche, its complexity, which Jung placed at the fundament of the psychic life. Our complexes are a twisting together of opposites. . . . We are twisted in soul because soul is by nature and of necessity in a tortuous condition. We cannot be explained, nor can we be straightened out. Psychopathological distortion is the primary condition given with our complexity, the crowning wreath of thorns or laurel garland we wear always on the tortuous path through the labyrinth that has no exit. For, as Jung said, the complexes are life itself; to be rid of them is to be rid of life.[8]

So, as a therapist, one concerned about how persons feel about themselves, about a sense of significance, Hillman can conclude that "the damaged and queer figures who emerge from our complexes do not indicate that something has gone wrong and that the ego should set it straight. These shapes are dynamic, and their pathological detail is a goad to vivacity and insight. They are the active agents of the imagination, its vanguard, leading to profounder psychological insights."[9] Speaking deconstructively before the formulation of Deconstruction, Hillman could say firmly that "soul-making entails soul-destroying."[10] Thus, the whole therapeutic procedure is a descent,[11] a viewpoint with which Jung concurred in advance, saying, "The scope of the integration [i.e., therapy] is suggested by the *descensus ad inferos,* the descent of Christ's soul to hell, its work of redemption embracing even the dead."[12] Put theologically, this therapeutic point of view implies that the eternal bliss of the blessed entails the simultaneously eternal torment of the ones who feel suffering. *In anima, ad inferos* these poles belong together, and they belong together, whether we will it or not, forever and forever.

This is why the old insight from theology regarding the *descensus ad inferos* is so crucial here and now to the contemporary man or woman in search of soul. What these depth psychologists have observed in terms of the ontology of self, I have already put theologically in the first part of this book: namely, the *descensus ad inferos* is itself an ascendancy of soul, and already. The way down *is* the way up, as Heraclitus said so long ago.[13] The function of the descent is, at least in part, to bring feeling into life, to life, and deeply so. Surely, to feel things deeply is to be, not dead, but alive—or, alive in death, in the death of ego's perspective. The dying is a being born.

So-called sadomasochism, then, viewed from this theological and archetypal perspective, is the imagined, but no less felt, experience of torturing that brings the self to its senses, to a sense of itself. The experience requires of self an imaginal way of seeing and being. It is now not that *I* am tormenting *someone* or that *someone* is giving *me* a bad time. It is now not a matter of ego at all. Rather, more fundamentally and with more fidelity to the experience, one might say, a torturing is happening, without reference to a torturer or to one tortured. The torment is not taken personally, from this point of view. Rather, the torturing is going on purely and simply, and it is happening because a self is descended *ad inferos,* into the depths, which is to say, into itself, that is, into a self which has many sides, a self in which there are indeed many *personae* who seem to occupy themselves (if one may speak in this way) by tormenting one another.

So it is that theology's "abominable fancy" forces one out of personal perspectives. From inside the fantasy, one can hardly view the God of the Hebrew Bible, the Gnostic Christ, and the blessed saints of Christendom as sadists. Nor may the damned who persist in their condition be seen as masochists. Rather, the belonging-together in some eternal "middle" of active energy and passive energy, of love and hate, of death and life, of sadness and anger—these simply are the way things are deeply in the self. And, according to the Christian tradition, apparently it is anathema—that is, damning—to imagine otherwise.

Indeed, it is not the theological imagination of Augustine and Aquinas which is "abominable." No. What would really be abominable, offensive, unthinkable, and lacking in faith, hope, and love, would be to have to imagine that there were no salvation *in* suffering, no depth here and now in life, no Paradise in Hades. Perhaps this is why the poet Charles Olson penned the lines we have already cited:

> ... hell now
> is not exterior, is not to be got out of, is
> the coat of your own self.[14]

How can one ever jump out of one's own two feet? How can one ever be saved from the self while still being the self? We suffer who we are and we are our sufferings. Sometimes, to be sure, we suffer deeply, which is to say *ad inferos*. But it is not to be got out of. Rather, like hell, it is to be gone into more deeply. There is "pleasure" there, but not a personal pleasure; rather, it is a joy that is, though "all too human," nonetheless beyond "me."

CHAPTER SEVEN

A Descent into the Hells of Modern Literature: The Dark Inference and Negative Theology

Even were the perspective to be made compelling, that hell is not to be got out of but is to be gone into, we still would surely be as reticent as the lines of Dylan Thomas say. "Though wise men at their end know dark is right," nonetheless "they do not go gentle into that good night."[1] To be sure, the conclusion of the last chapter is odd—that a going into the underworld imaginatively, implies a discovery that the way down is already the way up, that descents bring a deepening of life, that the sufferings of ego are a salvation for a deeper sense of self, that dying is always and already a being born! Yet the testimony persists.

Martin Heidegger, in one way, and Charles Baudelaire, in another, express the paradox succinctly. Heidegger writes:

> When we allow ourselves to fall into the depths [*den Abgrund*], we do not plunge into mere emptiness. We fall into the height, whose height opens a depth [*eine Tiefe*].[2]

Similarly, but on the topic of "beauty," Baudelaire said:

> Sometimes, too—and this is one of the most interesting characteristics of beauty—it will have mystery; and lastly ... it will have *unhappiness*. I do not claim that joy cannot associate with beauty; but I say that joy is one of beauty's most vulgar adornments, whereas melancholy is, so to speak, her illustrious companion—so much so that I can

scarcely imagine . . . a type of beauty in which there is
no unhappiness.[3]

Baudelaire's saying is reminiscent of Hölderlin's epigram concerning
Sophocles' *Antigone:*

> Many have attempted in vain with joy to express
>   the most joyful;
> Here I have found it at last, here, but in
>   sadness it speaks.[4]

The poets seem to know, as we have already noted in chapter 2, about
the *descensus ad inferos.*

What may seem abominable to theology, absurd and paradoxical
to philosophy, obnoxious and cruel to ego's sense of morality, is
nonetheless one of the experiences the deep self suffers, and not in
vain. It is the poets, particularly, who make articulate the "logic" of
why such wounding is not in vain.

Rilke's poem, "A Book for the Hours of Prayer," has already
been petitioned. His poetic "logic" concerning the value of darkness
is definite in part 5 of that work:

> You darkness, that I come from,
> I love you more than all the fires
> that fence in the world,
> for the fire makes
> a circle of light for everyone,
> and then no one outside learns of you.
>
> But the darkness pulls in everything:
> shapes and fires, animals and myself,
> how easily it gathers them!—
> powers and people—
>
> And it is possible a great energy
> is moving near me.
> I have faith in nights.[5]

Rilke sees the inclusive power of the imagination that comes with the darkness, the "shapes," "animals," and "people" that gather everything with renewed energy. And if he has "faith in nights," so does Donald Hall. The following is from the latter's work, *Seasons at Eagle Pond*:

> Some of us ... are darkness-lovers. We do not dislike the early and late daylight of June, whippoorwill's graytime, but we cherish the gradually increasing dark of November, which we wrap around ourselves in the prosperous warmth of woodstove, oil, electric blanket, storm window, and insulation. We are partly tuber, partly bear. Inside our warmth we fold ourselves in the dark and its cold—around us, outside us, safely away from us; we tuck ourselves up in the long sleep and comfort of cold's opposite, warming ourselves by thought of the cold, lighting ourselves by darkness's idea. Or we are Persephone gone underground again, cozy in the amenities of hell. Sheltered between stove and electric light, we hollow islands of safety within the cold and dark. As light grows less each day, our fur grows thicker.[6]

The poetic "logic" of the "coincidence of opposites" in Hall and Rilke—light in dark, warmth in cold—if not encouraging their going into the good night gently, at least gives them faith in its important function. Confirmation of their embrace of darkness for reasons of poetic logic, comes from a curious oriental source.

Makoto Ueda is attempting to explain one Japanese Noh dramatist's way of viewing "comedy" and "laughter." "The highest type of comedy," Ueda writes, "is austere in its outlook. Theoretically, to be funny is not the ultimate aim of comedy."[7] This is like saying that being "up" or ascendant is not the ultimate aim of religion or of psychotherapy. Like the *divina comoedia* of the soul, the laughter in the heavens is based, Ueda observes about Noh theater, in "pathos."[8] But the pathos is not merely pathological, not merely being "down." Like the Aristotelian tradition about Western comedy, the comic representation of the "pathos" involves a certain artistry.

HELLS AND HOLY GHOSTS

In Noh drama the "low," the comic, is achieved by a mood the Japanese call *yūgen*.[9] *Yūgen* was a stylistic ideal of poets of the Heian period. The meaning of this word, so difficult to translate, is something like the Latin word which Western Christian theologians chose to mean "underworld," that is, *inferos,* the word which would give to English the term "inference." *Yūgen,* like *inferos,* suggests a seeing of things inferentially, not in the sense of rational deduction, but rather in the sense of seeing as in a dream or in a haze. This is the same style and mode of understanding that is realized in Oriental scroll paintings which are shrouded in clouds and are full of subtle hints.

According to Richard Pilgrim, the root meaning of the syllable *gen* in *yūgen* is "the color of the universe," that is, deep black.[10] This is not the same as mere black, the blackness ego experiences when its history is deprived of underworldly depth. Rather, it is something more like the alchemical notion of *nigrum nigrius nigro,* the "black that is blacker than black."[11] It is fundamental "dark," prior to distinctions between black and white or dark and light, a perspective of "inference" (*inferos*) that is basic and immediate, the profound sense known to one always and already, as in these lines of the poet Saigyō:

> If it were not for loneliness,
> this would be a wretched place to live.[12]

This is *yūgen.* It is also *inferos.* Its poetic "logic" is dark, but not without a deep humor. Its meaning is inferential with the understanding coming between the words of the text. As in the subtle connections achieved by radical metaphor, the language of the poem descends, so to say, into the profundity of its own implications. In poetic "logic," it is language which descends *ad inferos,* into the text's interiority, into its underworld. Nor are Ueda and Pilgrim the only philosophers who are sensitive to this poetic mode of knowing and being.

In his presidential address for the sixth conference of the International Association of Buddhist Studies in 1983, Gadjin M.

Nagao spoke on the theme "ascent and descent." To anyone who may have thought that emphasis on descent or on underworld is somewhat perverse or nihilistic, Nagao's clear-headed common sense concerning human meaning will come as a surprise. It is ascensionalism in religion, rather than descensionalism, which is nihilistic, according to Nagao.

> The ascent [he explains] implies a negative movement, because to aspire to something higher implies a negation of the present state of existence in anticipation of a higher one in the future. Ascent is always nihilistic in character—through self-negating practice, a practitioner finally reaches the summit of negation, which [in Buddhism] may be called sūnyatā, "negated-ness," or "zero-ness." Descent, on the other hand, naturally implies an affirmative movement,[13]

since it moves, as in the ideal of compassion in Buddhism, "down" and "into" life and its sufferings lovingly. Though Nagao's "logic" is religious rather than poetic, the human insight is nonetheless like that of the poetry we have invoked.

Nor is a philosophical "logic" of the *descensus* limited to Oriental examples. Heidegger was mentioned at the beginning of this chapter, but three more-recent examples are also to the point. It may be too much to argue that Julia Kristeva has faith in "abjection," but her book *Powers of Horror* focuses on the cruciality of the descent modality in poetry, psychoanalysis, and feminism. Like the poets, she, too, identifies the postmodern "descent" into abjection as a descent into language. She calls this a "descent into naming," where the semiotics of a discourse provides what we have called inferences, but no "signifiable identities."[14] The function of such abjection is, in part, the humbling of egoic certainty, which was the theme of the last chapter.

In the Introduction, the work of David Krell was mentioned. Although his sources are thoroughly Occidental (Nietzsche and Heidegger) rather than Buddhist, the conclusions of his important essay "Descensional Reflection" accord completely with Nagao and stress linguisticality in the same way Kristeva does. "Ascensional reflection (which constitutes most of Western philosophy) is a matter of dying ahead of time," writes Krell, whereas descensional thinking "climbs back down into the nearness of the nearest."[15] It is the embrace of this "nearness" of things which a third philosopher, Alphonso Lingis, is monitoring in his remarkable book *Excesses.* Like the others, he refers to moving close to life as a "descent," a descent in which the eye, detached from its grasping, possessive style, becomes curious and voluptuous, caressing experience and being caressed by that which it sees, as if seeking the invisible. "The invisible that the eroticized eye seeks," says Lingis, "is no longer the substances, the principles, the causes of the alien; it is the alien look ... the look of the other."[16] Just here, in the eye, the perspective, eroticized and given feeling by the interior descent, by descensional reflection, is the locus of what Charles Winquist calls "epiphanies of darkness."[17]

So, the poet Theodore Roethke writes, "The dark showed me a face," and, "In a dark time, the eye begins to see."[18] The eye begins to see poetically, metaphorically, inferentially under the conditions of the *descensus ad inferos,* the descent into the interiority of the resonances of the language of its own poetizing. Wallace Stevens called this poetic self, which gives itself up to the language (Kristeva's "descent into the hell of naming"), a self "which night illumines, / Night and its midnight-minting fragrances." In this, the poetic self speaks from "below the tension of the lyre."[19] The testimony of Denise Levertov is the same when she calls poetry the "mind in the / act of plucking / truth from the dark surrounding nowhere."[20] In a poem about a lagoon, Levertov speaks of the water, in which

> long lines of beveled darkness
> draw the mind
> down to its own depths
> where the imagination swims,
> shining dark-scaled fish,

> swims and waits, flashes, waits and
> wavers, shining of its own light.[21]

The shine of the darkness in human life and meaning has been a traditional, if unpopular and neglected, theme of Western Christian mysticism, in which poetic "logic" never left theology. Nikolai Berdyaev describes Jakob Böhme's version of the superluminosity that is experienced in the "dark night of the soul." "Apophatically and by way of antinomy," writes Berdyaev, Böhme "describes the mystery which comes to pass within that depth of being which makes contact with the original nothingness. Fire flames up in the darkness. ... Nothingness is deeper down and more original than light."[22] And then Berdyaev quotes Böhme: "The ground of the tincture [an alchemical term analogous to our word 'inference'] is the wisdom of God; and the ground of the wisdom of God is the Trinity of the ungrounded divinity; and the ground of the Trinity is the will; and the ground of the will is nothing [*das Nichts*]."[23]

This fundamental "negative theology" (as opposed to a nihilistic fundamentalist theology) can be found also in Dionysius the Areopagite, Meister Eckhart, Nicholas of Cusa, and many others, but it is perhaps best known in John of the Cross. John is commenting theologically on the experience of the *descensus ad inferos* (which he calls the "dark night of the soul") in relation to a story in Exodus 14:19-20. In the biblical tale the Hebrew people were, according to the text, led through the night by a cloud which was itself dark. John says:

> How wonderful it was—a cloud dark in itself, could illumine the night! This is told to illustrate how faith, which is a dark and obscure cloud to people ..., illumines and pours light into the darkness of the soul by means of its own darkness. ... A person in darkness does not receive adequate enlightenment save by another darkness, according to David's teaching: ... "The day brims over and breathes speech to the day, and the night manifests knowledge to the night."[24]

So, John concludes that "since faith is a dark night, it illumines the soul that is in darkness."[25] To this end, he cites another psalm (139:12) to the effect that "night will be itself an illumination."

Others testify in the same manner. For example, there is this in a sermon of Meister Eckhart's:

> The light shines in the darkness and there a person becomes aware of it. . . . It is when people are in the dark, or suffering, that they are to see the light. Truth is that the more ourselves we are, the less [ego-] self is in us.[26]

These texts by John of the Cross and Eckhart are alluding to an idea based in traditional religious psychology, an idea which goes by the name "superluminous darkness." Bonaventure quotes Dionysius the Areopagite concerning this notion, saying that the "superluminous and most sublime summit of mystical eloquence, where new and absolute and unchangeable mysteries of theology are deeply hidden," is in "the superluminous darkness of instructive silence—darkness which is supermanifest and superresplendent, and in which all is aglow, pouring out upon the invisible intellect the splendors of invisible goodness."[27]

It is not that the *descensus* will feel good to the ego, nor that pain and suffering will be absent, nor that eternal torment of historical existence will end. The contrary is the case: no darkness, no light. But what poets and mystics and philosophers are inviting us to notice is that in fact a certain sheen or shine, an "epiphany," accompanies the darkness, as for example Goya managed to imagine and show dramatically in the use of black colors in his paintings. Nor is Goya idiosyncratic. John Updike has celebrated the chiaroscuro of other more recent artists in a poem called, "Gradations of Black (Third Floor, Whitney Museum)."[28] In the poem, Updike tells that "Ad Reinhardt's black" leads "the eye into / that darkness where, self-awakened ... we come to see that the corners of his square / black canvas are squares ..., slightly brown." It is Frank Stella's "dark gray, upon black ground" that is "lustrous and granular, like the shiny hide / of some hairless, geometrical reptile." "The black of Mark Rothko's

'Four Darks in Red,'" Updike goes on, "holds grief," but also "small lakes of sheen." While Franz Kline's "'Mahoning' ... lets leak through the dead white underneath."[29]

The light is *in* the darkness. It does not save us *from* the darkness. Such is the testimony of this circle, in which poetry reflects painting, which reflects religious experience, which is reflected in negative theology and philosophy, which is reflected in poetry—a round of inferences, concerning which, as Eric Voegelin once said, "The light that falls on the way does not come from an external source, but is the growing luminosity of the depth."[30] The poet Stevens calls this, making the jungle shine "as brilliant as a mystic ... the black sublime."[31] For Stevens—who also penned the phrase "chromatics in hilarious dark"[32]—"the true creator" is not the person of the poet, but "the shine / of darkness, creating from nothingness / such black constructions,"[33] a view of poetry echoed in these lines from a poem by Stanley Hopper entitled, "The Philosophy of No":

> It was an odd decease
>   like silence
>   underneath its wounds
> seeking darkness
>   where a healing
>   and the light
> might shine.[34]

This paradoxical, if no less real, poetic and inferential light of historical darknesses, accounts for the irony of Joseph Conrad's title: *The Heart of Darkness.*

That darkness has a heart, to which mystics and philosophers join poets in acknowledging, is confirmed by the psyche-logic of the last chapter. C. G. Jung, for example, out of his experience as a therapist, wrote:

> Filling the conscious mind with ideal conceptions is a characteristic feature of Western theosophy, but not the confrontation with the shadow and the world of darkness. One does not become enlightened by imagining figures

of light, but by making the darkness conscious. The latter procedure, however, is disagreeable and therefore not popular.[35]

Jung was speaking of the experience of a particular patient when he wrote that,

> by accepting the darkness, the patient has not, to be sure, changed it into light, but she has kindled a light that illuminates the darkness within. By day no light is needed, and if you don't know it is night you won't light one, nor will any light be lit for you unless you have suffered the horror of darkness. This is not [Jung insists] an edifying text but a mere statement of the psychological facts.[36]

The human facts are, to use Jung's words again, that "light from above makes the darkness still darker, but the light from within the darkness turns blackness bright."[37] This is surely known to anyone who, in deep grief, has experienced another person trying to be cheery!

It was known also, experientially and theoretically, to Freud, as well as to Jung. Norman O. Brown's aphoristic conclusion about Freud's therapeutic perspective resonates with theology's abominable fancy: "Go down and stay down, in the forbidden zone, a descent into hell."[38] Then Brown quotes Freud directly [from *History of the Psychoanalytic Movement*]:

> I can only conclude with the wish that fate may grant an easy ascension to those whose sojourn in the underworld of psychoanalysis has become uncomfortable. May it be vouchsafed to others to bring to happy conclusion their work in the depth.[39]

To which Brown adds, inferentially, and not without poetry:

> The revolution is from below, the lower classes, the underworld, the damned, the disreputable, the despised and rejected. Freud's revolutionary motto in *The Interpretation of Dreams*: ... "If I cannot bend the higher powers, I will stir up the lower depths." Freud's

> discovery: the universal underworld. Darkness at noon. A
> progressive darkening of the everyday world of common
> sense. *Finnegans Wake.* Second sight is the dark night.
> Night gives light unto night; the double dark, or negation
> of the negation. *Admirable cosa es que, siendo
> tenebrosa, alumbrase la noche.*[40]

(This last quotation, in Spanish, comprises the same lines we have
already quoted from John of the Cross.)

So, Freud and Jung concur. The *descensus ad inferos* of religion
and mythology, the metaphors of poets and mystics which tell of the
superluminous bliss of hell, even though they be difficult for at least
one aspect of the self to accept and embrace, are nonetheless purely
and straightforwardly the way it is in a person's history, if one could
allow oneself to see the chiaroscuro. Octavio Paz has struck the image
which tells that the "abominable fancy" is our reality. Paz' poetic line
is, "The black fruit bursts / in the flesh-colored blossoms."[41]

CHAPTER EIGHT

History As Hell

The *descensus ad inferos* is crucial for soul, whether ego likes it or not. It is *via crucis,* a "way of ego crucifixion," a sacrifice of ego's perspectives, its opinions, historical literalisms and fundamentalisms.[1] Such crucifixion is crucial in order that a person may have a way to imagine his or her history, for such experiences bring with them a "treasure house" and a "womb" full of imagination. The descent into whatever hells becomes an initiation in life, a "baptism" by burning and drowning in life (fire and water), a confrontation with "dragons" and "serpents" and other animality, an experience of "rumbling belly" and "gnashing teeth," of "swinging doors" and "clashing rocks," of "warring" and a "shaking of the foundations." Hell gives underworldly (deep) imagination to our histories. It provides our "is" with "as," telling us what life is like, offering ways to imagine the here and now, as well as how to go on.

So, in spite of what we may say in our anguished moments, history is not hell. Hell is far deeper, "blacker" than what white ego imagines black to be. But, though history is *not* hell, history may be viewed from the perspective of what shines forth ("epiphanizes") in the variety of our descents. This is the way that the hell of the descent illuminates the darkness. Or rather, it is a way to understand how the darkness itself provides a deepened perspective on life. Lacking the poetry, the as-structures, the images and imaginings of the underworld, one takes one's torments literally and personally, being thereby *merely* down, with no way to sense soul's ascendancy in the moment. This is different from being *really* "down," with a sense of the mystery in which so-called down is up and in which making one's torments conscious can give—strange to say—a dark comedic sense, a black sublime, a superluminous chiaroscuro.

The descent into the mystery of the article of the Christian creed, *descendit Christi ad inferos*, is not alone in sensing the cruciality and mystery of the inferential "as." The Eleusinian Mysteries in ancient Greece make the same affirmation in the images of their mythology. These ancient mysteries had to do with the depression experienced by the goddess Demeter when she lost her beloved daughter, Persephone, to the underworld of Hades. Apollodorus says that Demeter sat "agelastos petra," "not laughing, petrified, sitting on a rock."[2] Kerényi tells what happened to the goddess in her depression. "While sitting on that rock, Iambe came to her. The role of this hearty serving maid was to make Demeter laugh by jests and mockery, to turn her grief to tenderness. This she succeeded in doing," says Kerényi, "by means of obscene gestures, which the Homeric poet's style forbids him to describe."[3]

But where the Homeric tradition is reticent in the face of the mystery of the laughter in darkness (what Stevens called "chromatics of hilarious dark"), the Orphic tradition is bold. A fragment in the *Orphica* tells that Baubo, which is Iambe's other name, sits in front of the goddess with her legs wide apart, and she lifts her skirt, revealing her womb. *Mirabile dictu!*—there was in Baubo's womb the child Iakchos, whom some call Dionysos, laughing![4] Demeter's descent into darkness, which is prompted by her daughter's descent into the underworld, is transformed by sensual physicality into laughter.

Baubo's name means "belly," we are told by Kerényi,[5] which implies that her dance is a "belly dance." Her sensuality is, like Jonah's and Christ's, in the "belly." Baubo's other name, Iambe, means "foot," like the *iambs* of poetry, being the rhythm or meter of poetry, its "logic." Poetry's rhythm—its "logic"—may be thought

90

of as a third foot (recalling Origen's account of Christ's sandals); it is the "as" between history and hell, a way of "dancing in the dark."

So it was in ancient Greek ritual that the worshipers passed under a bridge as they processed from Athens to Eleusis in celebration of the mystery. Kerényi says that on a bridge under which the procession marched, there was a hetaera, a courtesan or prostitute, who greeted the worshipers with *gephyrismoi* ("bridge jests").[6] She was playing the role of Iambe or Baubo, and her function for the worshiper, like the function of her mythological counterpart for Demeter, was to relieve the seriousness, the literalism, of the religious practice. Baubo's humor breaks the fixation and idolatry, the ego identification and the personalizing, and it opens the possibility of embracing the descent.

Indeed, the various descents we have been tracing—the descent into theology and its ideas, the descent into mythology and its images and stories, the descent into poetry and its metaphoric way of seeing, the descent into literary theory and its drama, the descent into psychopathology and its complexes, and the descent into negative theology and its mystical understanding—all these are somehow, in the end, a descent into laughter ... not human laughter, but Baubo's laughter, the *divina comoedia* of the soul, which comes from the "belly," *ad inferos,* from the interior depths of meaning.

Such a "laughter" is in our descents. It is not a personal laughter to be enjoyed by ego, but a much darker laughter, mocking ego's identifications, inflations, and idolatries. This "laughter" is near when a woman or a man cries out in anguish, "My life is hell!" It is a laughter made possible by the "as" of the "is,"[7] the mystery of imagination in the profound metaphors of everyday life. The creed, indeed, tells it *as* it is.

PART THREE

Holy Ghosts

CHAPTER NINE

The Death of Ghosts

If—as we have seen in parts 1 and 2—there is mystery and paradox in that article of the Christian creed having to do with "descent," so equally is there irony and uncanniness implied in the article which affirms belief in the Holy Ghost. To be sure, ghosts are already uncanny. That is, the notion of the continuing powerful presence of some person or some event that one had assumed to be dead and gone is odd. But a further irony is implied if this notion were itself to "die" in the collective consciousness without its function failing. Then we would be in a position of being ghosted by our notion of ghosts, exorcized of the notion of ghosts but not of the need for exorcism. The awkwardness of the irony of the death of ghosts can perhaps be made concrete by way of two anecdotes.

The first story involves a conversation that took place during the present century, though both conversation-partners are now dead. The setting was the garden outside a villa, Casa Gabriella, overlooking Lake Maggiore in Southern Switzerland. The garden is still the site, as it was at the time of the conversation, for the gathering around a large round table of the speakers and guests of the Eranos Conferences, which have been held each year since 1933 during the last two weeks of August.

On one such occasion, the psychologist C. G. Jung and the historian of religions Henry Corbin were looking at a picture album that contained photographs from earlier conferences. They came upon one picture which stood out from the rest. In it there were no persons, only the round table, with sixteen empty chairs, a folded cloth and flowers on it, the great garden-tree at the edge, with the lake and the southern Swiss mountains in the background. A beautiful photograph, but somehow fearsome in its ability to recall all of the now-deceased scholars who had come together from all over the world to wrestle with ideas in troubled times. Jung turned to Corbin and said, *"L'image est parfaite. Ils sont tous là"* (The picture is perfect. They are all there.)[1] The figures are all present, and more uncannily so by virtue of their absence. In this case, the ghosts are hardly dead. But, the second anecdote has a different implication.

During the fortnight following All Souls' Day, in 1880, Matthew Arnold was moved to verse. This was a bit unusual for the poet, as he himself hints in the poem, saying, "There rise these lines of verse / On lips that rarely form them now."[2] Arnold is referring to the fact that he had not published a collection of poems in thirteen years. What had caused him to pick up his pen once again? The poem's title tells the story. It was called "Geist's Grave."

Geist—the word means "mind" or "spirit" or "ghost" in German—had died. Surely the death of "mind" or "spirit" would be proper provocation for an elegy. All the more is this the case since Arnold had passionately preached *Geist* to the British people in earlier works (for example, through the mouth of his fictive Prussian savant, Arminius, in the work, *Friendship's Garland* [1871]). The people, however, were resistant to Arnold's urging, producing thereby a situation for the culturally sensitive poet that could bring forth an elegy, just as certainly as would the proclamation of Nietzsche's madman that "God had died" or the pronouncement of Plutarch's Epitherses that the great god Pan had passed away.[3]

All the more grievous would be the loss of a *Geist* that matched the poet's description—

THE DEATH OF GHOSTS

That liquid, melancholy eye,
From whose pathetic, soul-fed springs
Seemed surging the Virgilian cry,
The sense of tears in mortal things.[4]

The allusion is to Virgil's *Aeneid,* 1.462: *"Sunt lacrimae rerum"* ("They are the tears of things"). The inclusion of this ancient phrase in the modern poem implies that the *Geist* Arnold mourns is one that sees and senses the depth of things, a profound sadness, not opposite to joy, but more like the Japanese sense of the beauty of a falling plum blossom, *mono no aware wo shiru,* "to be aware of the pity of things,"[5] or like Plotinus' sense of the *"anima mundi"* (the soul of the world), which gives *"sympathein allelois"* (a sympathy with all things).[6] It would, indeed, be cause for grief if this sense had gone, for this sense gives depth to life with death.

This much we have already argued earlier. But the irony enters, not so much in what Jung or Arnold says, as in that which they leave unsaid precisely in their sayings.

Jung's saying says that the image of absence carries a sense of real presence, that the ghosts of the Eranos circle are what give to present experience a motive-power. But the irony that may be implied, if not spoken, in such an observation is that what we may have thought of as "real" presences, the personalities imagined to be truly in the here and now, may in fact be in some sense absent. If the ghosts are the reality, then may not we historical persons be somehow and in some way ghostly precisely when we are present? The irony of the unsaid reflects on us as much as it does on those who we may have thought are not present.

There is a reversal (at least of mood), also, in the irony of what is unspoken in Arnold's poem. What the verse fails to tell us directly is that, in Arnold's case, "Geist" refers to a dog, to the pet dachshund owned by Arnold's son, Richard. This is hinted at only in the last line of the poem, which reads, "The dachshound, Geist, their little friend."[7] The "ghost" has died, to be sure. But it was just a little dog anyway!

97

So what is the point of the two anecdotes? Especially, what do they have to do with religious concern, in general, and with the Christian belief in the Holy Ghost, in particular?

To be sure, many in our time have complained about the death of "mind" and of "rationality" (*Geist, esprit*). Many, too, have expressed remorse concerning the demise of "spirit" (*Geist, esprit*). This twin regret should surely be enough to trouble postmodern men and women. But it is the passing of a third factor (if indeed it actually be a "third" different from "mind" and "spirit") which might properly trouble theology. I am speaking of "ghost" (*Geist, esprit*), a term in English which has been removed from serious theological vocabularies and, especially in the United States, relegated to realms of superstition and of children merely playing at Halloween. Does this imply that in postmodernity men and women no longer acknowledge the powerful sense of the presence of absent ones (as Jung did)? Does it mean that religion is no longer concerned about the death of the "ghost" (as was Arnold)? Indeed, could it be that if we lose the sense of "ghost," we lose our "mind" and "spirit" as well?—not to mention the religious sense of the uncanny and its accompanying irony, factors which could lend a bit of humility to existence.

The modern philosopher Gilbert Ryle published a book in 1949 called *The Concept of Mind.* In it he spoke of the "mind," as he himself said, "with deliberate abusiveness," calling it a "ghost in the machine." If Ryle's rhetoric is radical, his sentiment is nonetheless, I fear, not uncommon. He announced that the "concept of mind" is a superstition, and he denounced the notion of spiritual or nonmaterial "body," characterizing it by using the English word "ghost," as if everyone in our time would clearly recognize from associations with this term that "the concept of mind" belongs properly to the wastebasket of history's delusions. Arthur Koestler, commenting on Ryle's book, worried, however, that "by the very act of denying the existence of the ghost in the machine ... we incur the risk of turning it into a very nasty, malevolent ghost."[8]

98

THE DEATH OF GHOSTS

There are, of course, a great many theological matters of a philosophical and historical nature lurking in Koestler's worry about Ryle's dead ghost. Some of these have to do with whether or not there is actually such a "thing" as "mind," "spirit," and "ghost," and what the actual history of the idea of "mind," "spirit," and "ghost" has meant in its different permutations. The concern of this book is different. Here it is more a psychological or existential, rather than a philosophical or historical, matter that is at stake. What does it actually matter for a person or for a people to experience the death of the ghostly?

For example, in the English-speaking Christian tradition, after the phrase "Holy Ghost" was insisted on, perhaps wrongly, as in the translation for *to pneuma to hagion* (Luther's *der Heilige Geist*), why did there come a time, our time, when every effort is made to repress the very terminology earlier urged? Paul Tillich's admonition is typical: "The term 'Holy Ghost' must be purged from every liturgical or other use."[9] Strong words! What do they mean? And what does it matter?

However linguistically inapt the translation may have been in the King James Bible, could it *now* be—the anecdotes about Jung and Arnold prompt one to wonder—that when the term "ghost" is resisted, some deep human truth is being defended against in the name of rationality, a curious defeat of religious signification precisely by modern theology? This is the matter for exploration here in part 3.

The exploration will take the form of a sort of detective story in the chapters that follow, a search for an uncanny corpse, not for a person who has been murdered, not for a ghost, but for "the ghost of the ghost."[10] As is true in any detective story, there are some clues. But like those in most detective stories, the clues are scattered and may at first seem unconnected to the object of the search and to one another. It is not easy to find a ghost, let alone the ghost of a ghost; and, as Sherlock Holmes and Socrates have shown, in detective-work every clue needs to be followed until some picture emerges.

In this particular case, there are three clues. The first is linguistic, having to do with the meaning carried by linguistic associations surrounding the term "ghost" itself (chapter 10). The second is historical, having to do with British traditions at the time of the Reformation, the time of the appearance of the King James Version of the Bible (chapter 11). The third clue is folkloristic, having to do with a very ancient motif from myth and fairy tale, a motif which has in these latter days been appropriated somewhat unconsciously by a rock music group (chapter 12).

CHAPTER TEN

Ghastly, Guest, Host:
The Ghosts in Language

Young's Analytical Concordance of the Authorized Version (1611) of the Bible lists eighty-eight occurrences of the phrase "Holy Ghost" as the rendering of the Greek *hagion pneuma*.[1] It also gives nineteen other typical uses of the English term "ghost" by King James' translators where the Hebrew terms are *nephesh* and *gava,* and where the Greek terms are *pneuma, ekpneō,* and *ekpsychō* (these last two words being translated with the English phrase "give up the ghost").[2] But usage shifted considerably between the seventeenth century and our own.

According to an exhaustive concordance of the Revised Standard Version of the Bible (the New Testament of the RSV completed in 1946; the Old Testament in 1952), there are only three instances of the word "ghost" in the entire Bible, and none refers to God, the Holy Ghost.[3] One of the uses of "ghost" is in the prophecy of Isaiah (29:4), where the destruction of the city of David is proclaimed, and the people are told that their voice "shall come from the ground like the voice of a ghost." The other two uses, in Matthew 14:26 and in Mark 6:49, both chronicle the story of Jesus' walking on the water of the sea. The disciples are terrified by what they see, and they cry out in fear, saying, "It is a ghost!" It would seem that biblical translators in our time, like the disciples in their own time, have sufficient reticence about ghosts to warrant their following the admonition of Paul Tillich to avoid the use of the term.

101

To be sure, Tillich gave good reason for his strong view. In the third volume of his *Systematic Theology*, he noted that "the word 'spirit' ... raises an important problem of terminology. The Stoic term for spirit is *pneuma,* and the Latin, *spiritus,* with its derivations in modern languages—in German it is *Geist,* in Hebrew *ru'ach.* " Then Tillich noted that "there is no semantic problem in these languages, but there is one in English because of misuse of the word 'spirit' with a small 's'."[4]

Tillich is thinking of a particular misuse, one he explains in the following way:

> If spirit is a dimension of life, one can certainly speak of living beings in which this dimension is actualized, and one can call them beings with spirit. But it is extremely misleading to call them "spirits," because this implies the existence of a "spirit" realm apart from life. Spirit becomes somewhat like inorganic matter and loses its character as a dimension of life which is potentially or actually present in all life. It assumes a "ghostly" character. This is confirmed by the so-called spiritualistic ... movements which try to make contact with the "spirits" or "ghosts" of the deceased and to provoke physical effects from them (noises, words, physical movements, visual appearances). ... Just like the question of extra-sensory perception, it is a matter of empirical investigations the results of which, whether positive or negative, have no direct bearing on the problem of human spirit or God as Spirit.[5]

Tillich is suggesting theologically that the use of the word "ghost" to translate *pneuma* or *spiritus* or *Geist* unwittingly leads one to think of "spirit" literalistically rather than, as Paul urged, "interpreting spiritual truths in spiritual [i.e., nonliteral] language."[6]

The philological and semantic oddness of the translation of *hagion pneuma* with the phrase "Holy Ghost" is immediately apparent when one performs the linguistic experiment of translating backward English to other languages. "Holy Ghost" could be rendered in

German, *das Heilige Gespenst,* or in French, *le Saint Fantôme* or *Spectre,* or in Latin, *Sanctum Phantasma* or *Sancta Umbra,* or in Greek, *to eidōlon to hagion.* These would in fact mean "Holy Shade," "Holy Shadow," or even "Holy Idol"! Impossible!

But the translators of the Authorized Version (King James) were not ignorant persons. They knew the linguistic facts reviewed here. So one may wonder why they persisted in this apparent folly. Did they have intuition that transcended semantic reason? Perhaps a closer examination of the term "ghost" can lend some sort of sense to their error.

The word *ghost* and its cognate forms *(gást, gáest, gast, goste, goist, ghoste, ghoost, ghoast, ghest, ghaist)* are common in West Germanic and Anglo-Saxon, hence Old English, in the form of *gást* and *gáest.* The strong mode is equivalent to the Old Frisian *gást* and to the Old Saxon *gēst* as well as to the Dutch *geest* and the Old High German *geist.* The existence of this family has caused philologists to infer an Old Teutonic type, *gaisto-z.*

The meaning of a pre-Teutonic root, *ghoidzo-z,* also inferred, should be "fury" or "anger," if the conventional etymological research is accurate. This would mean that the modern English word *ghost* is ultimately related to the Sanskrit *hēdas,* meaning "anger," and to the Zend term *zōizda,* meaning "ugly." The root, *gheis-* or *ghois-,* appears in Old Norse as *geisa,* meaning "to rage," and in Gothic as *usgaisjan,* meaning "to terrify." Outside Teutonic the derivatives point to a primary meaning of "to wound," "to tear," and "to pull to pieces." No wonder there is religious reticence in our time concerning the word *ghost*! It carries a most numinous complex of meaning in its history.

In fact, the history of the term in English is relatively simple. The Old English form, *gáest,* appears commonly in The Exeter Book (*Codex Exoniensis*) in the late eleventh century. Before this, however, the word was used forty-nine times in the Hatton manuscript and three times in the Bodl manuscript of Aelfred's translation of Gregory's work, *Pastoral Care.* This would be in the late ninth century.

The spelling of the term with *gh-* is rare, and it may come from Flemish influence (*ghaest*). This spelling does not seem to exist until the middle of the sixteenth century, and according to the *Oxford English Dictionary,* whose lineage I have been following here, the form we now have was not finally established until about 1590.[7] This means that the word was new, or at least had a new form (just twenty-one years old), at the time the translators authorized by King James used it in their Bible.

Eight of the meanings of the word *ghost* listed in the *OED* are, for the most part, just what one today would suppose: (1) soul or principle of life, (2) the equivalent of the Latin *spiritus* when the sense is "breath" or "wind," (3) the spiritual dimension of a person as opposed to the bodily aspect, (4) a local ghost comparable to the Latin *genius loci,* or (5) the soul of one deceased appearing visibly to the living.

But two meanings, once important, are now obsolete. (6) The word *ghost* could be used, as indeed Spenser did use it in *The Faerie Queene* (1590), simply to mean a person, much as today one might refer to someone as "a fine spirit" or "one of the souls of the community." Spenser's line is, "No knight so rude, I weene, As to doen outrage to a sleeping ghost" (2.8.26). This means: No knight would be so unmannerly as to do violence to any person when she or he was not awake. The sense here is that we are all "ghosts," here and now, while alive. (7) A second traditional use that is now odd to modern ears suggests that a "ghost" is any person who is dead and dwells in the unseen world, not only such a one who appears in this world. So in the *Cursor Mundi* (c. 1300), one may read, "His body here, his ghost was there; his godhead wanted nobler quarters" (1. 18603, modernized spellings). This meaning suggests that we are all of us "ghosts," not only while alive, but also after death. Ghosts eternal!

That the Eternal One is also a "ghost," in traditional usage, is also implied by etymological study, even if that implication also begins to fade from modern use. (8) The *OED* tells that the word *ghost* was "formerly used in the sense of Spirit (of God)"—now only in liturgical and dogmatic language as reference to "the Third Person of the Trinity."[8] For example, in the *York Mystery Plays* (c. 1440) there occurs this line: "He shall give baptism [of God] entire in fire and ghost" (21.14, modernized spellings). Imagine! Baptism not only in water but also in ghost. George MacDonald's "Sonnet Concerning Jesus" (1871) supplies yet another striking example: "'Tis man himself, the temple of thy Ghost." The "ghost" within a human person is the Divinity within! And the interior "ghost" is, as the clues from language have here indicated, something which is "ugly," which "terrifies," "alarms," "wounds," and "tortures." Thus, the English word "ghastly" and the term "ghost" are one in sense—which makes even more strange the inclination of the translators who coined the phrase "Holy Ghost."

But we are by no means at the end of this odd story. Old English (Anglo-Saxon) had another use for *gáest*. It was not only the equivalent of the Germanic *geist,* but also the transformation of *giest* (Old High German *gast).* The West Aryan background lay in the term *ghosti-s,* which apparently was a rendering of the Latin *hostis,* meaning "stranger" and, in classical usage, "enemy." Of course, in modern English, this Latin root, by way of Anglo-Saxon transformation, became the word "guest," meaning "one who is entertained," a "stranger," or a "parasite."[9]

There is something strange about this history, an uncanniness to which J. Hillis Miller has already pointed and to which Sigmund Freud alerted his readers when he observed, in studying the terms *heimlich* and *unheimlich,* what he called the "antithetical sense of primal words."[10] The same Latin root (the root of *hostis, hospitem, hospes),* which in Northern Europe takes on the sense of "guest," in Southern European linguistic families takes on the meaning "host," and even sometimes carries the double meaning "host" and "guest" at the same time, as in the case of Old French *oste* and *hoste,* and in the modern French *hôte.*[11]

J. Hillis Miller summarizes the uncanny sense of meaning carried in this language. He writes that

a host is a guest, and a guest is a host. ... A host in the
sense of a guest, moreover, is both a friendly visitor in
the house and at the same time an alien presence who turns
the home into a hotel, a neutral territory. Perhaps the
guest is the first emissary of a host of enemies ... , the
first in the door, followed by a swarm of hostile strangers,
to be met by our own host, as the Christian deity is the
Lord God of Hosts.[12]

But there is yet even more that is strange in the language which
gives shape to our present sense of meaning, albeit in most instances
unconsciously. The Anglo-Saxon *gáest* is parent, as we have seen, to
the words "ghost" and "ghostly," as well as to the words "host" and
"guest." Could it be that when King James' translators rendered *der
Heilige Geist* and *to pneuma to hagion* with the English phrase "Holy
Ghost," they were, wittingly or unwittingly, implying an intimacy of
meanings, a complex of theological sense, in whose perspective God
is Guest as well as Host when God is a Ghost? That is, God is God
when being a Ghost, and God is Ghost when being Ghastly, the
Ghastly Anger which haunts, being at the same time the Host of the
human and its strange Guest—wounded and torn, shade and shadow,
present when absent, in life and death, forever. The Divine Host is
Ghost which is at the same time Ghastly Guest. Is this odd sense that
which is implied by an improper translation, one which is somehow
correct just the same? Can it be that "ghost" and "spirit," "ghost" and
"host" in fact do belong together in the fantasia of the eternal
mystery sustained by the word?—the Lord of Hosts a Ghost; the
Ghost our Host!

The answer to these idle speculations is a simple no. At least the
answer is negative and such word games are foolishness, if one is
inquiring rationalistically and intellectualistically from a philological
and semantic point of view. From such a perspective the words "ghost"
and "ghastly" belong to one family of terms (Teutonic) and "guest"
and "host" belong to quite another (Latinate). There is no linguistic
connection, historically speaking, and it is therefore quite "accidental"

106

that the same-sounding word is used in Anglo-Saxon terminology to name each of these differing families of words. From this perspective also, the translators of the Authorized Version of the Bible simply made a mistake, as Tillich has correctly observed.

But *meaning,* a deeply human sense of signification, is not always so direct and simple as reason's sort of reasoning. The saying of Martin Heidegger is to the deeper point:

> It is not we who play with words, but the nature of language plays with us. ... For language plays with our speech—it likes to let our speech drift away into the more obvious meanings of words. It is as though a person had to make an effort to live properly with language. It is as though such a dwelling were especially prone to succumb to the danger of commonness. ... This floundering in commonness is part of the high and dangerous game and gamble in which, by the nature of language, we are the stakes. Is it playing with words when we attempt to give heed to this game of language and to hear what language really says when it speaks? If we succeed in hearing that, then it may happen—provided we proceed carefully—that we get more truly to the matter that is expressed in any telling and asking.[13]

Heidegger is pointing to the possibility that some dimensions of meaning in language are carried autonomously by the language itself, apart from the conscious uses to which mortals put the words for purposes of communication. Thus, in spite of whatever historical human facts, there may yet be some further "reason" for the connection in sound between "ghost," "ghastly," "guest," and "host."

Paul Kugler has written a most remarkable book, which can perhaps assist with this "deeper reason." In *The Alchemy of Discourse,* Kugler has brought together the empirical researches of C. G. Jung's word-association experiments and twentieth-century postmodern studies of linguistics, giving a needed psychological depth to the philosophy and philology of language, and, at the same time, giving a linguistic and philosophical sophistication to the language of psychologists, who may otherwise remain naively naturalistic and positivistic about their terminologies of so-called depth.[14] What Kugler explains will help in understanding why Heidegger used the words, "if we succeed in *hearing*" (italics added), when he was speaking about the autonomous play of meaning in language.

Jung—as Kugler notes—discovered that apparently "faulty" associations (that is, responses made by patients to stimulus-words where the responses conflicted with the semantic "meaning" of the word) were of great psychological value, because they gave an understanding of the unconscious fantasies disturbing the patient. "Mistakes," Jung found, not unlike Freud, were not mistakes at all. At least, they were not mistakes from the perspective of hidden psychological meaning.

Jung also observed, in case after case, that when the response, so crucial to therapy, was illogical, it had a "logic" nonetheless. But, as Jung already noted, the "logic" was contained in phonetic rather than semantic associations. So Jung wrote, "It can ... be said that the more the attention of the patient decreases, the more the external and sound associations increase."[15] This observation led Jung to conclude that "subconscious association process takes place through *similarities of image and sound.*"[16]

Kugler summarizes Jung's findings by noting that they "suggest a fundamental law of imagination," namely, "that its mode of operation is sonorous, acoustic, and phonetic."[17] The contribution to psycholinguistic theory is clear: (1) the meanings of human speech are dominated by autonomous complexes of associations at whose core is a fundamental image; and (2) the process of associations in these complexes is directed, at least sometimes and in part, by phonetic consideration as much as or perhaps more than, by semantic connections.[18] As Kugler says, "Through words our fantasies move from image to sound."[19]

Jung identified "meaning" with traditional semantic understandings, and so he was forced to see an inverse ratio between "meaning" and the psychologically important sound-associations his patients experienced. Kugler, however, has more recent linguistic theory available to him than did Jung. He is therefore able to see the meaning precisely in the sound-association, a perspective already implied by, but never made explicit in, Jung's work.

So Kugler can conclude:

> On a deep [unconscious] level there is a meaning-relation between phonetically associated words; however, the connection is not via the literal lexical meaning, or syntactic relations, or common origin, but through the underlying archetypal image. The relation between phonetic associations is imagistic, not lexical, syntactic, or etymological. They are affiliated by a complex which is an acoustic image.[20]

The important contribution of Kugler may be just to the point of "success in *hearing*" (Heidegger) the autonomous play of meaning in the complex of the words "ghost" and "ghastly" and "guest" and "host." In spite of a lack of historical semantic connection between the Northern and Southern European lineages of this family of words, the phonetic and acoustic connection can be heard by everyone, even if that person knows no English.

So—in this detective quest for "the ghost of the ghost"—we once again ask: Can it be that there is a depth-theological significance, however unwitting, to the King James translation, which shades and nuances the meaning of God the Ghost?—an archetypal religious truth hidden in an "error"?—and that in some profound sense the Host is Ghost and the Ghost is Host?

The idea is speculative, to be sure. But we are only at the beginning of our story of detection. This is only a first clue. Indeed, Kugler warns his readers that "not all phonetic associations are archetypal, any more than all fantasies are archetypal."[21] The test of the speculation would be to discover whether or not there is an underlying archetypal image in the God-Ghost-Ghastly-Guest-Host acoustic complex.

A second clue in this detective quest for the ghost of the Holy Ghost may perhaps begin to give a bit of credence to the linguistic speculation and, in fact, lead somewhat nearer a more complete picture of so-called mistaken translation of *to hagion to pneuma.* We shall next pursue this second clue, a historical one.

CHAPTER ELEVEN

The Ghost of Old Mrs. Leakey:
The Ghosts of History

The historical clue in our quest for "the ghost of a ghost" has to do with a very particular piece of history: namely, the period of the Reformation in Great Britain, a period of a "general devaluation of the numinous," as one scholar, Theo Brown, has termed it.[1] The "incoming Puritanism [of that time] taught a doctrine of other-worldliness that contained only God and the Devil," and, as Brown tells the story, "from this stark, uncompromising, black-and-white cosmos, all intermediate beings were banished."[2] This included the holy virgin, the saints and angels, and—to be sure—the ghosts of Purgatory, who were neither here nor there, but were in between. Indeed, the "Romish Doctrine Concerning Purgatory," as it was called, was repudiated in the 1549 Prayer Book, and is still repudiated in the most recent Book of Common Prayer, being statement number twenty-two in the Thirty-Nine Articles of Religion:

> The Romish Doctrine concerning Purgatory, Pardons, Worshipping and Adoration, as well of Images as of Relics, and also invocation of Saints, is a fond thing, vainly invented, and grounded upon no warranty of Scripture, but rather repugnant to the Word of God.[3]

Thus the world in which restless ghosts dwell was banished in 1549, and yet the same Reformation responsible for its banishment sponsored in 1611 a translation of the Bible in which the Spirit of God was called a Holy Ghost!

It was into this world that Old Mrs. Leakey, as she came to be called, was born, subsequently died (5 November 1634), and finally came back to haunt (according to her daughter-in-law, Elizabeth). The tale and some of its history are well known in the English West Country (Susannah Leakey lived at Minehead, and the story of her haunting was investigated by a commission headed by the Bishop of Bath and Wells); but the account of her ghost, which could whistle up winds to sink the ships of her son, Alexander,[4] is a good deal more important than one more bogus ghost story of the people ... which it also turns out to be. Theo Brown's careful research and interpretation have shown it to have profound theological, not to mention literary and political import. It is Brown's accounts about Mrs. Leakey's ghost that are reported here as a second clue to the mystery story about the Holy Ghost.

The story is as simple as the history is complex. During the reign of Charles I, in the early seventeenth century, Susannah Leakey, a charming widow, lived with her merchant son, Alexander. This latter had a prosperous sea-trade with Waterford in Ireland. Old Mrs. Leakey, so-called to distinguish her from her son's wife, Elizabeth, was a faithful churchgoer and was apparently popular in the community. However, she warned neighbors that if she returned after death, as she might, they would not like her as much as they did in life. This turned out to be indeed the case.

Not many months after her autumn death in 1634, people began to talk about her haunting Alexander and Elizabeth's house. The only person who would testify to having seen the ghost of Old Mrs. Leakey was Elizabeth, the daughter-in-law, and sometimes that apparition was seen only in a mirror. Alexander denied ever seeing the ghost of his mother, yet his ships began to sink, one after another. No sailors' lives were lost, but Alexander's fortunes began to sink like his ships.

It might have all been ignored had not things come to such a pass that the Bishop of Bath and Wells, prompted perhaps by the

Privy Council, set up a small commission. It consisted of himself, Sir Robert Philips of Mantacute (a former head of the House of Commons), and Paul Godwin (a local magistrate). They filed their report with Archbishop Laud on 24 February 1638, and this report may still be consulted at the Public Record Office in London, according to Theo Brown.[5]

Two items prompted the investigation. First, the ghost of Old Mrs. Leakey was said to have strangled her grand-daughter while the latter lay in bed. Second, when Elizabeth asked the apparition what it wanted, Old Mrs. Leakey demanded that young Mrs. Leakey go to Ireland and deliver a message to the Bishop of Waterford. She was to tell him that if he did not repent of his sin, he would be hanged. When the Commission asked Elizabeth what the sin was, she would not reveal it, as she herself said, "to any body but only unto the Kinge, and not unlesse he commands her soe to doe." The Commission apparently was not very impressed by all this, since its conclusion was, "There was never any such Apparition but that it is an Imposture devised and framed for some particular End, but what they are wee know not."[6]

The report of the Commission should have put the matter to rest once and for all. But neither the people nor the scholars could rid themselves of Old Mrs. Leakey's ghost as clerics and judges might have wished. For the history behind the story is not only complex, but also, as Theo Brown has discovered, somewhat gruesome.

There was near anarchy in Ireland during the reign of Charles I, the time just before the Great Rebellion. Government was weak. Crime was rampant. And the church was being impoverished by Roman Catholic gentry, who were misappropriating its resources. The king responded by appointing a man named Wentworth to go to Ireland to remedy the situation. It was Wentworth's success, his strength as Lord Deputy and then Lord Lieutenant, that made him unpopular with many. He was executed in 1641.

One of the charges against Wentworth was that he had appointed a notoriously evil man, John Atherton, to be Bishop of Waterford and Lismore. Atherton was himself hanged six months prior to Wentworth's execution, thus distinguishing himself by being the only Anglican bishop known to have been hanged while holding sacred office.

It seems that Atherton, son of a prebendary of St. Paul's Cathedral in Bawdrip, achieved a fine reputation in canon law at Oxford, where he graduated in 1619. From Oxford he had gone to live at Huish Champflower about 1622, and this is the very place where Old Mrs. Leakey was living at the time. Atherton married one of the Leakeys' two daughters. They in turn had a daughter in 1623 and later another. But the young clergyman was attracted also to his sister-in-law, the other Leakey daughter, Susan. While Atherton was in Huish, she produced an illegitimate child of which he was the suspected father, since he was already a notorious womanizer. In fact, two years after Atherton had been sent to Ireland by Wentworth, the rogue returned to the West Country and made another sister-in-law pregnant, the widow of one of the Leakey sons, a Puritan with the remarkable name of Lordisneare. As Theo Brown tells the terrible tale, "Mrs. Leakey solved the embarrassing problem quite simply. After Atherton had baptised it, she smothered the infant and they concealed the body under the floorboards. The erring daughter was sent over to Wales for a very long holiday."[7] The reforming Bishop of Waterford hardly practiced the reform he preached!

Nor was his sin limited to sex. He was also attracted to money, and the main charge in his trial had to do with embezzlement of church funds he had recovered from others who had embezzled the same money earlier. His sins were many, but, as Brown points out, "If in fact the wretched man had committed half the crimes attributed to him we may well ask how he found the time to eat his meals, let alone carry out the vigorous campaign he did on behalf of the Church and King."[8] For example, it was said that during his short tenure as Bishop he seduced sixty-four women!

114

THE GHOSTS OF HISTORY

All this—and much more that is better forgotten—has led to speculation concerning the motive of young Mrs. Leakey in starting the phony ghost story and her making a futile visit to the Bishop of Waterford. For example, Douglas Stevens of Minehead, who has researched the case thoroughly, believes that she was a pious woman who wanted to urge Atherton to reform, not only others, but himself as well.[9] Brown, on the other hand, thinks that Elizabeth may have seen "the glowing possibility of a little discreet blackmail," the ghost story being a device for drawing attention with a false story of infanticide to a real murder that she was not going to let the Bishop forget.[10]

It is indeed difficult to forget the story of Old Mrs. Leakey's ghost once one has heard it. But it may also be equally difficult to see how it lends credence to the linguistic speculation concerning the word "ghost" as an errant translation, in the years just preceding Mrs. Leakey, for the Spirit of the Lord of Hosts. That these two matters may be linked will have to remain obscure until all our clues are in place and the whole picture begins to become clear on its own. Suffice it for the present moment to note the possibility that the Protestant Reformation may well have unintentionally provoked as many ghosts as it managed to exorcize, for tales similar to that of Mrs. Leakey are the rule rather than the exception in this period.[11]

One might have expected the history of immaterial bodies and intermediate beings to have been quite different in the period of the Protestant Reformation. Indeed, Linda-May Ballard cites from her research in Ulster what she calls a "typical Protestant reaction." One man told her, "Well, if he's in heaven he'll not want to get out, and if he's in the other place, he'll not be able to."[12] Indeed, it would seem that Roman Catholic belief in Purgatory would provide a more suitable context for ghost tales of the restless dead than does Protestant purgation of such belief. But the actual historical effect was exactly the opposite.

To be sure, it is not the case that ghost stories did not exist prior to the sixteenth century. For example, the presence of

115

"ghosts" in Greek and Roman civilization (though they are black rather than white) can easily be demonstrated by referring to Homeric literature, not to mention Pausanias, Plutarch, Pliny the Elder, Strabo, and Lucian, as well as others. E. R. Dodds, L. Collison-Morley, and W. M. S. Russell have each performed such demonstrations, and they are by no means alone in this work.[13] J. R. Porter, drawing on the earlier research of many others in our century, has provided interested readers with a similar proof of ghost stories, if not actual ghosts, in the cases of ancient Hebrew, as well as other Near Eastern, nations and peoples.[14] And R. A. Boyer—to give yet another instance of pre-Reformation literature about ghosts—has reported on the role of the ghost story in medieval Christian culture.[15]

Yet it is important not to be misled by such accounts as these. There are significant differences between the ghost literature prior to the Reformation and that which comes with the Reformation and after. E. R. Dodds writes that he has "never come across a recognizable pre-Christian tale of a poltergeist as distinct from the traditional 'haunt.'"[16] Russell acknowledges that Augustine already, in his book *The Care of the Dead,* says it is not really the dead who appear to the living, but rather an *image (imago, eidōlon).*[17] Porter notes that "the ghost-story, as we commonly understand it, was an unknown genre in the ancient Near East."[18] The matter is complicated even further by the fact that the English word "ghost," with the connotations we have already noted in chapter 10, poorly translates the meanings of such Ancient Near Eastern terms as *ilāni* and *elōhim* (which really mean "gods"), or *utukku* and *zaqiqu'* (which really mean "wind"), or *sabāru* or *haghāh* (which really mean "gibber" or "chirper"), or *muttalliku* (which really means "wanderer")—even though each of these has from time to time been translated with the English word "ghost."[19]

R. A. Boyer, in writing on the ghost story's role in medieval Christianity, admitted that

> the people of the Middle Ages did not share our concept
> of the "ghost," and indeed there is no mediaeval word

"ghost" with all its associations of distressed or malevolent "revenants"; the Middle English word "ghost" means merely "spirit" (it translates the Latin *spiritus*) and both the English and Latin words are of very general application, carrying no particularly sinister or spine-chilling nuances. ... While the modern "ghost" appears in a psychological vacuum, terrifyingly isolated from our normal, everyday experience, the mediaeval "ghost" or "spirit" appears as an integral part of an immense and ordered spiritual world which includes not merely tormented sinners and devils, but also guardian angels and benevolent saints.[20]

Boyer also notes that "there is no mediaeval word which means the same as the modern English 'haunt,' ... and mediaeval ghosts almost invariably appear for a specific purpose, and having achieved their end, go, or are sent, away. They do not hang about for centuries, rattling chains and worrying the visitors."[21]

The conclusions of Boyer's research, which differentiate modern ghost stories from seemingly similar literature from the past, have been corroborated literarily and psychologically by Patricia Berry in a study relating Hamlet's experience of a ghost, as told in a post-Reformation drama, with Orestes' experience of the god Apollo, who, in classical Greek literature, urged the young man to revenge his father's murder. Berry notes that "a god in the Greek imagination presented itself unambiguously. ... In Shakespeare's Elizabethan world, the gods have become 'pagan' ambiguous presences (fairies, witches, or ghosts), vague half-truths, apparitions, whirling fancy, wild imaginings."[22] The result of this difference is that Orestes knew what to do when an immaterial body presented itself, whereas in more modern times, a person, like Hamlet, is more perplexed by the ambiguous presence of a ghost. There may have been ghost stories before the Reformation, but beliefs became definitely different afterward, definitely different by virtue of being indefinite, at least with regard to ghosts.

Theo Brown's work concerning the "difference," or what Brown calls "the colossal change of faith that took place around the

Reformation,"[23] is noteworthy to this history because it gives a compelling explanation from common sense. There were, Brown argues, three "unexpected problems" which accompanied the repudiation of Roman Catholic "superstition," as it was called, concerning Purgatory. (1) It produced a dreariness in orthodox Protestantism. In the mid–seventeenth century, John Seldon wrote: "There never was a merry world since the fairies left dancing and the parson left conjuring."[24] (2) Despite the attempts at demythologization by the Reformers, England in the 1600s experienced an extraordinary upsurge of millennial cults and tales about ghosts, of which the story of Old Mrs. Leakey is indicative and typical. (3) Because Purgatory was denied, a hiatus developed, there being no "buffer world" intermediate between heaven and hell. Concepts and images pertaining to such a "between"-realm were repressed, at least officially.[25]

But, as we have already seen and as Theo Brown has so dramatically put, "The ghosts themselves were oblivious to official opinion and continued to come and go at their own sweet will."[26] Two beliefs developed: One was held officially, and, because of the circumstances of the Reformation, was kept within the confines of religion; but a very different sense was held privately, and, since denied by religion, was necessarily absorbed into secular folk tradition in tales and in pagan holiday practice, like the American Halloween.[27]

Brown suggests a reason for the private retention of the sense repressed by official religion:

> The doctrine of Purgatory [argues Brown], however debatable on theological grounds, actually filled a very important area in people's lives and gave great emotional satisfaction. When a person died, the relatives had a clear and purposive picture of the condition of the dead loved one. This enabled them to integrate the experience of bereavement, eventually to put it at the back of their minds and to get on with their ordinary lives. ... Hence when a ghost appeared ..., it meant the deceased was not at rest, and then "the old church" had a remedy for it which settled the matter to the satisfaction of all concerned.[28]

This much of Brown's argument seems sensible.

But now add to the matter of the collective psychological function of Catholic theology another dimension of common sense. Brown puts the matter this way:

> The vastest gulfs must exist between the extremes of Heaven and Hell, but souls do not usually extend to these limits. Few of us are so wicked or so good: most of us lie somewhere in between. ... On the borders of Heaven we can picture the intermediary spirits, saints, and angels; on the edge of Hell come the demons and perhaps those pagan gods that have not been absorbed or obliterated. Between these there lies an innumerable profusion of spirits, monsters, dragons, fairies, the semi-lineated creatures of the bestiaries, and nightmares and bogeys of every kind, besides all manner of hallucination— in fact, the whole shadowy, unknown hinterland of the human psyche.[29]

Before the Reformation, collective religion provided a "place" for such imaginal "bodies." And in so doing, it provided a dwelling for us women and men as well—creatures dwelling "between" the extremes, as we do. So goes the argument of Theo Brown.

It makes a good deal of sense. It implies that if the official religion provides no cultic location for our spirit and spirits, indeed, for us, we people will find another way to locate our being, a being forever and always "in the middle." And if the form taken by such secular attempts on the part of the people seems sometimes to be a parody or mistaking of traditional religious myth or cult, a "mistranslation" of belief or liturgy; if, for example, the attempts invoke or provoke ghosts and ghost stories, which are themselves "ghosts," so to say, or spirits once thought holy—then this would hardly be surprising. There must be some manner, one might have thought, by which women and men, in whatever times and places, can give "body" to feeling; and, doubtless, imagination will provide the way to that "body"; indeed, it will perhaps *be* that embodiment itself.

The ghost of Old Mrs. Leakey may be such an instance. And if Elizabeth Leakey's tale does not yield much direct information concerning the mistaken translation of "Holy Spirit" in the King James Bible, or concerning recent rejection of that translation, the historical context of this ghost story does nonetheless contain a clue about the so-called Holy Ghost. It calls attention to the people and the people's stories as important for theological ideas and historical process, as has been noted recently in the burgeoning of interest in so-called narrative theology.[30] This history of the Reformation leads one to see the importance of folklore in the study of religion, since it is precisely in folklore, rather than in orthodox theology, that one may find, after the seventeenth century, evidence having to do with immaterial beings of an intermediate nature. It is as if folklore were the true "theology" of the people. Therefore, let us stay with folklore, entering it even more deeply, in our continuing quest for "the ghost of a ghost."

CHAPTER TWELVE

The Grateful Dead:
The Ghosts of Folklore

There is a particular characteristic of folktales in Protestant contexts that is noteworthy. Richard Boyer calls attention to this characteristic when he observes, in picturesque rhetoric, that "when the Reformation came to northern Europe ... the church formally severed diplomatic relations with the Other World, ceasing to invoke the aid of the saints in heaven, and ceasing to recognize its responsibility toward the souls of the dead in Purgatory."[1] As the "spirit" world was forced ineluctably into the secular domain, ghosts took on a ghastly tone, as did the term which names such specters. Boyer notes "that the idea of a spirit returning from the Other World did not necessarily mean to the people of the Middle Ages, as it does for us, something sinister, malevolent, or frightening, but could equally well mean something holy, joyful, and benevolent"[2]—that is, something "religious" or "spiritual." Ghosts in folktales after the Reformation in the West, being no longer sanctioned officially as a part of religion, tended to be one-dimensional in value, and that largely negative; whereas prior to the Reformation the ghosts in folktales could be, not only either evil or good, but also both evil and good, or even "beyond good and evil." Ghosts could be of help formerly, as much as Old Mrs. Leakey's ghost could be of harm. Formerly ghosts were spirits, as now even spirits are ghosts.

There are, of course, many traditional instances of the sense among women and men that ghosts are as helpful as they are harmful, and sometimes both at once. Plotinus, for example, when speaking in *The Enneads* about the psychē in its epiphany both as "individual soul" and as "world soul" (*anima mundi*), reminds his hearers that "there are also the oracles of the gods ordering the appeasing of wronged souls and the honoring of the dead as still sentient," and he notes that this is "a practice common to all mankind." Then Plotinus adds, "Not a few souls, once among the living, have continued to serve them after quitting the body and by revelations practically helpful."[3] That Plotinus' observation is, as he says, "common to all mankind"— that is, that the dead who return can be of help to the living—is attested by many, and by many who hold very different perspectives otherwise, as for instance W. K. C. Guthrie, on the one hand, and Theodor Gaster, on the other.[4]

Gaster's examples come not only from Greek and ancient Near Eastern sources, but also from the folklore of the Iroquois, the Australians, the Burmese, the Thai, and others. He observes that ghosts are often revenant or errant or wandering, according to the tales, because they have not received proper burial, and it is to the achievement of that particular end that they return. It is Gaster's view that "the main purpose of burial rites is precisely to tuck the dead away comfortably so that they do not become a nuisance to the living—or, in broader terms, so that the past does not haunt and invade the present."[5] But, of course, if the ghost—or the past—is as helpful as it is harmful, then one might wish for its presence precisely in its absence. Such is the force of a particular type of folktale: namely, that one which has, since at least 1856, gone by the name "The Grateful Dead."

"The grateful dead" is type numbers 505-508 in the classification by Aarne and Thompson,[6] and it is motif number E341 in the Motif-Index edited by the latter of these two scholars.[7] In the Motif-Index, Category E includes stories about "the dead," and Section 340 collects the specific stories about "the return of the dead to repay obligations."

More particularly, the theme of "the grateful dead" is expressed in tales where the ghost is grateful because his or her corpse was ransomed from unpaid debts, or where the ghost is grateful for having been spared indignity in regard to the treatment of the corpse, or where the ghost is grateful for having received food, or clothes, or prayers. In return, the ghost will take the form of a specter, or an animal, or a knight, or a saint, or an angel, or—in one tale—even God. The returned ghost will then aid in rescue from shipwreck, or will help to achieve an impossible object, or will give advice on the magical manner in which to rescue a captive woman, often a princess or bride.[8] The Israeli story, "The Box with Bones" and the French story "John of Calais" are well-known and typical examples of this motif.[9]

It was Karl Simrock who, in 1856, discovered the importance of the theme of "the grateful dead" in the history of literature and legend, although the romance he was studying, *Der gute Gerhard*, may finally not belong to the type, as Gordon Gerould subsequently argued.[10] Many ethnologists have picked up the motif, adding tales to it and amplifying the research historically and geographically: Benfy in 1859, Stephens in 1860, Kohler in 1858, Liebrecht in 1868, Sepp in 1876, Cosquin in 1886, Hippe in 1885, Dutz in 1894, Wilhelmi in 1894, Groome in 1898, and—finally—Gerould in 1907.[11]

Gerould's study is monumental. His book, *The Grateful Dead: The History of a Folk Story*, summarizes and corrects the earlier studies. The particular genius of Gerould's work is in demonstrating how the simple motif of "the grateful dead" has tended to combine with other motifs in the folktales of the Russian, the Near Eastern, and the Western traditions. Particularly, the account of "the grateful dead" seems commonly to be linked to stories of "the poison maiden" and "the ransomed woman," to tales of Assyrio-Babylonian and Semitic origin, such as "the water of life," and to folk themes of "the spendthrift knight," "the two friends," and "the thankful beasts" (recall that the *Geist* of Matthew Arnold was a pet dog).

Gerould studied more than one hundred folktales. The geographical scope of occurrence is remarkable, although it may be significant that Gerould found no instances from the Orient. The tales came from ancient Palestine and modern Israel, from Greece and Rome, from Siberia and Russia, from Poland, Bulgaria, and Lithuania, from Hungary and Rumania, from Finland, Sweden, Iceland, and Denmark, from Italy, France, and Spain, and from England and Ireland—nor is this the end of the list.[12] The fantasy, one might conclude, is pervasive and perduring, at least in the West.

One of the most ancient versions of the simple and uncombined form of the tale of "the grateful dead" is reported by Cicero in his work *De divinatione* ("On Divination").[13] The story, in this case, refers to Simonides, a Greek poet of the sixth century B.C.E., about whom the people told the following. One day Simonides saw a dead man who had not received proper burial. Being a pious man, Simonides performed the appropriate rites. Later, when he was about to go on a sea journey, the dead man's ghost appeared to him in a dream and warned him against the voyage. Simonides took the advice, and, as it turned out, the ship was lost and everyone with it. Simonides was, of course, saved by "the grateful dead."

A second version from antiquity is the story contained in the apocryphal book of Tobit. This account is perhaps better known than Cicero's tale of Simonides, since Tobit was an extremely popular love story in the ancient world, even though it is somewhat more complex than the tale about Simonides. (The Jewish text of Tobit, dating from perhaps the time of the emperor Hadrian [second century C.E.] nearly two hundred years after Cicero, may well be taken from a Chaldean source, which antedates Cicero by approximately that same number of years.)

Tobit—according to the account—was a devout Jew in exile. His piety compelled him to the unhappy task of burying those of his people who had been slain and thrown outside the city wall of

124

Nineveh, first by Shalmaneser and then by Sennacherib in their anti-Semitic atrocities. Tobit's "reward" for being a holy and righteous man was that he was blinded by the excrement of sparrows, which fell on his eyes as he performed his pieties in the city scrap heap.

But it happened that Tobit's son, Tobias, going with his faithful dog in quest of the family fortune, as his father had directed, met a person who was not exactly a ghost, but was rather the angel Raphael. The angel of the dead whom Tobit had buried had taken note of the piety and he aided the son. Raphael advised Tobias to use the heart and liver of a magical fish in order to free a kinsman's daughter from a demon, Asmodeus. The ghastly one had caused the daughter's first seven husbands to die on the wedding night.

Tobias took the woman, Sarah, in marriage, and returned with her and the family treasure. He used the gall of the fish to heal his father's eyes of their films, just as he had used the heart and liver to cure his loved one, all on the advice of the angelic companion, Raphael. So, in this ancient version of the tale of "the grateful dead," the ghost is an angel and the hero is doubled, appearing both as an old man and as a young man, the names indicating their unity (Tobit, Tobias).

It would seem that later folktale traditions tend to fuse complex motifs that are differentiated in ancient texts.[14] This can happen in two ways: (1) by combining a clear and distinct ghost tale, such as Cicero's, with a romantic story, such as one of the tales of "the ransomed maiden," thereby giving the ghost story a sentimental and heroic point (the ghost helps the hero free the woman from her wicked captor so that the former can have her for his own wife); or (2) by joining a *senex*-figure and a *puer*-figure into one hero, and demythologizing (or perhaps remythologizing) an angel with the notion of ghost, thereby secularizing a tale that is fundamentally religious. This tendency by the folktale tradition to make of a complex motif something that is monovalent and heroic can be seen dramatically in the case of a story curiously neglected in the otherwise exhaustive research of the stories of "the grateful dead" by Gerould.

Collison-Morley and Russell have already noted the omission of this narrative, which is actually mythic rather than folkloric.[15] It is a story of divine and semi-divine figures, rather than one involving human heroes. And it is a myth that likely antedates both Tobit and Simonides, being attributed to the ancient oral tradition in Greece according to Pausanias, Strabo, Apollodorus, and other later writers.[16] It is the story of Pelops and Cillas, who was Pelops' charioteer.

That Pelops was a son of Tantalus already indicates the tone of the tale. Like Tobit, Pelops was an exile from his native land; like Tobias, he desired a woman, Hippodamia, who, like Sarah, had been death to earlier suitors. Unlike Sarah, however, Hippodamia's problem was her father, Oenomaus.

It is not clear whether Oenomaus, who was a son of Ares, incestuously wanted his daughter for himself or whether he feared an oracle who prophesied his death by the hand of a son-in-law. In any case, Oenomaus schemed to prevent Hippodamia's marriage. He announced that any suitor would be welcome to his daughter if such could defeat him in a chariot race. But there could be no winner over Oenomaus, since his chariot was powered by the wind-begotten mares of his father, Ares, and also because his charioteer was Myrtilus, a son of Hermes, the crafty one. Twelve heads hanging in Oenomaus' hall demonstrated the futility of pursuing the hand of Hippodamia.

But Poseidon, who was not a ghost, but a god, and who had been a lover of Pelops, was more than delighted to be of assistance. This god of horses provided Pelops with a winged gold chariot, which was so swift that Cillas, Pelops' driver, perished from the speed on a trial run. Cillas' ghost asked Pelops for heroic (rather than a servant's) burial, as if the ghost were the real hero in these tales by being the servant of the living. Pelops complied and was hardly sorry—or perhaps he was!

THE GHOSTS OF FOLKLORE

Cillas' ghost—according to one variant of the myth—told Pelops to bribe Myrtilus, Oenomaus' charioteer, who had something of a crush on Hippodamia himself. Myrtilus was to have half the fortune that would come to Pelops from Oenomaus' kingdom, and he was also to have the opportunity of spending the wedding night with the bride. This would be in return for sabotaging the chariot of Oenomaus, which he did easily by replacing the wheel-and-axle pins with wax so that when the race got "hot," Oenomaus would be thrown from his vehicle and killed ... which is exactly what happened.

In all later folktale versions of this mythic story of "the grateful dead," the hero is happy to keep the bargain, as an honest person should. In these accounts, the ghost then reveals at the last moment its true identity and relinquishes its claim so that the hero gets girl and gold alike. But in the Greek mythic version, Pelops, for whatever reason, kicked Myrtilus into the sea when he came for his riches and for his night of sex with the woman. The result of not keeping the bargain (which some may wonder why the hero agreed to in the first place) was that the ghost of Myrtilus, a second ghost of a second charioteer in this tale, cursed the house of Pelops. The curse was so potent that it made Pelops' family the source for a great amount of dramatic tragedy in later Greek literature.

The myth, therefore, does not end "happily ever after," as is typical of later folktales of "the grateful dead," especially in their heroic combinations with other more romantic themes. Nor is there a single ghost. Furthermore, the second ghost does not make the hero more heroic, but just the reverse. The ghost is doubled, and the tale is not heroic in tone. Rather, it is the story of a judgment on a people.

There is something in all of this that is of importance in our quest for "the ghost of a ghost." We have taken note of a folktale tradition in the predominantly Catholic Christian West (from after the time of Tobit and Cicero to the sixteenth century). In this tradition there is carried a perspective according to which ghosts, properly tended, are helpers—"the grateful dead." But in apparent opposition to this Christianized pagan and Jewish perspective (Simonides and Tobit), we have also noted a Northern European and British Protestant historical context from a later period, which produced, outside official religion, but clearly dependent on Christian theological reform, a folklore about ghastly haunting figures. Both of these religious perspectives (Roman Catholic and Protestant) seem to be carrying a notion about the spirit realm which implies that it is monolithic, not possessing a shadow and shade (which is what the Greek word for "ghost," *eidōlon,* means). Roman Catholic contexts express the one-sidedness by including spirit stories in the theological tradition, stories which that tradition valences positively. Protestant ecclesiastical contexts express their one-sidedness by excluding the intermediate ghost realm altogether, implying that this realm is negative from a religious perspective. In this latter, the positive realm of the Spirit (as opposed to "ghost") is reserved for the sanctity of the church and its theology, leaving no place for the "ghost" except in the secular domain.

Meanwhile, in the ancient, pre-Christian Greek world, we have seen that there existed a single myth, which carried both sides at once. The side of the Catholic "helper" is represented in Pelops' story by Cillas, the ghost who aids his master gratefully. The side of the Protestant "revenant" is represented by Myrtilus, the ghost who hangs around rattling all the skeletons in the family's closets. The existence in antiquity of the mythology of Pelops may imply that any later folkloric expression that is one-sided expresses only a portion of a total complex of meaning. It is as if the mythology of Pelops itself "haunts" the later Christian tradition. Indeed, it shadows any expression where so-called good (Cillas) and so-called evil (Myrtilus) are severed by a perspective that insists on an "infinite qualitative distinction" between divine and human, which is to say, by a perspective that believes it can differentiate between the sacred (light) and the secular (dark) realms of human life and meaning.

128

THE GHOSTS OF FOLKLORE

It is this sort of shift in perspective, and its implications for human signification, for which we have been looking. Indeed, the linguistic, historical, and folkloric clues are now all in place. If no clear picture has yet appeared concerning the reason for the death of ghosts in modern Western religion, it is because the clues from language, history, and folklore have not yet been properly applied to the problem itself. In every detective story it is not sufficient to gather clues; they must in addition be applied to the mystery, so that a case may be erected or, one might say, so that the dead may be resurrected. In our own theological story of detection, it is the dead ideas concerning ghosts whose resurrection presents us with a mystery. In part 4, the clues discovered here in part 3 will be applied to the Bible (chapter 13), to human psychology (chapter 14), and to the literate expressions of the people (chapter 15).

PART FOUR

Resurrections of the Dead

CHAPTER THIRTEEN

The Paraclete:
Ghosts of Scripture

We have already noted Gerould's omission of the myth of Pelops from the folkloric tradition of "the grateful dead." But though at least Collison-Morley and Russell also observed *this* neglect, no folklorist at all, to my knowledge, has bothered to include in the canon of the fantasy of "the grateful dead" a rather obvious narrative from Christian Scripture, just as, on the other hand, no biblical scholar, to my knowledge, has deigned to draw upon secular folkloric evidence for the solution to a particular enigma in the language of the Fourth Gospel. Applying to the Bible the folkloric evidence given in chapter 12 can bring closer a conclusion concerning the disappearance of the word "ghost" from Scripture, if not from religion altogether.

It is not that folklore has not been taken seriously by serious biblical scholars. The contrary is the case. An entire "school" of biblical criticism in our century has been engaged in applying the conclusions reached by folklorists to the traditions of early Christianity as preserved in the New Testament and particularly the Gospels. Two names have been associated especially with this *Formgeschichte,* "Form Criticism," as it came to be called. Martin Dibelius of Heidelberg published a first contribution, *From Tradition to Gospel,* in 1919, and Rudolf Bultmann's thoroughgoing analysis of the Gospel materials, *The History of the Synoptic Tradition,* appeared two years later.

The guiding idea in Form Criticism is quite simple: namely, (1) that folk literature tends to be expressed in more or less fixed forms, which are transmitted with little change; (2) that these forms are shaped by the situation in which the tradition was fixed; and (3) that the history of a tradition can therefore be discerned by a close reading of the forms, as distinguished from attending merely to what the material in the content of those forms seems to be saying.[1]

The interpretive insight of Form Criticism may be summarized in the saying coined by a Canadian literary and culture critic, Marshall McLuhan: "The medium is the message."[2] In a different context, that of depth psychology, a similar view is expressed in an essay written by James Hillman. He urges therapists to attend to the style and genre that a patient unconsciously selects as the appropriate manner in which to tell his or her sufferings, as if the *way* we tell our stories is as revealing as *what* we tell.[3]

So Bultmann, for example, shows the functional "meaning" of the form of certain apophthegms uttered by Jesus, such as his asking, in Luke 7:41-44, which debtor will love the creditor more, one who is forgiven a debt of five hundred denarii or one who is forgiven a debt of fifty denarii. The "meaning" is demonstrated form-critically by reference to Indian, Greek, and Turkish folktales that employ the same formal device of a trick question. Or, to give one other example, Bultmann is able to interpret the historical-traditional sense of Jesus' parables that end with a question (such as the one concerning the good Samaritan in Luke 10:29-37), by showing the function of this same form in a German folktale.[4] It is clear from work such as this by Form Critics that secular folkloristic studies can be of significant assistance in dealing with certain conundrums of biblical interpretation.

It is all the more surprising, therefore, that when Bultmann (not to mention others) approached the problems of the Fourth Gospel, he did not petition folktales for help. In Bultmann's more than seven-hundred-page work on the Gospel of John, there are only three references to "legendary motifs," and each of these is in a footnote.[5] That this abandonment of the folkloristic resource may be a not insignificant omission in the case of the Fourth Gospel may become clear by examining a particular problematic: namely, that of the Paraclete.

In the sixteenth chapter of the Gospel of John, Jesus says a very strange thing, especially strange since those in the so-called Upper Room to whom he is speaking, his beloved disciples, are considerably concerned over the ghastly possibility of losing their Christ. Jesus says, "Sorrow has filled your hearts. Nevertheless I tell you the truth: it is to your advantage that I go away, for if I do not go away, the [Paraclete] will not come to you" (John 16:6*b*-7, RSV). Why, one might wonder, is it an advantage to let go the historical Jesus? for him to be dead and buried?

The answer Jesus gives is, so that the Paraclete may come. But who or what is the Paraclete? This word, *paraklētos,* is used in no other book in the New Testament, save for one instance in the First Epistle of John (I John 2:1), where it is applied to the exalted Christ in heaven. All textual clues, therefore, must of necessity come from the Fourth Gospel itself, and there are indeed enough uses of the term *paraklētos* in this Gospel to form something of a picture.

Four times in the farewell discourses Jesus emphasizes that the Paraclete will not come until he dies (John 15:26; 16:7, 8, 13). Jesus calls this figure *allon paraklēton,* "another [Paraclete]" (John 14:16), as if he himself had been a "first Paraclete," coming after John the Baptist had gone away, like Joshua coming after Moses, or Elisha coming after Elijah. That the presence of the Paraclete will be an advantage to the disciples in their teaching, preaching, and healing ministries is made clear by Jesus in his description of the Paraclete's function: namely, its remaining within them (John 14:17), its help in teaching (John 14:26), and, generally, its guiding them on their way (John 16:13). However, this helpful Paraclete will not be received without considerable personal cost to the disciples, a "cost" that will include being mocked by the world in suffering and persecution and hatred (John 15:18-26).

Jesus also identifies the Paraclete with the Holy Ghost, saying, according to the King James translation, "But the [Paraclete], which is the Holy Ghost, ... shall teach you all things, and bring all things to your remembrance" (John 14:26).[6] Jesus adds the information that others of the world will not be able to "see or recognize" the Paraclete. Only those who love and remember him will receive this Helper (John 14:17).

The word the author of the Fourth Gospel used to name these functions—*paraklētos*—is not a little problematic. Scientific linguistic scholarship has not yet found either a Hebrew or an Aramaic title for which this term is equivalent.[7] It does not occur in the Septuagint (the Greek version of the Hebrew Scriptures).[8] The King James Version of the Bible translates it into the English "Comforter," whereas the Revised Standard Version uses "Counselor." The Old Latin Bible uses both *advocatus* and *consolator.* But none of these carries quite the same sense as does the Greek word in the Hellenistic world.

Para-kalein, in its most elementary sense, means "to call alongside." Presumably, the noun formed on this verb depicts a person "called alongside to help," that is, a "helper." For example, the Stoic philosopher Heraclitus, in his *Homeric Allegories,* used the term in this simple and straightforward manner when he called Priam's pathetic saying to Achilles *"tēs hiketeias paraklēton* ("the helper of a suppliant").[9] Priam was talking about the ransom of the abused body of his dead son, Hector, which body he wished to give proper burial. Diogenes Laertius uses the word similarly when he is telling how Bion rid himself of a persistent petitioner by calling a "helper."[10] This much seems uncomplicated.

But in classical Greek usage, from the fourth century B.C.E. through the time of Philo, a legalistic meaning became attached to *paraklētos* so that the "one called to help" was often a "witness" at court or an "advocate," as is surely the significance of *paraklētos* in I John 2:1, where the risen Christ is pictured as an "advocate" for mortals in the heavenly court, and it is also surely the meaning intended by the translators who rendered *paraklētos* in the Fourth

136

Gospel with the Latin word *advocatus* or with the English word "counselor," like a legal counselor or lawyer.[11]

But it was another fantasy altogether which guided those other translators who used the Latin *consolator* or the English "comforter" for *paraklētos*. Perhaps these persons, drawn not to legalistic meanings but to therapeutic ones, drawn—that is to say—to subjective rather than to objective ways of seeing, were depending on an unorthodox translation (and one that occurs in only two manuscripts) of Job 16:2. There Job says to his discomforting "friends," "You are all miserable comforters!" But even about this, one scholar notes that it would be "unusual in Jewish usage."[12]

Translation—as is so often the case, if not always—is interpretation: "*Traditore traduttore*" (a translator is a betrayer), puns an Italian proverb. A word says what it wants to say, but the people who use words often want its meaning made objective or subjective, legalistic or psychological. So, as time goes by, and as theologies develop this way and that, dogmatically and then pietistically, *parakletos,* "helper," takes on the meaning of "advocate" in dogmatic traditions and of "comforter" in more pietistic contexts.

Where apparently faithful translators have been victimized by their language, by the unconscious meaning carried in diction, which overdetermines sense, theologians are eager to rush in with interpretations. The present case is no exception. The problematic Paraclete has provided much opportunity for theological and historical fancy.

For example, Bultmann believed that he had found the source of the Johannine *parakletos* in a Proto-Mandaean source he somewhat uncritically called "gnostic."[13] In Mandaean literature the *Yawar,* or "Helper," seems to be an independent mythological figure, an immaterial body. So, in that literature we find texts such as these:

> Yes, I have come to love my Lord Manda d'Haije, and hope
> That in him there will come to be a *helper* for me,
> A *helper* and a sustainer,
> From the place of darkness to the place of light.[14]

Or there is this:

> Endure the world's persecutions,
> With genuine, believing hearts.
> Revere me in uprightness,
> That I may present myself
> And be to you a *helper*,
> A *helper* and a sustainer.[15]

However, in spite of the fact that the Mandaean Revealer-figure shows himself to be also *Yawar,* "Helper," and in a way that very much resembles some of the farewell discourses of Jesus in the Fourth Gospel, Bultmann's critics find his history of religions and comparativist methods too fanciful.

Mowinckel, Johansson, and Cross—to give the names of only three examples—believe the source of *parakletos* in John's Gospel is from the community of Qumran.[16] Still different views concerning the Jewish, rather than so-called gnostic, backgrounds of the concept of Paraclete are developed by Michaelis and Behm.[17] Their notion is especially dependent on the comparison of John the Baptist and Jesus with, say, Moses and Joshua, or Elijah and Elisha, where, as it is put in Deuteronomy 34:9, Joshua receives Moses' spirit, or, as is said in II Kings 2:9 and 15, Elisha receives Elijah's spirit after the latter has departed. Furthermore, since the word *an-angel-lein* is used in the Fourth Gospel to characterize the Paraclete (John 16:13-14), those arguing for a Jewish background of the *parakletos*-idea see the Jewish angelology of Zechariah and Daniel as pertinent, not to mention the dualistic angelology of the Qumranic literature. Angels are ghosts, this view seems to imply; and the Holy Ghost is an angel.[18] But, of course, all of this is speculative and in dispute.

By far and away the most compelling historical interpretation of the function of the Paraclete texts has been given in an extremely careful study made by Morton Smith.[19] His thoroughly documented thesis that Jesus was viewed as a magician *(goes)* in his own time, gives an easy access to the meaning of Jesus' sayings concerning the Paraclete.

Smith's argument goes like this. It was a common view in the ancient world that magicians performed their "miracles" by virtue of the power which came to them from spirit-possession, sometimes by the possession of the spirit of another person who had formerly been a healer or "helper," and sometimes by the possession of a spirit or *daimōn* of one who had been wrongfully killed. The Johannine literature seems to picture the relation of John the Baptist to Jesus in this fashion, since John said of Jesus that the latter was one who would come after he (John) had left and do greater works than he (John) had done. As the King James Version says:

> This is he of whom I said, After me cometh a man which
> is preferred before me. ... He that sent me to baptize with
> water, the same said unto me, Upon whom thou shalt see
> the Spirit descending, and remaining on him, the same is
> he which baptizeth with the Holy Ghost. (John 1:30, 33)

In this context, then, it is not so surprising that the ghost of Jesus would be passed on to the disciples, dwelling in them as John the Baptist did in Jesus, so that they might be empowered to continue the magic of teaching and healing. Indeed, in the telling of the Fourth Gospel, when Jesus had died and was buried by Joseph of Arimathea, and when the tomb turned out to be empty, Jesus appeared to those who loved him and remembered him and said, "Receive ye the Holy Ghost" (John 20:22*b*, KJV).

In the light of the ancient perspective that Jesus' work was that of a magician, the promise of a helper ghost makes perfect historical-textual sense.[20] It would, in fact, be to the disciples' advantage for Jesus to go away, because then they could have "him" inside rather than outside, and they could get on with their own wonderful work, which is, of course, ultimately not theirs but his.

However accurate this reading, and the evidence seems very much on its side, we may be confronted in this case with an instance of historical significance that is not very relevant to modern human meaning. Modernity does not much believe in magic—at least not literally. Can there be some sense, beyond the magical and ghostly historical, which can be seen to reside in the Johannine account of the Paraclete?—a sense, to be sure, that does not contradict, but is aided by, historical interpretations? It is with existential questions, such as this one, that Form Criticism can sometimes be of help.

Nor do we have to look far or speculate wildly. The form and plot of the Johannine text is simple and clear. Whatever meaning was intended historically by the author, the form he chose, wittingly or unwittingly, in which to tell that meaning, and expressively so, is stunningly like the form of the tale of "the grateful dead." That the form was known at the time of the writing of the Fourth Gospel is demonstrated by the dating of the nearly contemporary book of Tobit.

The motifs of the simple form of "the grateful dead" are in fact all present in the last pericopes of the Gospel of John. A man (Jesus) dies. He is improperly treated, but then is properly buried by his friends (which here means "remembered" and "loved," improper burial being a "forgetting" of the dead or a "neglecting" of the ghost). The dead man (Jesus as the Christ) then returns, according to the Scripture's story, in the form of a Ghost (Paraclete) in order to help those who have remembered him. Just as a ghost is a helper in the folktale form of "the grateful dead" stories, so in the King James Version of the Fourth Gospel, Jesus calls the Holy Ghost by the name Paraclete (Helper), and he implies that the Paraclete-Helper is a Ghost, that it is the deep and holy power of an Other Paraclete, that is, Jesus himself, which will in that day be then *within* the disciples as a loving remembrance properly buried, that is, not repressed or forgotten.

Gerould, in his report on the secular folkloric material of "the grateful dead," complained about "how easily," as he put it, "such a narrative may be adapted, whether consciously or not, to a religious purpose."[21] But could it be that, in the case of "the grateful dead," Gerould has things backward: namely, that the folktale was *originally religious,* and that it was later adapted by the people, as any archetypal pattern might be, to be a way of expressing and viewing secular situations?

Indeed, the people seem to have *this* sense rather than that of the ethnologist. They may in fact corroborate our reading of the Fourth Gospel as an earlier theological form of the tale of "the grateful dead" by the fact that they allow this ghostly religious background to surface, from time to time, in their folktales. Three examples will serve to indicate the *people's* sense. Each of these examples comes from a social and religious cultural context that is either Eastern Orthodox or Roman Catholic Christian.

(1) Gerould cites a Siberian variant of "the grateful dead" in which a soldier buys a picture of the Christ from a peasant and then maltreats it. Out of proper piety, a merchant's son buys it and rescues it. Later, a mysterious old man helps the young man. When the young man thanks him, he reveals that he is God.[22]

(2) In another version, one which is Rumanian, a shepherd boy gives a sheep to Christ when the latter asks for food. Christ gives him a knife with three blades in return. Later, however, when the young man needs help in a matter of mistaken identity concerning a bridegroom, Christ comes back and helps the young shepherd.[23]

(3) Can it then come as a complete surprise, in yet a third tale which has the form of "the grateful dead," that the ghost of the dead appears in the form of a snow-white dove (that is, the symbol of the Holy Ghost)? This variant is Oldenburgian, and it begins with a merchant's son giving all that he has while on a voyage—namely thirty dollars—to give a dead man proper burial.[24]

In these three examples, not only the form, but even the content, of the folkloric stories of "the grateful dead" resembles the Paraclete material in the Fourth Gospel. If this still seems "coincidental," perhaps one additional factor, this time in Scripture itself, should be recalled.

We have already seen, thanks to the research of Gerould, that the simple tale of "the grateful dead" tends to combine with other typical story-forms, and that one of these is that form which ethnologists refer to as "the water of life," an example of which, under this very title, occurs in the collection made by the Brothers Grimm. Now, the Fourth Gospel, and the Fourth Gospel *alone,* contains a story concerned precisely with "the water of life" *(hydōr zōn.)*

In the fourth chapter of John's Gospel, Jesus not only identifies himself as a Helper (Paraclete), and says that when he is buried properly, that is, remembered, he will send another Helper (the Holy Ghost), but he also tells a Samaritan woman that he will give her the water of life *, (hydōr zōn* "living water"). She asks him where he will get this water of life. And Jesus says, "The water that I shall give ... will become *in* him a spring of water welling up" (John 4:10-14, emphasis mine).

Later in the Gospel, and again uniquely in this Gospel, Jesus is quoted as having said, "He who believes in me, ... Out of his *heart* shall flow rivers of living water." And the author of this Gospel adds (in the translation of the King James Version): "This spake he of the Spirit, which they that believe on him should receive: for the Holy Ghost was not yet given; because that Jesus was not yet glorified," that is, he was not yet dead and buried properly (John 7:38-39 emphasis mine).

So, the connection between the stories of "the grateful dead" and "the water of life" is made in the scriptural text itself. The Ghost is Holy. It is the Water of Life. The Water of Life is a Holy Ghost. The application of folkloric evidence to this portion of Christian Scripture makes the so-called mistranslation by the King James translators seem right on the mark. It is the word *Ghost* (not *Spirit)* which is appropriate to the meaning implied in the *form* of the story ("the grateful dead").

But we were speaking about the particular word *paraklētos.* What have the stunning coincidences between early sacred and later secular stories to do with that term? Perhaps the author's choice of words was guided by the unique form of the Fourth Gospel, in which he expressed his religious message, including the choice, conscious or

142

unconscious, of the problematic term *paraklētos,* "helper," this being a term that would not have come to expression appropriately in the other Gospels, since those versions of the story of Jesus are cast in considerably different genres, as Bultmann has already shown.[25]

Even were this the case, the further question concerning the relevance of all this to a person today would still remain unanswered. How does noticing the folkloristic form of a portion of sacred Scripture help one to see the modern significance and sense of the language of the text? What, specifically, does it have to do with the modern resistance to a word ("ghost"), which may now seem not altogether inappropriate? Why are we today afraid, if not of ghosts, at least of the word "ghost"? What does this application of folkloric understanding to the Bible have to do with our original quest—the search for the ghost of the Holy Ghost, not in the ancient world, but in the seventeenth and in the twentieth centuries?

According to the Fourth Gospel, the location both of the Water of Life and of the Holy Ghost may point in a direction worth stressing. The Water of Life is "in" a person; it flows "out of the heart" (John 4:14; 7:38). And the Holy Ghost, according to Jesus, will be "within" the disciples and "remain" within them (John 14:17, 16).

It would seem that the Ghost according to this scriptural account is a psychological factor within the self of a person who does not forget (repress?) the dead. The "helper," to put it another way, is expressed in this portion of the Bible as the sacred power and energy which dwells deep within the self as a result of something that might have been taken to be dead and absent (a ghastly possibility), but which is in fact very much alive and present (albeit not literally or externally). As Jung said to Corbin about the photograph: "They are all there," precisely because they were absent.

If this reading is accurate, then one source of *theological* insight concerning the present meaning of the ghostly mystery should come from the realm of *depth psychology,* which realm we now petition for aid in completing our account of the mystery of the ghost of the Holy Ghost.

CHAPTER FOURTEEN

Proper Burial:
Ghosts of Depth Psychology

The field of depth psychology hardly disappoints our turn toward it. On the contrary, it may be surprising to the minds of some persons to discover, in the very time when official religion seems eager to repress "ghost"-language in favor of "spirit"-terminology, that the secular science of depth psychology is laden with references to "ghosts," not in ways incidental to theological interest. In fact, the ghost-literature is so extensive in depth psychology that we shall in this chapter need to remain content by indicating simply an interesting correspondence in ideas between Jung and Freud, and also between Jungians and Freudians. It is this coincidence of perspective that will serve the present argument *theologically*.

Spurred perhaps by his conversations with Jung about the relation between psychology and religion,[1] Sigmund Freud, in the book *Totem and Taboo* (1912-13), constructed a truly elegant argument concerning "the fear of ghosts," which was, as Freud believed, "a superstition of primitive savages."[2]

Why—Freud wondered—are people afraid of ghosts? It would seem according to normal common sense, that such a fear is completely irrational, especially in the particular case of a fear of the ghost of a person well known and loved during that person's life. Such a fear would have to be based, as Freud reasoned, "on a supposition so extraordinary that it seems at first sight incredible."[3] The supposition is this: "That a dearly loved relative at the moment of death changes into a demon, from whom his survivors can expect nothing but hostility and against whose evil desires they must protect themselves by every possible means."[4] It is, indeed, a strange fantasy! From where does this imagined hostility of the ghost come?

Freud's response to this question is not without compelling reason. The source of the hostility of the ghost could be accounted for, he argued, by way of the psycho-logic of projection. Normally, Freud had found, a person's deep feelings are fundamentally ambivalent; they are, as Jung was later to say, *a complexio oppositorum,* a "complex of opposites." Some negative emotion attaches, however marginally, to every affection. During the lifetime of our dearest acquaintances, and for very good social reason, the negative emotion may be repressed. But when such a one dies, as Freud observes, "the conflict becomes acute." So "the mourning which derives from an intensification of the affectionate feelings becomes on the one hand more impatient of the latent hostility and, on the other hand, will not allow it to give rise to any sense of satisfaction."[5] One way of satisfying such a deep sense, this unconscious shadow of emotion, would be unconsciously to project it onto the person now deceased. Then, instead of facing the ambivalence of one's own shaded emotion, which one may fear lurks deep within, one now fears the emotion of the shade, the ghost which one may have to face.[6]

Such an argument surely contains more sense than does the supposition that those who would do us no harm in life will somehow suddenly change their attitude in death. Indeed, it led Freud to the conclusion that the fear of ghosts and the religious rituals of appropriate burial both point to a simply psychological insight: the fundamental ambivalence of all emotions.[7]

Jung agreed about this, and his agreement remained long after the break with Freud. In 1944, thirty-two years after *Totem and Taboo* first appeared, Jung published a work, *Psychology and Alchemy,* based on lectures he had first given at Eranos Conferences in 1935 and 1936.

It is in the second of these lectures that Jung spoke of "the fear of ghosts," calling it, not unlike Freud, "primitive man's greatest dread."[8] Jung's explanation concurs with Freud's. He says: "The fear of ghosts means, psychologically speaking, the overpowering of consciousness by the autonomous contents of the unconscious." And then he adds: "This is equivalent to mental derangement."[9] (Could one deduce that Protestantism's apparent "fear of ghosts," symbolized by its renunciation of the realm of intermediate immaterial bodies, though this made good reformational sense in its historical context, is tantamount in the longer range of meaning to a sort of theological pathology, a Protestant "derangement"?)

That a fear of ghosts is a "derangement" was explained by Jung in his Terry Lectures at Yale University in 1938, two years after his talk at Eranos. Ghosts—he argued at Yale—are complexes that, like all complexes, are autonomous, going and coming as *they* will, and "being capable of interfering with the intentions of the ego."[10] In the particular case of a ghost, the complex, as Jung put it, is experienced as "split off," a phrase indicating a psychodynamic that is parallel to "projection," which was Freud's explanation. Jung notes: "Many complexes are split off from consciousness because the latter preferred to get rid of them by repression."[11] "People are afraid," then, not of ghosts, but "of becoming conscious of themselves," Jung said.[12]

These insights of Freud and Jung concerning the ambivalence of emotion and the split-off complex are so fundamental to a psychology that transcends subjectivism and ego, that is, to a *depth* psychology, that it is no surprise that the followers of these seminal thinkers continued to express the perspective, in part, by attending to the matter of ghosts. Works by Edgar Herzog, Aniela Jaffé, Marie-Louise von Franz, and Erich Neumann are noteworthy in this regard.[13]

In fact, the psychological insights coming from attention to ghostly matters were so successful in the actual therapeutic work that it was perhaps inevitable that a subtle shift would occur. There would come a time, as indeed there has, when the transpersonal insights of Freud and Jung would be used in the helping professions to solve ego's problems *on behalf of* the personal ego, strengthening ego and securing ego precisely against split-off complexes and against emotion and its ambivalences, thereby once again neglecting the ghosts of self, not to mention neglecting the ghosts of Freud and Jung. Therapy on behalf of ego would then have become a new repression, or itself a sublimation. The "dead" were being "buried," but their burial was not psychologically a *proper* burial, which, in therapy as in religion, should function, not as a forgetting, but as a remembering.

The loss of the deep power of the original insight of Freud and Jung was fated to produce later revisionists, those who wished properly to remember the dead, the dead in the psychological tradition and the dead in the self. Norman O. Brown, to give only one example from the Freudian side, performed this function with his book, *Life Against Death,* by stressing once again the radicalness of Freud's original insight. Brown's controlling metaphor is the word "dialectical," which over and over again makes Freud's point about fundamental ambivalence, the belonging-together of life and death. Nor is it astonishing that Brown stresses the crucial nature of Freud's "discovery" of a death instinct, a matter that some Freudians would like to bury once and for all, that is, to suppress and forget. Brown quotes Freud's own words: "Subordinating sense-perception to an abstract idea was a triumph of spirituality [*Geistigkeit*] over the senses; more precisely an instinctual renunciation accompanied by its psychologically necessary consequences."[14] The "necessary consequences" of abstraction and spirituality are, in Freud's view, neurosis. And, to Brown, it is an irony that psychoanalysis itself has become an abstraction and that therapy has become a spirituality—which is to say, Freud's theory and practice have become, in the hands of some of his followers, a part of the human dilemma rather than its help.

This statement of Brown's Freudian revisionism is strikingly like a statement of Jungian revisionism made by Patricia Berry, precisely when she is speaking about ghosts. She suggests that therapy ought to function, not to repress further the repressed dimensions of the human spirit, but rather to allow, as she puts it, "the ghost to speak."[15] "To sense this ghost and to create with it form the art of psychological work," she writes.[16] Like Brown, she warns against abstraction, whether in theory or practice. "The ghost is an imaginal presence," she notes. That is, it is something concrete. Thus, psychology should be attuned to *hearing* (recall Kugler) the "nuance, metaphor, double meanings, irony and so on, as it destroys naive, commonplace, and platitudinous talk."[17] So Berry concludes that

> the psychological art is ghostly, based on a ghost. It is not founded by fiat as a kingdom or system. Its real limitation is given not by a conceptual scheme from above, no matter how revealing or supposedly "psychological." Rather, the work is secured by a half-visible presence, a deeper ground with darker demands. Let us beware of kingdoms, systems, and structures. ... Let us be on about our ghostly work, a work bound less to kingdom and rule than to that grounding in an intangible presence. If the "psychological" be anything at all, it is just this making, re-making activity, which is at once a remembering in service of the ghost.[18]

In such a view, Jungian (Berry) and Freudian (Brown) concur, and emphatically so, just as did Jung and Freud themselves.

Psychology, here, is reporting something it has discovered about *proper burial.* Its insight, though psychological, may not be less a theological one. Apparently, according to depth psychology, there are two ways, not one, in which *improper burial* of the dead can occur, whether of objectively dead persons or of subjectively dead factors of the self, feelings or thoughts imagined to be in the past. One, of course, is by repression, the conscious or unconscious attempt to "bury" something by not giving it proper burial. But another way of improper psychological burial would be to refuse to "bury" the dead, holding on to them, being possessed by the dispossessed, obsessed by the objectively fixated egoic reality. Psychologically speaking, this form of remembrance is not remembrance at all, but a forgetting of the factor, loved or hated, deep in the heart of the self, hanging it instead on the dead. Remembering taken literally is as much a forgetting as is literal forgetting. One is improper *burial,* and the other is *improper* burial. Both are different from proper burial, which remembers in a manner that allows the dead to be dead, the ghosts to be ghosts, rather than substances.

It is this matter of proper burial and that of the graceful, if ghastly, dead that interest perhaps the most radical of Freudians and Jungians, and in a way that once again bring these two camps into collusion. Jacques Lacan and James Hillman, for present purposes, may be taken as the representatives, since in their writings "ghosts" have figured prominently, and constantly. Both urge patients to "entertain"[19] the ghost, as a host would entertain a guest, an act of hospitality owed the self as much as others, and an act in which the ego-host may discover herself or himself to be guest to the guest now become host, the ghost become helper in a total therapeutic experience.

Lacan, for example, remembers that Freud said that neurotic persons suffer mainly from reminiscences, that is, "from a past that has not been dealt with, from a mourning process that has not reached its term, from the unburied dead." So, "the hysteric may try to forget the dead but the dead do not forget her."[20] Therapy, this would imply, "has as its major task the repairing of the relationships people have, not with other people, but with the dead."[21]

Stuart Schneiderman has expressed a problem in this radical perspective of therapy. He writes, "How can we deal with the dead without the mediating functions of ego?"[22] That is, how can *we* bury the dead without an egoic repression or a fixated egoic remembering, neither of which is proper burial. The religious answer would be that "we bury them according to rituals" that are not personal. This resituates the grief in a symbolic act, in myth and metaphor, which transcend ego and its historical sensibility. So, too, Lacan observes psychologically, "It is through the symbolic order and through the rituals it prescribes that the object is truly given up, truly buried," which is to say, remembered truly and in a manner appropriate to the past.[23] In therapy the symbolic order is language, the language in which dream and fantasy, mood and emotion, symptom and complaint are ritually expressed in "the talking cure" of the therapy session. Our language is filled with our ghosts, and it is there that they can live their death powerfully.[24]

How like this Lacanian perspective is that of James Hillman when he is speaking of ghosts. For example, Hillman states the aim of therapy in diction precisely like that of Lacan's: "The ability to live life in the company of ghosts, familiars, ancestors, guides—the populace of the metaxy—are ... aims of an archetypal therapy."[25] Indeed, Hillman dedicated an entire lecture at an Eranos Conference in 1973, and later a book which was an amplification of that lecture, not only to a viewing of death and the underworld of ghosts from a psychological perspective, but also, like Lacan, to a viewing of psychology from the perspective of death and the ghostly underworld.[26] It is just this—a *perspective*—that psychology gives to a theology of ghosts and that ghosts give to a theological psychology.

What is this perspective? Hillman calls it imaginal, archetypal, a poetic basis of mind, just as Lacan has called it symbolic and linguistic.[27] This poetic-linguistic perspective, according to these postmodern psychologists, provides a way properly to deal with the dead in the self, giving proper burial to the buried, a remembering which is not a further fixation of ego, not an idolatry of the dead. It would be difficult to know, without glancing at the endnote, whether Lacan or Hillman had written this line: "Human beings are defined by language, and letting your word determine your acts is one of the essential ways we have of recognizing our debt to the dead."[28]

Just here is where a contemporary theology of ghosts and of the Holy Ghost may be able to recognize a perspectival debt to depth psychology. It was a problem of language, the ghost in our language about the Holy Ghost, concerning which we initially sought clues. And now, finally, Lacan and Hillman suggest that it may be in the language of the problem where the real ghost we seek may be found, perhaps just in that acoustic complex of ghost-ghastly-guest-host whose archetypal core, if we could believe Scripture, may have been located in the folkloric motif of "the grateful dead." But we must not move too quickly to uncalled-for abstract conclusions. That is, we must try to avoid making substantial theological sense out of that which is truly a set of ghosts, shadows, and shades of former meanings.

Freud warned against resolving the matter of ghosts one way or the other. Such supposed resolutions may result, he noted, in simple projections of clear meaning where there are in fact basic ambivalences. Jung, too, worried that in matters of ghosts there may emerge a one-sidedness. He went so far as to say forthrightly that "the Holy Ghost is a *complexio oppositorum.*"[29] Brown's word is "dialectical," and Berry's is "half-visible" or "nuanced." Lacan and Hillman have gone even farther. They have attempted to write a psychology *for* ghosts rather than *about* ghosts, a psychology written in the language of ghosts—ambivalent, imaginal, dialectical, and poetic—rather than written in a language of the historical ego: a depth psychology of depth.

This psychological bout with the ghosts of the self is theologically striking. It is striking, for example, that Tillich, one of the very persons resisting the use of the phrase "Holy Ghost," and for good theological reasons, constructs a theology of the Holy Spirit (as he calls it), in the third volume of his *Systematic Theology,* which very closely parallels the depth-psychological findings about ghosts. Tillich insists (he calls it a "theological necessity"[30]) on understanding the "spirit" as "a dimension of life."[31] This is tantamount in theology to withdrawing the projection or the split-off complex in psychology, and to discovering the proper location of the ghost to be within the self, where the Fourth Gospel said one would discover the Holy Ghost.

Furthermore, Tillich takes three hundred pages to demonstrate that the primary characteristic of the spirit, whether divine or human, is, as he calls it, "ambiguity."[32] How like Freud and Jung, Brown and Berry! Tillich then notes that the only appropriate way to give theological honor to this "multidimensional unity of life" in all its full "ambiguity" is by retaining a symbolic perspective on the language we use concerning it. Anything else would be one-sided. It would not be "interpreting spiritual truths in spiritual language," as Paul urges (I Cor. 2:13, alt. reading).

It is as if, not only psychologists, but also at least this theologian (Tillich), cherishes a speaking about the Holy Ghost that will convey the whole ghostly pleroma itself—guest and host, finite and infinite, male and female, full of fury and helper, legalistic counselor and therapeutic comforter, heaven and hell, wounding and healing, the "sense of tears in mortal things" and the sense of mortality in things imagined to be eternal—as if, from the perspective of the Holy Ghost, these somehow belong together.

But just here is the problem, is it not? Theological discourse tends to be one-sided, unambivalent, unimaginative, not poetic. It wants to aim at historical clarity and certainty. It is theistic when speaking about God and christocentric when speaking about Jesus, tending thereby, if taken literally, to be Theolatry or Jesusolatry. And we have seen what happens in theological discourse to the poor Holy Ghost! In Catholic contexts prior to the Reformation, talk about ghosts enters a fairy-tale world, in which the spirit helps the human ego to be heroic. This is one-sidedly positive, as in so many combined stories of "the grateful dead." But on the other hand, in Protestant precincts, as for example in the case of Old Mrs. Leakey, the ghost is exiled to the secular world, a world it haunts negatively, since it is no longer accepted as religious. This is, of course, one-sided in the other direction. To be sure, behind these traditions lies the Greek one (Pelops and Cillas) in which the ghost is, as psychologists today have also noticed, double—the ghosts of Cillas and of Myrtilus representing the ambivalence, not of a hero's egoic relation to the ghost, but of the deep complexity residing within the ghost itself. This ambiguity, however, seems to have been somewhat neglected in theoretical Christendom at least until the time of the advent of depth psychology.

We say "seems" since there still remains the unsolved case of the improper translation of *to hagion to pneuma* in the King James Version of the Bible. Could it be that the translators, who of course knew the languages well, wittingly or unwittingly also knew that the English word "spirit," though right, was wrong, precisely because it deprived Divinity of its full doubleness? To call the Holy Ghost by the phrase Holy Spirit would "spiritualize" the meaning, rendering the transpersonal Divine, which is beyond distinctions, with a word that clearly carries only positive significance in English. Did these translators see that the word "ghost," though wrong, was right, because it reunited in one complex of ultimate meaning what had been severed in Christendom's theology, and was being further severed by the Protestant one-sided overreaction to Catholic "spirituality" gone awry? Did the English Reformation rid the theological world of intermediate immaterial bodies, only because they had come to be believed in substantialistically and fundamentalistically, which is to say, not spiritually? And did the Reformers perform this exorcism so that they could bring back this imaginal ghastly helper, guest and host, in the clearly fantastic translation "Holy Ghost"? Is not the word "ghost" more in the spirit of spirit than is the word "spirit"?—and still?[33]

If any of this be in any way compelling, then the *semantic* error of the King James translation is not *theologically* a mistake, since it gives proper burial to the biblical text: remembering the Divine without fixating upon it idolatrously. It turns religion into ghost story, folktale, myth; and, as we have seen, it makes religion psychologically to the point of persons' real-life suffering today. It deprives the believer of Counselor and legalistic counsel, of Comforter and comfort; but it offers a Paraclete, and it makes divine the Ghost, making a proper place for that which may seem ghastly from another perspective.

Is this, then, the "solution" to our detective story? Surely, by applying the "clues" from linguistics, history, and folklore, we have discovered in the text of the Bible and in the "text" of the human psyche, some insights concerning the use of the word "ghost" to translate "spirit" in an appropriately powerful way. But the "Holy Ghost" of Elizabethan usage is dead and gone, even if the people's folktales and their psychology attest to its subtle perdurance. Ghosts— we are told—do not give up easily. If that to which the term "ghost" points is archetypally human, then where has "the ghost of the ghost" gone since the seventeenth century? Will there be a resurrection of *this* dead? There are still unanswered questions. The case is not quite closed.

CHAPTER FIFTEEN

Our Dark Alphabet:
Ghosts of Modern Literature

In an actual detective story it would be an embarrassment to the plot were the corpse to be discovered to be very much alive. Where it had been assumed that a crime had been committed, a ghastly murder, there would need to be a new sense of things.

In the case of our particular "detective story"—the quest for the ghost of the Holy Ghost—this is just what has happened. If the Holy Ghost has been forgotten ("murdered") in religious circles and progressively so since the seventeenth century, its "ghost," so to say, has appeared alive and well in literature, properly "buried," which is to say, not fixated on idolatrously (as in the literalism of Catholic Spiritualism and Protestant Pentecostalism) and not forgotten (as in orthodox Christendom), but remembered and loved with the detachment deserved by any loved one. If, as we have seen earlier, the *religion* of ghosts is in folklore (the people's stories) and in depth psychology (the people's psyche), the *theology* of this religious dimension is taking place in modern literature and postmodern literary theory.

Christian Scripture alerted people to the fact that the Holy Ghost would not "leave [it]self without witness" (Acts 14:17; cf. The Wisdom of Solomon 1:6). And Charles Péguy warned that "grace is insidious, it twists and is full of surprises."[1] So, if the Holy Ghost is banned from official religion, it is not unthinkable that it might find another medium. The Fourth Gospel says, *"to pneuma hopou thelei penei,"* which might be translated, "The Holy Ghost ghosts wherever it wishes" (John 3:8, author's translation). Indeed, the image (ghost?) of "ghost" is alive and well in the work of recent writers.

Laura Hofrichter, in her fine study on Heinrich Heine, has noted that "although ghosts are among the most widespread symbols in the world's literature," their imagery is "especially prominent in the literature and painting of the Western world in the nineteenth and twentieth centuries," a fact about which she complains that it does "not seem to have met with adequate treatment." Hofrichter explains a bit about the burgeoning prominence of the ghost theme in modern literature:

> The ghost-world was only too well known to many, including Goethe, Hoffmann, Byron, Poe, D. H. Lawrence, Musset, Barlach, Dostoevski, Picasso, Benn, Kokoschka, Hauptmann. Goethe's repeated concern about the ghost-world ... at the time of writing *Faust I* is part of the phenomenon. But Goethe among others made himself the master of it, by converting ghosts, which were a symbol to begin with—a symbol of the inexplicable, the unclarified, the mysterious, with an uncanniness and a fascination of their own—into new symbols and investing them with an individual meaning. Lawrence [Hofrichter concludes] even makes the ghost into the Holy Ghost, by which he means "the plurality of gods" a person has within—a symbol, then, for the complex personality.[2]

A single chapter can hardly satisfy Hofrichter's proper complaint that the resurrection of the "ghost" in contemporary literature has not been met with adequate notice. But perhaps we can get a sense for the tone and the anatomy of meaning which accompany the "ghostlier demarcations" of recent literature and literary theory. The attempt of this chapter is to be indicative rather than exhaustive, inferential (see chapter 7) rather than decisive.

GHOSTS OF MODERN LITERATURE

Foreign Ghosts

To be sure, literature has always been a favorite haunt of ghosts, not only in folklore and not only in recent times. This much Hofrichter has intimated already. And in chapter 11 we invoked the names of Shakespeare, Coleridge, Scott, and Wordsworth when speaking about the importance of the story of Old Mrs. Leakey. Chaucer might also have been mentioned, not only because of the ghosts in his literature generally, but also specifically because his "Nun's Priest's Tale" seems to be taken from Cicero's account of Simonides' encounter with "the grateful dead." There are also Thomas Hardy, Charles Dickens, and William Butler Yeats, the last of whom conjured an entire world of immaterial bodies in which ghosts are crucial. But ghosts somehow become more persistent at the end of the last century and, as Hofrichter has indicated in the cases of Goethe and Lawrence, ghost imagery begins to implicate the uncanniness of the everyday human sense of things.

Instances of the beginnings of a transformed valuation of the ghost in modern and postmodern literary imaginations are not difficult to find. In drama there are Ibsen's play *Ghosts* and Strindberg's play *The Ghost Sonata*. These lead to Samuel Beckett's play *Ghost Trio* (named after a composition by Beethoven commonly called *The Ghost,* because he took the main theme of the second movement from a sketch he was making for a proposed opera based on Shakespeare's *Macbeth*). Beckett's play called *Play* also shows forth the notion of the ghost. The three figures of the cast are all ghosts, and are situated during the entire drama on the stage in large gray funeral urns with heads protruding.

Harold Pinter, whose plays are often compared to those of Beckett, invokes the notion of ghost centrally. In his work *Old Times,* not only does one of the characters sing the line from an old popular song, "Oh how the ghost of you clings," but this same character later complains that the others speak about her "as if I am dead—now."[3]

Indeed, there is some doubt in this drama about the status of all three characters. Like the characters in Beckett's play, they may all be ghosts.

There is little doubt, however, concerning the status of the ghost image in another of Pinter's plays. In *No Man's Land,* an old man, Hirst, says to Briggs, who is twenty years his junior:

> I might even show you my photograph album. You might even see a face in it which might remind you of your own, of what you once were. You might see faces of others, in shadow, or cheeks of others, turning, or jaws, or backs of necks, or eyes, dark under hats, which might remind you of others, whom once you knew, whom you thought long dead, but from whom you will still receive a sidelong glance, if you can face the good ghost. Allow the love of the good ghost.[4]

But why should Briggs look the ghost in the face? Why should he embrace the ghostly and the ghastly in his own life? Hirst explains:

> They possess all that emotion ... trapped. Bow to it. It will assuredly never release them, but who knows ... what relief ... it may give to them ... who knows how they may quicken ... in their chains, in their glass jars. You think it cruel ... to quicken them, when they are fixed, imprisoned? No ... no. Deeply, deeply, they wish to respond to your touch, to your look, and when you smile, their joy ... is unbounded. And I say to you, tender the dead, as you would yourself be tendered, now, in what you would describe as your life.[5]

The ghost gives emotion, deep feeling. It gives life, by way of memory's love. So, according to Pinter's character, one should "tender the dead," allowing "the love of the good ghost." This is, of course, reminiscent of the advice from depth psychologists petitioned in the last chapter, and it prompted Pinter to write in an earlier play, *The Dwarfs,* that "giving up the ghost isn't so much a failure as a tactical error."[6]

If dramatists have not "given up the ghost" in our time, neither have poets. For example, in Germany, the literature of the last two centuries seems to have favored ghosts as much as the theology of the same period seems to have abjured them. Goethe was already especially fond of the poem by Johann Peter Hebel called "The Ghost of Kanderer Street." Novalis' famous *Hymns to the Night* has been mentioned in chapter 2 as expressing the theme of the "descent into hell." The poet speaks there of going "down into the earth's womb, / Away from Light's kingdom" where "I've felt an unchangeable, eternal faith in the heaven of Night and its Light, the beloved."[7] But that which makes the descent potentially salvific is Novalis' notion in *Hymns to the Night* of *Nachtbegeisterung.* This German term means "night's inspiration," but the image in the word which empowers its meaning is that of "ghost" (*Geist*), so that the term could be translated, awkwardly to be sure, "the ghostification of night."[8]

The romanticization of night and its "ghostification" is matched by Novalis' fellow countryman, Heinrich Heine. Like the former, the ghosts of the latter's poetry are linked with dream-state and love. In *Dream-images,* Heine wrote:

> I sat musing and dreaming
> And thinking of my love,
> When three ghosts came nodding
> At my carriage window.
>
> They hopped about
> And made such mocking faces,
> And they melted into mist
> And were gone with a chuckle.[9]

Such figures are not all moonlight and roses, as one can plainly see from the threatening quality of Heine's lines in *Almansor*: "I see nothing of this earth but ugly forms and sickly ghosts; I don't know whether it is a madhouse or a hospital."[10] Yet the threatening quality of ghosts is all the more reason, from Heine's perspective, to deal with them. Heine wrote a satire (*Die Harzreise*) making fun of those who do not acknowledge the importance of the figure of the ghost. In the satire, the ghost of a modern rationalist, Saul Ascher, a man who does not believe in ghosts, returns and proves by the rules of reason and logic that ghosts do not exist. It is the story of a ghost proving there are not ghosts![11] It seemed that Heine knew, again like the depth psychologists of a century later, that "now my own ghosts are pulling me into the misty house."[12]

Georg Trakl also expressed this awareness, and the ghosts of his poetry's encounters, like those of Novalis, are the result of a "descent into hell." As Trakl said, "It is the abyss [*der Untergang*] toward which we steer."[13] This *Untergang,* a "going under," will become the title-image of a later work of "crisis."[14] Nor is it too surprising that the crisis of war would conjure ghost imagery. So, in the poem "In the East," we read:

> With shattered eyebrows, silvery arms,
> The night signals dying soldiers.
> In the shade of the autumn ash
> Sigh ghosts of those waiting.[15]

And in the poem "Grodek" there appear these lines:

> Under the golden branches of the night and stars
> The sister's shadow staggers through the silent grove,
> Greeting the ghosts of heroes, the bleeding heads.[16]

An earlier poem entitled "Ghostly Twilight" links this female voice ("sister") with the moon and, as the title indicates, with twilight—not with darkness, but with the blue coloration experienced in the darkening of the light. The poet writes, "Always the sister's lunar voice / Sounds through the ghostly night."[17] In "Seven Songs of Death" and "Transfigured Autumn," this coloration is made explicit when the poet writes in the former, "Would that the blue wild game were to recall its paths, / the music of its ghostly years," and in the latter, "Something strange is the soul on earth. / Ghostly the twilight dusk / Bluing above the mishewn forest."[18]

Because of the associations in Trakl's poetry with the image of "ghost"—namely: twilight, night, a stranger's years and paths—Martin Heidegger thinks that the meaning of "ghost" implied by Trakl's poetry is that of "apartness" (*Abgeschiedenheit*). Heidegger reflects on the question of why the poet used the word "ghostly" rather than "spiritual" when he wanted to suggest "apartness." He thinks it is because the "spiritual" has come to mean the opposite of the material in Western thinking and imagination. So, "spiritual," understood in this oppositional manner, has come to mean "rational, intellectual, ideological." The ghostly is different:

> The "dark journey" of the "blue soul" parts company with this kind [of spirituality]. The twilight leading toward the night in which the strangeness goes under deserves as little to be called "of the spirit, intellectual" as does the stranger's path. Apartness is spiritual, determined by the spirit, and ghostly, but it is not "of the spirit" in the sense of the language of metaphysics[19]

—or of metaphysical understandings of religion. Apartness is the site of the poetic art, of poetic living, and this site is inhabited by the ghostly. "Ghost" is the right word because its original meaning, as we have earlier seen and as Heidegger insists on behalf of the poet, carries connotations of being "terrified, beside itself, *ek-static*"—which is to say, "apart." The muse in the time of the "death of God" is the blue ghost, the trace of the absent one.[20] "Soul," says Trakl in a poem called "Childhood," "is a purely blue moment."[21]

This ghostly, ghastly muse does not appear solely in Northern, Protestant Europe or only in Romanticism. Modern and postmodern Spanish literature has also affirmed the ghost and ghostliness as crucial to creative understandings and expressions. The popular novel *House of the Spirits,* by the Chilean writer Isabel Allende, should, with its more than three hundred and fifty pages of ghosts, make the point all by itself! But perhaps Federico

163

García Lorca's notion of the *duende* is more to the point of the present argument.

To be sure, *duende* is not the same as "ghost." The Spanish word is taken from *duen de casa,* meaning "lord of the house," and it refers to a "household spirit fond of hiding things, breaking dishes, causing noise, and making a general nuisance of itself."[22] Yet, the description of the *duende* by the Spanish poet in his lecture in South America in 1933 is very close to the notion of "ghost" that has been developing in this work.

Lorca began his account anecdotally. He said:

> Manuel Torre, great artist of the Andalusian people, once told a singer, "You have a voice, you know the styles, but you will never triumph, because you have no duende." ... The marvelous singer El Lebrijano, creator of the debla, used to say, "On days when I sing with duende, no one can touch me." The old Gypsy dancer La Malena once heard Brailowsky play a fragment of Bach and exclaimed, "Olé! That has duende!" ... Manuel Torre, who had more culture in the blood than any man I have ever known, pronounced this splendid sentence on hearing Falla play his own *Nocturno del Generalife*: "All that has black sounds has duende." And [Lorca added] there is no greater truth.[23]

The poet distinguished the *duende* and its "black sounds" from Christian concepts. He said that he did "not want anyone to confuse the duende with the theological demon of doubt at whom Luther, with bacchic feeling, hurled a pot of ink ..., nor with the destructive and rather stupid Catholic devil who disguises himself as a bitch to get into convents."[24]

Furthermore, according to Lorca, *duende* is different from the romantically aesthetic notions of "muse" and "angel."

> The angel dazzles, but flies high over a person's head, shedding grace, and the person effortlessly realizes the work or the charm or the dance. ... The muse dictates and sometimes prompts. She can do relatively

little, for she is distant and so tired ... that one would
have to give her half a heart of marble. Poets who have
muses hear voices and do not know where they are
coming from. ... The muse and angel come from without;
the angel gives lights, and the muse gives forms.[25]

Lorca's advice was therefore to "reject the angel, and give the muse
a kick in the seat of the pants, and conquer our fear of the smile of
violets exhaled by eighteenth-century poetry and of the great telescope
in whose lens the muse, sickened by limits, is sleeping. The true fight,"
he said, "is with the duende."[26]

"Every person and every artist," said Lorca, "climbs each step
in the tower of perfection by fighting the duende, not the angel, as
has been said, nor the muse."[27] When Lorca was a student at Columbia
University, he discovered Harlem. For the Spanish poet, the struggles
of blacks against the crushing oppression of the white megalopolis was
a manifestation of the fight of *duende,* the black soul.[28] Where *duende*
is, death is near. Lorca says that "the duende does not come at all
unless it sees that death is possible."[29] And the presence of "the dead"
prompts, as Lorca puts it, "a radical change in forms."[30] It is its
creative characteristic and quality that links the Spanish *duende*
to the Northern European "ghost" (but not to the less physical and
more ethereal "spirit" of Romanticism and orthodox Religion). For
Lorca, all great literature has *duende*; all poetry, we may say, is
"of the ghost."

American Ghosts

In some sense or another, the notion of "ghost" carries with it a sense
of "foreignness," but it also implies, and forcefully so, a sense of
"nearness"; otherwise, it would not "haunt." So, it is not unimaginable
that the ghost imagery of modern European literature might be seen
in the literature of our own shores. And this is indeed the case.

Conrad Aiken's work is to the point. In both "Preludes for
Memnon" and "Time in the Rock," two of the most substantial and
important of Aiken's poems, ghost imagery figures crucially. Examples

165

from each poem will make the point. The first is from "Preludes for Memnon."

> You and I
> Are things compounded of time's heart-beats, stretching
> The vascular instant from the vascular past;
> You, with forgotten worlds, and I with worlds
> Forgotten and remembered. Yet the leaf,
> With all its bleeding veins, is not more torn
> Than you are torn, this moment, from the last.
> Can you rejoin it? Is it here, or there?
> Where is that drop of blood you knew last year?
> Where is that image which you loved, that frame
> Of ghostly apparitions in your thought,
> Alchemic mystery of your childhood, lost
> With all its dizzy colors? ... It is gone.
> Only the echo's echo can be heard,
> Thrice-mirrored, the ghost-pales.[31]

This poetic expression of memory, of the haunting of what was thought past, dead and gone, is emphasized in Aiken's poem "Hallowe'en," which he wrote after reading an article by a psychoanalyst on the practices of Halloween.

> But now none remembers, now they become
> the forgotten, the lost and forgotten. O lost and forgotten,
> you homeless and hearthless, you maskers and dancers,
> masquerading as witches, as wild beasts, as robbers,
> jack-o'-lantern leaping in the shadows of walls,
> bells thrilling at the touch of bone fingers,
> you come back to abuse and to haunt us,
> you, grandfather, and my brother, and the others:
> to the forgetful house, yourselves not forgetful,
> (for the dead do not forget us, in our hearts
> the dead never forget us).[32]

But it is not only the experience of memory that is indicated by ghost imagery in Aiken's poetry. More profoundly, "ghost" indicates the nature of the language used to utter the deepest sense of the heart and mind, what "ghosts" one the most. Earlier, in "Preludes for Memnon," Aiken had spoken about this feelingly:

> Despair, that seeking for the ding-an-sich,
> The feeling itself, the round bright dark emotion,
> The color, the light, the depth, the feathery swiftness
> Of you and the thought of you, I fall and fall
> From precipice word to chasm word, and shatter
> Heart, brain, and spirit on the maddening fact:
> If poetry says it, it must speak with a symbol.
>
> What is a symbol? It is the 'man stoops sharp
> To clutch a paper that blows in the wind';
> It is the 'bed of crocuses bending in the wind,' the
> Light, that 'breaks on the water with waves,' the
> Wings that 'achieve in the gust the unexpected.'
> These, and less than these, and more than these.
> The thought, the ghost of thought, the ghost in the mirror.[33]

So, poetry is itself a "ghost," the ghost of experience, or memory, of former words. In "Time in the Rock," Aiken puts the insight this way, retaining the imagery of "ghost":

> What you have thought and cannot think again
> prevented thought that would have found its word—
> word prevented by the forbidden thought—
> deliver us from this, deep alphabet
>
> the word walks with us, is a ghost of word—
> the thought walks with us, is a ghost of thought
> thus to the world's end in a silence brought
> and to a babel our dark alphabet
>
> come heart, invent a new word a new alphabet.[34]

American poetry in our century has continued both of Aiken's uses of the ghost image: as cipher for memory and as a figure of poetic figuration itself. W. H. Auden is a noteworthy example of the former.[35] His poem "Family Ghosts" already makes the point in its title. It tells that "out of [a] cloud the ancestral face may come" as we make important decisions concerning love and death in history, such that we will have the uncanny sense of the "ghost's approval of the choice."[36] It is as if, in some Freudian sense, we are each fated by what "ghosts" us. In the poem whose title tells that it poses "The Question," the answer, the reader is told, "is hard to remember" unless she or he remembers the past, because "ghosts must do again / What gives them pain."[37] It is as if we ignore our ghosts at our own peril.

That time and history (which may, indeed, be hell for some or sometimes for all) are the world of ghosts is made plain by Auden in two other poems. In "This Loved One," he writes:

> Before this loved one
> Was that one and that one
> A family
> And history
> And ghost's adversity
> Whose pleasing name
> Was neighbourly shame.[38]

Similarly, in "This Lunar Beauty," when speaking of absolute beauty, which "has no history," he says that it is a realm that "was never / A ghost's endeavour." But he warns that attempts to dwell in such "purity" will not put the "ghost at ease," because "time" is the place of "heart changes, / Where ghost has haunted."[39] Ghosts, then, though other-worldly are nonetheless this-worldly. For Auden, poetry sensitizes people realistically to life in time and history precisely by recalling the function of ghosts therein.

Wallace Stevens, on the other hand, focuses more on the second of Aiken's two themes than on the first. For Stevens, the image of "ghost" is not so much a cipher for the haunting return of dead ideas and images, but is more an image of poetic figurations which speak with feeling, and deeply, but disappear like phantoms and shadows, refusing idolatrous fixation. The image of the "ghost" makes its appearances in numerous of Stevens' poems. In "Comedian as the Letter C," the phrase "sovereign ghost" is used ironically to refer to human intelligence.[40] Two of Stevens' poems have the word "ghost" in the title—"A Rabbit as King of the Ghosts" and "Ghosts as Cocoons"—the latter of which contains the stunning image of a "ghost of fragrance falling on dung."[41] But the use of the ghost image as the metaphor of the art of poetry itself is found, briefly, in "Like Decorations in a Nigger Cemetery" and, in a more extended manner, in "Examination of the Hero in a Time of War."

In the latter poem there are these lines:

> These letters of him for the little,
> The imaginative, ghosts that dally
> With life's salt upon their lips and savor
> The taste of it, secrete within them
> Too many references.[42]

Like Aiken's image of ghosts, "our dark alphabet," Stevens' letters of the concrete imagination are the minutely concrete plurality of references which haunt our lives, giving it savor and salt. Why "ghost" is an appropriate image for this poetic perception of everyday human reality becomes apparent in Stevens' "Idea of Order at Key West."

The setting, as the title suggests, is just off the coast of Florida. The poem's quest has to do with "order," with our "ideas of order." How is it possible to put the experience of the vastness and depth of the Atlantic Ocean, of the various seas of our life's voyages, into language that will give appropriate shape and form to their fluid magnitude? The poet turns to the sea itself for an answer, and he hears a ghostly feminine voice:

> She sang beyond the genius of the sea.
> The water never formed to mind or voice,
> Like a body wholly body, fluttering
> Its empty sleeves.[43]

Yet when the poet looks for the figure behind the voice, that which gives "body" to the nothingness, the poem says "no more was she."[44]

The quest of this poem, then, is for the ghostly voice that gives "body" to meaningful expression.

> Whose spirit is this? we said, because we knew
> It was the spirit that we sought and knew
> That we should ask this often.[45]

But in spite of constant askings (or perhaps just because of them), all that seemed to come was "the dark voice of the sea,"[46] not unlike Aiken's "dark alphabet" or Lorca's *duende*. This is to say that the poetic voice that is sought comes in darkness, in emptiness. It gives "body" in its singing, but is not itself a body. As the poem puts it, "There never was a world for her / Except the one she sang and, singing, made."[47]

The poem concludes, then, by suggesting that our "blessed rage for order," "the maker's rage to order words of the sea," will fail. At least it will fail unless it can come by way of a ghostly voice, something ghastly and real that is nonetheless not present to mind or sense. Poetic utterance, Stevens said elsewhere, is like "a pheasant disappearing in the brush."[48] It is iconoclastic rather than idolatrous, not given to single meanings but to "too many references." One cannot fixate on a ghost, or it's gone. Literalism is impossible. So, Stevens summarizes his poem's sense by saying, in the last line, that the language appropriate to the "idea of order at Key West" will be in "ghostlier demarcations, keener sounds."[49] The implicit theology of the ghost in this poem about poetry suggests that it would be to our advantage were the words which express our deepest meanings to go away after their saying—like the pheasant and like Jesus. Then the *paraclete* can come, the spirit of the meaning, the ghost.

Unlike theologians in our time, poets are not reticent to use the word "ghost" and to affirm the importance of its meaning. Nor are Aiken, Auden, and Stevens (among American writers) atypical instances. Robert Penn Warren, in a poem about his mother and father, complained about the behavior of ghosts: "They must learn to / stay in their graves. / That is what graves / are for."[50] As if in response to Warren's complaint, Delmore Schwartz wrote: "All ghosts come back. They do not like it there, / No silky water and no big brown bear, / No beer and no siestas up above."[51] Hayden Carruth affirms the usefulness of the ghosts' return in these lines:

> When I went looking for you
>   in the place of darkness that was like a house
> I came first to the voices I could not see
>   in discourse of great importance
> to me, to everyone
>   as if I were hearing waves wash along a shore
> on a telephone, having dialed the wrong number.[52]

It is the ghostly voice that moves the poetic understanding for George Oppen as well as for Hayden Carruth. Oppen, writing about the memory of his adolescence with his father, says that "lights have entered / us it is a music more powerful / than music / till other voices wake / us or we drown."[53] Although the tone is different, the sentiment is similar in Charles Olson's lines: "As the dead prey upon us / they are the dead in ourselves, / awake, my sleeping ones, I cry out to you, / disentangle the nets of being!"[54] The very title of one collection of poetry by William Pitt Root, *Invisible Guests,* brings ghostly overtones with it, as do the figures about whom the poems are written (a beloved Afghan hound, a truck driver in West Texas, the poet's father, a motorcycle gang, a boy who died in a cave-in, a waitress in an all-night diner, a man who uses words without emotion, etc.). But the powerful interiority of these ghost figures of otherness is affirmed when Root writes in yet another book about having two impulses within himself ("the blood of two men trying / to be born runs / crazed through my heart"): "In the silence of the night / we lie together, ghost / clinging ghost for warmth, / haunting this house / with cries that do not come."[55] The ghosts here do not bring a poetic voice, but indicate "the indefiniteness of a missing discourse," as Robin Blaser has put it about the use of the word "ghost" in the poetry of Jack Spicer.[56] But this does not keep Blaser from noting also that, in Spicer's work, "the voice of the poem is a ghostly other and outside of meaning."[57] So, Spicer writes, "There is no excuse for bad ghosts / or

171

bad thoughts,"[58] as if the two were connected. Yet it is a different human connection affirmed when Spicer writes, reminiscent of Stevens' "A Rabbit as King of the Ghosts," "Rabbits do not know what they are. Ghosts are very similar. They are frightened and do not know what they are, but they can go where the rabbits cannot go. All the way to the heart."[59] So, in Spicer's view, we would do well to "hold to the future. With firm hands. The future of each afterlife, of each ghost, of each word that is about to be mentioned."[60] And, as if explaining why this is important advice, Spicer says, "What I am, I want, asks everything of everyone, is by degrees a ghost. ... The eye in the weeds (I am, I was, I will be, I am not). The eyes the ghosts have seeing. Our eyes."[61] Without such vision as ghosts provide, we may find ourselves "ghostlessly / leaving the story."[62] It is clear that poets have not hesitated to step in where theologians today have feared to tread.

Nor is it only poets. The novelist Alice Walker invokes powerful ghosts, as well as ghostly power, in her novel, *The Color Purple,* just as she had already done in the poetry of her work, *Revolutionary Petunias.*[63] And the memory of this novel may, in turn, serve to remind one of Maxine Hong Kingston's memoir of a girlhood among "ghosts" entitled *The Woman Warrior,* and Toni Morrison's Pulitzer Prize winning novel, *Beloved,* whose ghostly strategy may be without equal. That this litany of prose-ghosts names female writers may not be accidental. Alfred Bendixen has edited a magnificent collection of ghost stories by American women writers. Not only the title of his collection, *Haunted Women,* but also Bendixen's introduction, makes plain the importance of the ghost to women's writing. But it is surely a point that applies also to writing in general, if in a different context.

Bendixen argues that

> by portraying a world filled with uncertainty, mystery, and danger, supernatural fiction challenged complacency and emphasized the essential fragility of human life. In the haunted realms of these tales, the reader's safe and cozy

172

world would have to give way to new and disturbing visions. The unimaginable suddenly became real. The unspeakable was given form.

Thus, ghost stories

> empowered women authors to ask troubling questions about the nature of sexuality, love, and marriage. ... Supernatural fiction opened doors for American women writers, allowing them to move into otherwise forbidden regions. ... The supernatural tale allowed women writers to bring their doubts and fears into the open and into print. It even enabled them to deny that marriage was an unequivocal blessing and to suggest that a woman who surrenders herself to the conventions of society may wind up becoming a ghost.[64]

Bendixen's collection includes Harriet Prescott Spofford, Elizabeth Stuart Phelps, Harriet Beecher Stowe, Charlotte Perkins Gilman, Grace King, Madelene Yale Wynne, Kate Chopin, Sarah Orne Jewett, Mary E. Wilkins Freeman, Gertrude Atherton, and Edith Wharton. Bendixen believes that after the Second World War women writers may have felt that they did not need the image of the ghost to speak about what they could now address openly and directly. But the importance of the work of Maxine Hong Kingston, Alice Walker, and Toni Morrison may make one wonder whether ghosts can be given up, whether we egos have control over ghosts, and whether there will ever be a time when we can give up the ghost without peril to society and the individual soul.

Postmodern Ghosts

Heinrich Heine thought the French had surely attempted to exorcise the ghosts. He once said: "If there were really ghosts in Paris, I am convinced, the French being so sociable, they would get together even as ghosts, we should soon have ghost reunions, they would start a ghost café, issue a ghost newspaper; a Parisian death revue; there would soon be death soirées ... ," and so on.[65] But even French sociability would not be able to succeed in ridding daily life of ghosts. A century after Heine was to write these words about the French to a friend, there would arise in that country a movement in literary theory—"postmodernism,""deconstructionism"—in which ghost language and ghost imagery would play a significant role.

The notion of "postmodernism" is itself ghostly. Postmodernism can be viewed as the ghost of modernism. So it is not surprising to find postmodern literary theorists allying themselves with poets, dramatists, and novelists (and against theologians) in using the word "ghost" to signify important aspects of three of their major ideas: *reading, intertextuality, and otherness ("alterité")*.

Reading. Shoshana Felman, Professor of French Literature at Yale, has written a remarkable essay on Henry James' novel *The Turn of the Screw*. Felman's piece is called "Turning the Screw of Interpretation," and it is a mixing of insights from the novel itself and from the work of the French psychoanalyst Jacques Lacan, such that a view of reading-interpretation emerges.

The Turn of the Screw is a novel in which a woman hired to take care of two children tries to save them from ghosts. But since the governess is the only person in the story who actually "sees" the ghosts, some doubt is cast concerning their "reality." A whole body of psychological interpretation of James' work has arisen that reads the so-called ghosts in the novel as a projection of the governess. This reading makes it seem as if the children need to be saved from the governess and her psychology, rather than from ghosts.

But, as Felman acutely observes, the critical debate over the "reality" of the "ghosts" in *Turn of the Screw* has itself had a ghost-effect. Since a cultural awareness of psychoanalytic insight about human projection, generally, and the debate over the proper reading of this novel, particularly, have become more important than questions about ghosts, a person's reading of the text is haunted. It is haunted by what has been said by the psychoanalytic critics (and by those arguing against them); and, even more, this novel is haunted by the ghost of Sigmund Freud.[66]

Reading, then, is the act of being haunted. Portions of the novel, Felman says, are themselves like ghosts; they are "ambiguous and contradictory signifiers."[67] Thus, "It is here no longer fiction which interprets ghostly apparitions, but rather the ghost itself which constitutes a possible interpretation of the novel just read."[68] The reading of the novel is not an interpretation of ghosts, but the "ghosts" of the novel ghosting the reading are an interpretation of the reader and his or her reading. So the reading is constitutive of the meaning of the text rather than the reverse. Reading is seeing, not "reality," but a ghost. It is also, however, seeing by means of a ghost.[69]

This author (James) and this critic (Felman) are not alone in turning the "screw" of reader and text. Nor are they the only ones to petition ghost language in making the postmodern point about deconstructive reading. In an essay on Shelley's poem "The Triumph of Life," Jacques Derrida traces the narrative of the poem, noting that the narrator "quotes himself in a narrative," which is "a narrative of a dream, a vision, or a hallucination," which is itself "within a narrative, in addition to all his ghosts, his *hallucinations of ghosts*," and so on.[70] The effect of this narrative-strategy is to place the reader in a position of raising a question about the narrative, demanding a narrative, and being left either to supply the answer or to begin to understand the asking of the question about narrative as itself the "narrative" of the poem.[71]

Similarly, in Maurice Blanchot's book *The Space of Literature* the ghostly point about text and reader made by Felman and Derrida is again noted. Although Blanchot does not use ghost imagery, his sections on "Rilke and Death" and "Orpheus' Gaze" articulate a view of reading in which the text gives a reading of the reader's reading of the text as much as the reader gives a reading of the text's meaning. Blanchot says that "when Orpheus descends toward Eurydice, art is the power by which night opens."[72] This is like saying that when the reader "descends" into a text, the text makes possible an "opening" of the eyes to "dark" meanings of the reader. Blanchot almost uses the term "ghost" for this when he quotes André Breton as saying that, in reading, "one no longer has an ear for anything except what the shadow mouth says."[73]

Intertextuality. Related to the deconstructive "turn" of reader and text in notions about the act of reading, is the postmodern linguistic view of the intertextuality of the text itself. This view is summarized in the phrase which is the title of one of Harold Bloom's books, "the anxiety of influence," and it points to the possibility that, in a most fundamental way, books and words refer to other books and words which refer to others, before they refer to "things" in the world or in human history. This possible way of understanding texts and their intertextual texture makes—as Bloom puts it in another book—"every ambivalent identification with another self, writer or reader, ... an agon that makes ghostlier the demarcations between self and other."[74] Bloom is clearly not reticent to use Stevens' ghost imagery to stress the literary theoretical point: namely, there are ghosts haunting every text, and those ghosts are "ghosts" because they are themselves texts, which are haunted by the dead, and so on.

Other so-called deconstructive critics emphasize the same or a similar view. J. Hillis Miller, in an essay titled "The Critic as Host," uses the imagery of "host" and "parasitical guest" to make the intertextual point in a poem by Shelley. But when he writes that in a text "the host is a guest, and a guest is a host,"[75] the idea of multiple hauntings by a variety of ghosts is not far away. On the other hand, Geoffrey Hartman does invoke ghost language when he writes about the continuous weave and interweave of signifiers in a text of Wordsworth's. Although—Hartman says— "the intertextual referent delimits the ghostliness as we see *through* the text," nonetheless the answer to the question of referentiality is finally deferred in the lines of Wordsworth's *Prelude* (bk 2, ll. 6, 8-9): "I would stand ... / Beneath some rock, listening to notes that are / The ghostly language of the ancient earth."[76]

It may also be worth noting that Roland Barthes, in advance of these others, had already raised the "intertextual" point to a larger aesthetic principle in observing how one art haunts another. Barthes was writing about photography when he said that "photography has been, and is still, tormented by the ghost of painting."[77] This much may seem obvious, but it may be less clear why Barthes argues also that theater, too, "haunts" photography. He explains:

> We know the original relation of the theater and the cult of the Dead: the first actors separated themselves from the community by playing the role of the Dead: to make oneself up was to designate oneself as a body simultaneously living and dead: the whitened bust of the totemic theater, the man with the painted face in the Chinese theater, the rice-paste makeup of the Indian Katha-Kali, the Japanese No[h] mask. ... Now it is this same relation which I find in the photograph; however "lifelike" we strive to make it (and this frenzy to be lifelike can only be our mythic denial of an apprehension of death), photography is a kind of primitive theater, a kind of *Tableau Vivant,* a figuration of the motionless and made-up face beneath which we see the dead.[78]

All photographs on this view are pictures of ghosts; all prints, "negatives"!

Otherness. Postmodern philosophies of language have spotted one other ghost in the texts we readers read, besides the ghosts of the reader and of other texts: namely, the ghost of the "otherness" of meaning itself. There has seemed to have been a "natural attitude" in the Occident that some "meaning" exists "outside" texts, a "meaning" to which the text points or which it symbolizes, and a "meaning" toward which every reading is aimed, like a carrot in front of a donkey. This conventional, if unconscious, view of the meaning of "meaning" as metaphysical (as "outside" or "wholly other") may have its roots in Platonic philosophy and in Christian theology. Whatever the source, if source there be at all, it would now seem that such a view is less than useful, especially if the "meaning" is by definition "other" and can therefore, like the carrot, never in principle be attained. Western metaphysics (philosophical and theological) haunts our texts, whether we know it or not.

It is the problem of how to speak of "meaning" or "otherness" in other than metaphysical ways that Heidegger was addressing when he made use of the poet's *image* of "ghost" to speak of the *idea* of "apartness," rather than using unconscious philosophical *ideas* of "otherness" to interpret a poetic *image* (see the discussion of Trakl's poetry, above). "The language that the work [of Trakl] speaks," says Heidegger, "stems from the passage across and through the ghostly night's nocturnal pond. This language sings the song of the homecoming in apartness."[79]

Heidegger's notion of "apartness" *(Abgeschiedenheit)* has been modified by Jacques Derrida in the latter's notion of *différance* (the German word for "difference" is *Unterschied,* and is cognate to the word for "apartness"). Derrida's neologism in French yields a double meaning, a pun, by which he can speak of the meaning of "meaning" apart from metaphysical and theological senses. *Différance* carries both the sense of "differ" (i.e., "other") and the sense of "defer" (i.e., constantly to stop short of deciding the ultimate, the "other," meaning of any given text's "meaning"). J. Hillis Miller, drawing on both Heidegger and Derrida, like Heidegger, makes the same point with ghost language taken from the imagery of literature.

Miller is writing about the ghosts of Virginia Woolf and Thomas Hardy. In Woolf, Miller sees "repetition" as the strategy in her work *Mrs. Dalloway,* in which "the day of the action is to be seen," according to Miller, "as the occasion of a resurrection of ghosts from the past."[80] He goes on:

> The novel is a double resurrection. The characters exist
> for themselves as alive in a present which is a
> resuscitation of their dead pasts. In the all-embracing

mind of the narrator the characters exist as dead men and women whose continued existence depends on her words. When the circle of narration is complete, past joining present, the apparently living characters reveal themselves to be already dwellers among the dead.[81]

So, the book is about ghosts, but its meaning is in a sense also a "ghost" of those ghosts since "repetition in the narrative is the representation of ... a realm of the perpetual resurrection of the dead."[82] Otherness—whether in the form of "meaning," "God," "truth," "beauty," or "goodness"—is a ghost, and no less "real" for being of such a nature, but defers forever in the repetitions of its account the blessed assurance of resting in a fixated end.

In writing about Thomas Hardy's poetry, Miller makes a mockery of attempts to "name" the ghosts of Hardy's text in an effort to exorcise them, to fix the poem's meaning. The very beauty of the poetry, its power, says Miller, is that its "dead are haunted by the dead," or as Hardy puts it, they are "hands behind hands, growing paler and paler, / As in a mirror, a candle-flame / Shows images of itself, each frailer, / As it recedes, though the eye may frame / Its shape the same."[83] All attempts to "shape [it] the same" (as opposed to noting the differences and continually deferring definiteness or closure) will fail because of the ghostly nature of its "meaning." The "Other" (God) may not exist in Hardy's poems,[84] but there are plenty of ghosts to be found: traces of the Divine in a time of demise, ghosts of the Other whose nature gives image to the shape of otherness ... the Holy as Ghost.

Michel de Certeau has written an entire book dedicated to tracing the postmodern "logic" of this sort of "otherness" in a time of the absence of the Other. The title of his work, *Heterologies,* gives away its agenda. The word means "discourse on the other," as de Certeau's subtitle indeed indicates. Its content has to do with the literary quality of the writing of history (i.e., with narrative), but the "ghost" to whom the author is grateful is neither a historian nor a poet. Freud haunts de Certeau's argument.

179

The argument is that Freud's psychology showed postmodernity something about the nature of historical thinking by "injecting suspense and uncanniness" into the understanding of any narrative.[85] For Freud—according to de Certeau— "There is a ghost in the house" of the narrative patients tell their analysts; "the dead haunt the living," that is, the patients; and, in the analysis, "the dead are beginning to speak."[86] For de Certeau, what is true of the case histories told by Freud's patients is equally true of the histories written by historians. So, Freud makes possible a historiography in which the "narrative is a relationship between a system (be it explicit or not) and its alteration by an otherness."[87] Thus, there is an "otherness" in every telling of history; not only is it about what it seems to be about, but also it is about some "other." During the course of de Certeau's chapters, the reader confronts the ghosts of mysticism,[88] monotheistic belief in one god,[89] and so on, as "others" in our Occidental history. Reading this otherness of history is to be able to see the poetry of history.[90]

De Certeau—like the other postmodern and deconstructionist thinkers—is in the position of Madame du Deffant, about whom de Certeau says, "She did not believe in ghosts, but she was afraid of them."[91] Theologians in these postmodern times might take a lesson from the literary theorists, not to mention the poets, and have a little more respect for ghosts. Perhaps, in so doing, they would be a little less unconsciously haunted by ghosts in their notions of Otherness.

This is just the point, one might have thought: in facing the ghost, imagining it in its uncanniness, embracing its language and imagery, we remember the ghost and fear it, *mysterium tremendum et fascinosum*, so that, in the words of Umberto Eco, "we would not become slaves of our own ghosts."[92]

CHAPTER SIXTEEN

Conclusion:
Wimsey or Whimsy?

Are we now at the conclusion of this theological "detective story"? Having located the corpse in the body of modern literature and literary theory, is the quest for the "ghost" of the Holy Ghost complete? In the last chapter we saw that postmodern literary theorists warn against closure. Theological conclusions have always been risky (the risk being unwitting or witless idolatry), and in the case of the Holy Ghost perhaps conclusions are doubly difficult. Emil Brunner pointed to the problem in his book *The Misunderstanding of the Church:*

> The Holy Ghost seizes the heart, not merely the *nous* [Greek *nous, noos,* means "mind" or "intelligence"]: it pierces the heart until it reaches the depths of the unconscious and even the very physical constituents of personality. Theology is not the instrument best adapted to elucidate just *this* aspect of pneumatic manifestations. For theo-*logy* has to do with the Logos and therefore is only qualified to deal with matters which are in some way logical, not with the dynamic in its a-logical characteristics. Therefore the Holy Ghost has always been more or less the stepchild of theology and the dynamism of the Spirit a bugbear for theologians; on the other hand, theology through its unconscious intellectualism has often proved a significant restrictive influence, stifling the operations of the Holy Ghost, or at least their full creative manifestation.[1]

181

Perhaps it would be to our advantage were all constructive (as opposed to deconstructive, negative, apophatic, mythopoetic, and inferential) theological formulations to go away leaving the stories and myths, the folktales and ghosts, the Bible and language, the deep human psyche and its poetries. Theology, too, needs proper burial, else it can never function paracletically, as "helper." Indeed, if the Ghost be allowed to come, theological language, like Christ, may need to disappear, in the manner of Wallace Stevens' pheasant. Surely one must imagine that the Ghost could help theology more than theology could ever help the Holy Ghost.

Such are the frustrations of the constructive theological work. Indeed, the detection of solutions to theological problems is bound to be frustrating, especially if and when the detective story is taken, consciously or unconsciously, to be a model for the task, and most especially if, say, Sherlock Holmes or Monsieur Poirot is taken to be a typical instance of the model. Is it not the case that in a proper detective story the clues are supposed to produce a picture at the end? But the results of the clues in the quest for the "ghost" of the Holy Ghost have presented no clear total picture, even if they have given many concrete and definite images along the way. By now, patience at an end, all these forays into the ghostly images of language and history, folklore and myth, poetry and fantasy, may seem more like mere whimsy, rather than like the work of some theological Lord Peter Wimsey, that wondrous problem-solving sleuth of Dorothy Sayers' fiction.

But even in the case of Lord Peter Wimsey, there is the acoustical suggestion in the name of the sleuth that "whimsy" may not be entirely beside the point of the detective work. In fact, this suggestion is indirectly confirmed, albeit in fiction, by Lord Peter Wimsey's family crest, on which is emblazoned, "As my whimsey takes me."[2] It is as if Dorothy Sayers were at least suggesting that "whimsy" may be one mode of arriving at so-called solutions to so-called problems, that is, one manner of arriving at a clear, if imaginal, picture.

CONCLUSION: WIMSEY OR WHIMSY?

Something like this may be implied in William Spanos'
description of the postmodern adventure into human meaning as
an "anti-detective" story. Unlike the conventional notion of
detection and story, the idea of an "anti-detective" narrative would
be to evoke the "impulse to detect" precisely "in order violently
to frustrate by refusing to solve the crime," as if certain questions
of deep meaning do not admit to solution in the problem-solving
sense.[3] This experience would be like that expressed by the lines
of the poet Robert Penn Warren, when he wrote, "All day, I had
wandered in the glittering metaphor / For which I could find no
referent."[4] Or perhaps it is like the feeling in the saying of Italo
Calvino: "In Italy there are many mysterious stories which never
end—perhaps because the beginnings remain obscure."[5]

Such sayings as these by Spanos, Warren, and Calvino are
reminiscent of the distinction made some years ago by the French
philosopher Gabriel Marcel. He pointed to the difference between
two roses, one that appears in a seed catalog and one that is
written about in a poem. The presence of the former is a problem,
whereas the presence of the latter is a mystery. Marcel explained
this difference, saying:

> A problem is something which I meet, which I find
> complete before me, but which I can therefore lay siege
> to and reduce. But a mystery is something in which I
> myself am involved, and it can therefore only be thought
> of as "a sphere where the distinction between what is
> in me and what is before me loses its meaning and its
> initial validity." A genuine problem is subject to an
> appropriate technique by the exercise of which it is
> defined,

which would be like the problem in a normal detective story,
one in which Holmes, Poirot, or Wimsey would be hero,
"whereas a mystery [as Marcel goes on to say] by definition
transcends every conceivable technique."[6] Indeed, by
definition, theological "problems," so called, like the

183

"problem" of the Holy Ghost, deal not with problems, but rather with mysteries, and so transcend "solution" in the conventional sense.

It would then seem that were we to have arrived at a clear picture in this case of our quest for the "ghost" of the Holy Ghost, it would have been precisely *not* the Holy Ghost we would have discovered. Marcel puts the matter this way: "It is, no doubt, always possible ... to degrade a mystery so as to turn it into a problem. But this is a fundamentally vicious proceeding, whose springs might perhaps be discovered in a kind of corruption of the intelligence."[7] Marcel's language is strong: To think that one has "solved" a mystery is a vicious corruption in the mind. It would be to imagine that one could turn a mystery into a problem to be solved, but this would be merely to have degraded it.

Can it be that this is what happens in the Western theological imagination when it tries to defend against the use of the language of "ghosts" in the case of its Divinity? Could it be that we people, including we theologians, or the "theologian" in each of us, prefer certainty to mystery, detective heroes to anti-detectives? Does not the detective-impulse in religious sensibility prefer a God of the Law (Counselor) or a Christ of History (Comforter) to a Ghost (Paraclete)?

It may be that the English-speaking religious imagination has dealt with the mystery of the Paraclete by translating it into something which can be intellectually understood: Counselor or Comforter. In so doing it may have unwittingly degraded the spirit of its Deity, translating it, on the one hand, legalistically and, on the other hand, pietistically, rendering it objectively into dogma (the Counsel of belief) or subjectively into sentiment (the Comfort of a "strange warmth in the heart" or "Jesus Christ as my *personal* Lord and Savior"). Theologically this transforms the *Spirit* of Ultimate Reality, the Holy Ghost, into a theologism (theism) or a christologism, into Theolatry or Jesusolatry. In this manner, the theological tradition of orthodoxy does not solve a problem in pneumatology and spirituality; rather, it merely manages to demonstrate two ways by which we attempt to rid ourselves of the mystery of the Ghost.

But Scripture implies that it may be to our advantage for such attempts at dogmatism and pietism to go away, so that the Paraclete may permeate life with all of its mystery. Indeed, the testimony of Scripture concerning this matter is even stronger than that of Marcel. Turning mystery into problem, in the case of the Holy Ghost, is not just a vicious degradation, an intellectual corruption; according to Christian Scripture, it is the one sin that will not be forgiven! All three of the Synoptic Gospels witness to the saying of Jesus: "Wherefore I say unto you, All manner of sin and blasphemy shall be forgiven unto men; but the blasphemy against the Holy Ghost shall not be forgiven unto men. ... Whosoever speaketh against the Holy Ghost, it shall not be forgiven him, neither in this world, neither in the world to come."[8]

Legalizing or pietizing the Paraclete, implying or promising that the Holy Ghost will give a person Counsel or Comfort, spiritualizes the Holy Ghost, as does translating *to hagion to pneuma* with the now one-sided English word "Spirit." Is this not a form of blasphemy within theology itself? Does any "ghost," whether in literature or in life, really give a person doctrinal counsel or sentimental comfort? The "help" of the Paraclete is of an altogether different sort, more humbling than heroic. So attempts to deprive the Holy Ghost of its *tremendum* by repudiating the word "ghost" may merely serve to deprive Divinity of its *fascinosum* as well, in which case the entire *mysterium* would be lost and the modern concept of "God" would then "die," and not inappropriately.

It is precisely into this situation of the "death of God" that the poets of our time move with boldness. And if our secular writers may be petitioned for a clue to theological strategy, then it may be said, after the testimony of chapter 15, that "ghost"-language may be able to put more spirit into theology than can "spirit"-talk. "Ghost" lends the mystery theology is supposed to serve, and the ghost is "Holy" by virtue of its ability to transform theological detection into an anti-detective story whose purpose is served if no-thing is discovered, that is, nothing upon which persons may commit idolatry sensing closure and conclusion.

It is in this wise, then, that it would be to our religious advantage were theology to go away, at least, were theology of a certain sort to go away, the one with detective-story expectations, the one which is intellectualistic and rationalistic, whether by way of dogmatism or by way of experiential pietism. Were such perspective to vanish in some "proper burial" of the theological dead, perhaps then the Ghost could come, like one of the grateful dead, a "helper" by virtue of remythologizing a rationalist theological tradition, transforming religious problems with expected solutions into mystery, before which a person is humbled by facing images that haunt him or her.

To be sure, such a "conclusion" would be a justice deemed not only poetic, but also ironic. It would be ironic were a detective story, which goes in quest of the "ghost" of the Holy Ghost, to end by suggesting an end to detective stories of a certain sort. Perhaps it could mean that the Ghost would have won precisely in the moment that the detective (author) loses and goes away. With the detective-theologian as now one of the dead, having now become a ghost in the theological machine, the true Ghost who is no detective at all could appear as more real than so-called real reality.

Lafcadio Hern once wrote, "Like the single stroke of a bell, the perfect poem [or literary work] should set murmuring and undulating, in the mind of the hearer, many a ghostly aftertone of long duration."[9] Should a theology be any different? Should it not, too, produce a Ghost? If so, it would need be an odd theology, from a detective perspective, one whose function followed the path indicated by Stanley Hopper:

> It was an odd decease
>   like silence
>   underneath its wounds
> seeking darkness
>   where a healing
>   and the light
> might shine.[10]

NOTES

INTRODUCTION: ON NOT GIVING UP THE GHOST

1. Mircea Eliade, *No Souvenirs* (New York: Harper & Row, Publishers, 1977), p. 92.
2. Lucian, *Verae historiae,* 2.23.
3. Plato, *Apology,* 41A, tr. B. Jowett, *Dialogues of Plato* (New York: Random House, 1937), vol. 1, p. 422.
4. Steven Simmer, "The Academy of the Dead," *Spring 1981* (Dallas), 96 and passim.
5. Ibid., 97.
6. David L. Miller, *Christs: Meditations on Archetypal Images in Christian Theology* (New York: Seabury Press, 1981; marketed by Harper & Row, Publishers).
7. David L. Miller, *Three Faces of God: Traces of the Trinity in Literature and Life* (Philadelphia: Fortress Press, 1986).
8. David L. Miller, *The New Polytheism: Rebirth of the Gods and Goddesses* (New York: Harper & Row, Publishers, 1974; Dallas: Spring Publications, 1981).
9. Thomas J. J. Altizer, *The Descent into Hell: A Study of the Radical Reversal of the Christian Consciousness* (New York: Seabury Press, 1979).
10. Charles E. Winquist, *Epiphanies of Darkness: Deconstruction in Theology* (Philadelphia: Fortress Press, 1986).
11. D. P. Walker, *The Decline of Hell: Seventeenth-Century Discussions of Eternal Torment* (Chicago: University of Chicago Press, 1964).
12. Julia Kristeva, *Powers of Horror: An Essay on Abjection* (New York: Columbia University Press, 1982).
13. Wendy Lesser, *The Life Below the Ground: A Study of the Subterranean in Literature and History* (Boston: Faber and Faber, 1987).
14. David Farrell Krell, "Descensional Reflection," in John Sallis, ed., *Philosophy and Archaic Experience* (Pittsburgh: Duquesne University Press, 1982), pp. 3-13.
15. Erich Heller, *The Artist's Journey into the Interior and Other Essays* (New York: Vintage Books, 1965).
16. Walter A. Strauss, *Descent and Return: The Orphic Theme in Modern Literature* (Cambridge: Harvard University Press, 1971).

187

17. James Hillman, *The Dream and the Underworld* (New York: Harper & Row, Publishers, 1979).
18. Rudolph Binion, *After Christianity: Christian Survivals in a Post-Christian Culture* (Durango: Logbridge-Rhodes, 1986).
19. The poem is by Théophile Gautier, and it is quoted in ibid., p. 27.
20. Ibid., p. 34.
21. Michael Ventura, *Shadow Dancing in the U.S.A.* (New York: St. Martin's Press, 1985), p. 19.

1. HISTORY IS HELL

1. The Nag Hammadi library, 13.1.41 ("Trimorphic Protennoia") (New York: Harper & Row, Publishers, 1977), p. 465. Cf. 2.1 (The Fall of Pistis Sophia, in "Apocryphon of John") and 7.4 ("The Teachings of Silvanus").
2. Wilhelm Bousset, *Kyrios Christos,* tr. John E. Steely (Nashville: Abingdon Press, 1970), p. 61 and n. 84 (attributed to the Naasenes, according to Hippolytus, 5.8).
3. Frederic Huidekoper, *The Belief of the First Three Centuries Concerning Christ's Mission to the Underworld* (Boston: Crosby, Nichols and Co., 1854), p. 27, referring to Irenaeus, *Adv. haer.,* 1.5.4.
4. Josef Kroll, *Gott und Hölle: Der Mythos vom Descensus-kampfe,* my translation (Darmstadt: Wissenschaftliche Buchgesellschaft, 1963), p. 271.
5. J. A. MacCulloch, *The Harrowing of Hell* (Edinburgh: T. & T. Clark, 1930), pp. 149-51; cf. Allison Coudert, *Alchemy: The Philosopher's Stone* (Boulder: Shambhala, 1980), p. 135; and R. Joseph Hoffman, "Confluence in Early Christian and Gnostic Literature, the *descensus christi ad inferos (Acta Pilati* 17-27)," *Journal for Studies in the New Testament* 10 (1981): 42-60.
6. Origen, *Comm. in Ioh.,* 6.35.174; cf. Origène, *Commentaire sur Saint Jean,* tome 2, ed. Cecile Blanc, *Sources Chrétiennes,* no. 157 (Paris: Les Editions du Cerf, 1970), pp. 40-43, 261-63; and F. J. Dölger, "Das Schuhausziehen in der altchristlichen Taufliturgie," *Antike und Christentum,* 5 (1936): 98-100, where it is argued that the sandals signify the mortality and humanity of Christ.
7. Karl Kerényi, *Dionysos: Archetypal Image of the Indestructable Life,* tr. R. Manheim (Princeton: Princeton University Press, 1976), p. 360.

8. James Frazer, *The Golden Bough,* vol. 3: *Taboo and Perils of the Soul* (New York: St. Martin's Press, 1955), pp. 311-13; and Apollodorus, *The Library,* tr. J. Frazer (London: William Heinemann, 1967), pp. 94-95 n. 1.
9. Apollodorus, *Library,* 1.9.16.
10. Thucydides, 3.2.
11. Scholiast on Pindar, *Pyth,* 4.133.
12. Virgil, *Aen.,* 7.689ff.
13. Artemidorus, *Oneirocrit.,* 4.63.
14. Virgil, *Aen.,* 4.517ff.
15. Frazer, *Golden Bough,* p. 313.
16. C. G. Jung, *Collected Works* (hereafter *CW*), tr. R. F. C. Hull (Princeton: Princeton University Press, 1955—), 14.788 (indicating vol. and para. no. here and hereafter).
17. Ibid., 16.462.
18. Edward Edinger, *The Anatomy of the Psyche* (LaSalle, Ill.: Open Court, 1985), p. 172.
19. Wallace Stevens, "The Rock," *Collected Poems* (New York: Knopf, 1975), p. 528.
20. T. S. Eliot, "The Love Song of J. Alfred Prufrock," *Collected Poems and Plays, 1909—50* (New York: Harcourt, Brace and Co., 1952), p. 4.
21. Franz Kafka, *The Complete Stories,* ed. N. Glatzer (New York: Schocken Books, 1971), p. 456.

2. A DESCENT INTO HISTORY:
THE STORY OF THE DESCENT MOTIF

1. Cited in J. A. MacCulloch, *Harrowing of Hell,* p. 71.
2. See ibid., p. 67: "Though belief in our Lord's descent to Hades existed in the Church from the apostolic age, it did not expressly appear in the Baptismal creeds at an early date." Werner Bieder, *Die Vorstellung von der Höllenfahrt Jesu Christi* (Zürich: Zwingli-Verlag, 1949), p. 195: "So kam ins Credo der Kirche, was mit dem Credo der Urchistenheit innerlich im Widerspruch stand." J. Galot, "La descente du Christ aux enfers," *Nouvelle revue théologique* 83 (1961): 471: "Le 'descendit ad inferos' est certain, bien que l'affirmation n'en ait été introduite dans les formules du Credo qu'à une époque relativement tardive. C'est en 359 qu'on la recontre pour la première fois dans un Credo arien, et bientôt après on la trouve dans le symbole d'Aquilée, si

bien que son entrée officielle dans les formules de foi date de la seconde moitié du IV siècle." H. Leclercq et F. Cabrol, "La descente du Christ aux enfers," *Dictionnaire d'archéologie chrétienne et de liturgie,* 4.1, 684: "L'insertion de l'article du *descensus ad inferos* est considerée comme le problème le plus difficile (avec l'article sur la communion des saints) dans l'histoire du symbole de foi. Si la doctrine de la descente du Christ aux enfers remonte aux temps apostoliques ..., ce n'est qu'assez tartivement, au IV siècle, qu'elle fait son apparition dans les symboles. ... En tout cas, le *descensus ad inferos* ne se trouve ni dans la vieille formule romaine, ni dans aucun des symboles des trois premiers siècles."

3. This list is only partial. For more detailed information on these sources, see MacCulloch, *Harrowing of Hell,* pp. 131ff.; Heinz-Jurgen Vogels, *Christi Abstieg ins Totenreich und das Läuterungsgericht an den Toten* (Freiburg: Herder, 1976); Martha Himmelfarb, *Tours of Hell: An Apocalyptic Form in Jewish and Christian Literature* (Philadelphia: Fortress Press, 1987); and Werner Bieder, *Die Vorstellung.*

4. *Ep. ad Magn.: Ep. ad Philad.*

5. Ep. ad. Phil.

6. *Dial.,* 72.4.

7. *Adv. haer.,* 3.20; 4.22.1; 4.33.1; 4.38.12; 4.27.1-2; 5.31.1.

8. *De anim.,* 7, 55, 57; *De resur. carnis,* 44; *De pent.,* 12.

9. *Strom.,* 2.5.9.43; 6.44.6.14; 7.6.10.12.

10. *De prin.,* 2.2.6; *Comm. in Matt.,* 2, 3; *C. Cels.,* 2.56; 2.43; *Hom., in Luc.* 24; *Hom., in Ex.* 6.6.

11. *Test. adv. Iud.,* 2.24, 25, 27.

12. *De antichr.,* 26, 45.

13. *Ep. ad Dardanum,* 187. And note Augustine's saying in book 1 of the *Confessions:* "Why then do I ask Thee to come unto me ...? For I am not, after all, in hell" (1.2.2); and then in book 5 having a different sentiment: "I was very near to falling into hell" (5.9.16).

14. *De fide,* 3.4, 14, 27, 28.

15. This list, though long, is not exhaustive. See MacCulloch, *Harrowing of Hell,* pp. 83ff.; Huidekoper, *Christ's Mission,* passim; Bieder, *Die Vorstellung.*

16. In one work Augustine concurs with the opinion of Tertullian and Irenaeus (Ep., 188, *Depraesentia Dei Liber),* whereas in another work he rejects the view of zones of hell (Ep., 164,

Augustinus Evodio, respondens ad duos questions, quorum altera est de loco obscuro prima Petri). See also Ralph Turner, *"Descendit ad inferos:* Medieval Views of Christ's Descent into Hell and the Salvation of the Ancient Just," *Journal of the History of Ideas* 27 (1966): 176.

17. Friedrich Loofs, "Descent to Hades (Christ's)," *Encyclopaedia of Religion and Ethics,* ed. James Hastings (New York: Scribner's, 1912), 4:661; cf. Galot, "Descente du Christ," p. 489; and Huidekoper, *Christ's Mission, pp.* 144-45.

18. Besides the ones given above, there are also: Mark 3:27; 16:4; Matt. 12:29; 12:40; 16:18; 27:51-55; Luke 23:42; Rom. 6:3ff; 10:7; Phil. 2:10; Col. 2:14; and Heb. 2:14.

19. Cf. I Sam. 11:6; Isa. 14:11; Ezek. 31:15; Jon. 2:2; Dan. 12:2; Job 21:26; 26:5; Ps. 115:16; 29:10; 6:6; 87:6; 21:22; 29:10; etc.

20. Enoch 10:4; 12:13; 11:22; 12:14; 13:1; 18:2, 6, 11, 14; 21:3f.; etc.

21. This connection between the descent of Enoch and the *descensus Christi ad inferos,* by way of the I Pet. 3:19 interpretation, has been much debated. For some of the discussion, see Vogels, *Christi Abstieg,* pp. 74-85; MacCulloch, *Harrowing of Hell,* p. 53; W. J. Dalton, "Christ's Proclamation to the Spirits," *An. Bio.,* 23 (1965); and B. Reicke, "The Disobedient Spirits and Christian Baptism," *Acta seminarii Neotestamentici Upsaliensis* 13 (1946): 93.

22. There has been no end of debate concerning whether the *descensus Christi ad inferos* is better interpreted *historically* and theologically, giving special attention to the uniqueness of Christianity, or by using the tools of *comparative mythology* and the history of religions, where the universal human significance and the psychological power of the notion are seen. MacCulloch, for example, agrees with Clemen (*Primitive Christianity and its Non-Jewish Sources* [Edinburgh, 1912]) and Loofs ("Descent to Hades," p. 661) concerning the uniqueness of the Christian notion in spite of apparent similarities in world mythological traditions (see *Harrowing of Hell,* p. 322). These researchers stand against, say, P. Gardner (*Exploratio evangelica* [London, 1899]), who derives the Christian notion from Orphic backgrounds; and W. Bousset (*Hauptprobleme der Gnosis*), O. Pfleiderer (*Early Christian Conceptions of Christ*), T. Cheyne (*Bible Problems*), and H. Gunkel (*Zum Religionsgeschichtlichen Verständnis des Neuen Testaments*), each of whom derives the

Christian notion from Babylonian myth as filtered through Mandaeanism and Gnosticism. No matter which side one takes in this dispute, most seem agreed, as MacCulloch puts it, that "the *form* and *coloring* of the doctrine are largely *mythological"* (*Harrowing of Hell,* p. 322, emphasis added).

23. This typology (which has here been given a psychological slant) has been formulated by MacCulloch, "Descent to Hades (Ethnic)," in *The Encyclopaedia of Religion and Ethics,* ed. James Hastings (New York: Scribner's, 1912), 4:648-54.

24. For example, C. G. Jung, *CW,* 18.80: "Another version of the motif of the Hero and the Dragon is the Katabasis, the Descent into the Cave, the Nekyia. You remember in the Odyssey where Ulysses descends *ad inferos* to consult Tiresias, the seer. This motif of the Nekyia is found everywhere in antiquity and practically all over the world. It expresses the psychological mechanism of introversion of the conscious mind into the deeper layers of the unconscious psyche. From these layers derive the contents of an impersonal mythological character, in other words, the archetypes, and I call them therefore the impersonal or *collective unconscious."* See also the many index entries of "Christ—descent into hell," "ad inferos," "descensus ad inferos," "descent/descensus" in *CW,* 20. For other studies and sources of the comparative mythography of the *descensus ad inferos,* see Albrecht Dieterich, *Nekyia* (Leipzig: Teubner, 1893), esp. pp. 19-162; James Frazer, *The New Golden Bough,* ed. T. Gaster (New York: Mentor, 1964), p. 341 and passim; MacCulloch, *Harrowing of Hell,* pp. 1-60; and Kroll, *Gott und Hölle,* pp. 183ff. As Kroll says, "Der ganze Komplex ... ist frühzeitig verkümmert" (ibid., p. 523).

25. This brief history omits an important part of the story, namely, that which spans the time from the fourth century to the Renaissance, which includes, for example, how the conversation between Christ, Satan, and Hades in the Gospel of Nicodemus influenced Byzantine art; how it was rendered into the vernacular (Anglo-Saxon, English, French, German, and Italian); how it influenced Dante and was expressed in one of the most popular of Medieval Mystery Plays, "The Harrowing of Hell." For this, see MacCulloch, *Harrowing of Hell,* pp. 150-70. There is also the work on this topic by later church theologians: Pope Gregory, Peter Abelard, Bernard of Clairvaux, Alain of Lille, Peter Lombard, and Thomas Aquinas *(Summa theologica,* 4.3.53, "De

descensus Christi ad inferos in octo articulos divisa"). For this history, see Ralph Turner, "Views of Christ's Descent," 173-94.

26. Cited in Loofs, "Descent to Hades," 657.
27. Ibid.
28. Ibid.
29. Ibid., p. 658.
30. Herbert Vorgrimler, "Christ's Descent into Hell—Is It Important?" *Concilium,* 1, no. 2 (1966): 75.
31. Cf. the opinion of Huidekoper, *Christ's Mission,* p. v: "Christ's descent to the Underworld must in its most uninteresting shape, namely, as a point of doctrine, have occasioned an unusual amount of controversy, whilst its interesting . . . bearings have been overlooked."
32. Ibid., pp. 148, 177.
33. Loofs, "Descent to Hades," 662-63.
34. p. 526 (my translation). Cf. MacCulloch, *Harrowing of Hell,* pp. 322-23: "The form and coloring of the doctrine are largely mythological . . . [and] need not be taken literally."
35. Erich Heller, *Artist's Journey.* Other important literary critical studies of Heller's point include, Walter A. Strauss, *Descent and Return;* John J. White, *Mythology in the Modern Novel* (Princeton: Princeton University Press, 1971), pp. 175ff.; Lillian Feder, *Ancient Myth in Modern Poetry* (Princeton: Princeton University Press, 1971), pp. 90ff. ("Ezra Pound: The Voice from Hades"); Elizabeth Sewell, *The Orphic Voice* (New Haven: Yale University Press, 1960); Nathan A. Scott, Jr., "Eliot and the Orphic Way," *Journal of the American Academy of Religion* 42 (June 1974): 203ff.; and Stanley R. Hopper, "The Problem of Moral Isolation in Contemporary Literature," in *Spiritual Problems in Contemporary Literature* (New York: Harper & Bros., 1952), pp. 153ff. Hopper writes: "The quest is not outward, but inward. It is a descent into the void of contemporary lostness. . . . It is the raw descent of ego into itself" (ibid., pp. 154-55).
36. Northrop Frye, *Fables of Identity: Studies in Poetic Mythology* (New York: Harcourt, Brace and World, 1963), p. 62, and see the entire chapter entitled "New Directions from Old," in which the author treats the motif of the descent in contemporary literature. Cf. also David L. Miller, "Hades and Dionysos: The Poetry of Soul," *Journal of the American Academy of Religion* 46 (September 1978): 331-35.

37. The lines are from Rilke's poem, *Wendung* ("Turning"), cited in German in Heller, *Artist's Journey,* p. 155 (my translation).

38. R. M. Rilke, *Selected Poems,* tr. R. Bly (New York: Harper & Row, Publishers, 1981), p. 15. Excerpted from A *Book for the Hours of Prayer,* nos. 2, 4, and 5, from *Selected Poems* of Rainer Maria Rilke, tr. Robert Bly, copyright © 1981 by Robert Bly. Reprinted by permission of Harper & Row, Publishers, Inc.

39. Ibid., p. 19.

40. Geoffrey Hartman, *The Unmediated Vision* (New York: Harcourt, Brace and World, 1966), pp. 134ff.

41. Arthur Rimbaud, A *Season in Hell,* tr. L. Varese (New York: New Directions, 1961), p. 5.

42. See Strauss, *Descent and Return,* passim.

43. Reprinted from *Tulips & Chimneys* by E. E. Cummings, ed. George James Firmage, by permission of Liveright Publishing Corporation. Copyright 1923, 1925 and renewed 1951, 1953 by E. E. Cummings. Copyright © 1973, 1976 by the Trustees for the E. E. Cummings Trust. Copyright © 1973, 1976 by George James Firmage.

44. Theodore Roethke, *The Collected Poems* (Garden City, N.Y.: Doubleday, 1975), p. 211. From "The Abyss" from *The Collected Poems* of Theodore Roethke by Theodore Roethke. Copyright © 1963 by Beatrice Roethke, administratrix of the estate of Theodore Roethke. Reprinted by permission of Doubleday, a division of Bantam Doubleday Dell Publishing Group, Inc.

45. Charles Olson, *Selected Writings,* ed. Robert Creeley (New York: New Directions, 1966), p. 185. Copyright © 1960 by Charles Olson. Reprinted by permission of New Directions Pub. Corp.

46. Robinson Jeffers, *The Selected Poetry* (New York: Random House, 1938), p. 473.

47. Jack Gilbert, "County Musician," *Views of Jeopardy* (New Haven: Yale University Press, 1962), p. 14.

48. "Orpheus in Greenwich Village," Ibid., p. 17.

49. Stanley Kunitz, "The Poet's Quest for the Father," in *New York Times Book Review* (February 22, 1987), p. 1.

50. On the *Cantos,* by Ezra Pound, see Feder, *Ancient Myth,* pp. 90ff.

51. Origen, *De prin.,* 10.1, 6, 8. Cf. Origen, *Comm. in Cant.,* 3 (4).15, where he interprets the phrase "depths of the earth" (Ps. 63:9) metaphorically as referring to the "depths of [human] folly."

52. See MacCulloch, *Harrowing of Hell,* pp. 67ff.

53. Macarius Magnus, *Hom.* 11, par. 11, cited in Bieder, *Die Vorstellung,* p. 176 n. 198 (my translation).
54. Delmore Schwartz, *The World Is a Wedding* (Norfolk, Conn.: New Directions, 1948), p. 43.
55. Charles Williams, *Descent into Hell* (London: Faber & Faber, 1937), pp. 218, 220, 222.

3. A DESCENT INTO IMAGINATION: IMAGES OF THE DESCENT IN THE IDEAS OF THEOLOGY

1. Rainer Maria Rilke, *Duino Elegies,* 10.107 (my translation).
2. Cited in Vorgrimler, "Christ's Descent," p. 77; and MacCulloch, *Harrowing of Hell,* p. 71.
3. Origen, *C. Cels.,* 2.43: "After this he [Celsus] says to us: 'You will not say of him [Christ], I presume, that having failed to convince men on earth, he traveled to Hades to convince them there.' Even if he dislikes it, we maintain this, that when he was in the body he convinced not merely a few ... and then when he was in *psyche...* conversed with souls."
4. Regarding the relation of "hell" and "hole" and "pit," note the etymology of the English word "hell." It is cognate to "hall," "hole," "hold [of a ship]," "hollow," "howe" (i.e., a depressed land area), "hull," "cell," "cellar," "occult," and "clandestine." The Indo-European root of the family of the words is *kel-,* meaning "to hide," connecting thereby to Greek *kaluptein* and to Latin *celare,* both meaning "to hide." But the family also relates to Greek *kalia,* "hut," and Latin *cella,* a "small room." See Eric Partridge, *Origins* (New York: Macmillan, 1958), pp. 275ff. It should be noted also that the perspective developing here out of Christian theological materials has already been addressed and argued by James Hillman, *Dream and the Underworld,* ch. 3.
5. See MacCulloch, *Harrowing of Hell,* pp. 125-26, 130.
6. See ibid., pp. 110-11.
7. See ibid.
8. See ibid., p. 132.
9. This is from the *Epistle of Pilate to Herod* (fourth or fifth century). See MacCulloch, *Harrowing of Hell,* p. 132.
10. See ibid., p. 226.
11. Cf. the Nag Hammadi library, 7.1.19 ("The Paraphrase of Shem"); 202 and Patricia Cox, "Adam Ate from the Animal Tree," *Dionysius* 5 (1981): 165-80.

12. Edgar Hennecke, *New Testament Apocrypha,* ed. W. Schneemelcher, tr. R. Wilson (Philadelphia: Westminster Press, 1963), vol. 1, p. 473 (The Gospel of Bartholomew); cf. MacCulloch, *Harrowing of Hell,* p. 146.

13. Hennecke, *Apocrypha,* p. 489; cf. MacCulloch, *Harrowing of Hell,* p. 146.

14. See MacCulloch, pp. 125-26.

15. The metaphor of descent into the "heart" is commonly associated with a "descent into the heart of the earth." For example, see Galot, "Descente du Christ," p. 475: "Le Fils de l'homme serait pendant trois jours et trois nuits 'dans le coeur de la terre.'"

16. See Alan Watts, *Myth and Ritual in Christianity* (Boston: Beacon Press, 1968), p. 169. Cf. materials on "jaws" from Venantius Fortunatus, in MacCulloch, *Harrowing of Hell,* pp. 125ff.; and from homilies ascribed to Eusebius of Alexandria and to The Gospel of Nicodemus, where Hades is described as a monster who eats everyone, in ibid., p. 179.

17. For a fuller treatment of this motif, see the reference to the essay by A. K. Coomaraswamy on "Symplegades," in Alan Watts, *Myth and Ritual in Christianity* (Boston: Beacon Press, 1968), p. 169n.

18. Cf. David L. Miller, *Christs,* pp. 154-58.

19. See MacCulloch, *Harrowing of Hell,* p. 224.

20. Tertullian, *De resur. carnis,* 44, and note that the English word "adamant/adamantine," which means "hard stone" or "hard as steel," comes from the Greek *a-* ("not") + *daman* ("subdue"), and from Latin *adamas, adamantis* ("the hardest metal"). For similar descriptions of the underworld, cf. Athanasius, *De virginitate,* col. 16; also, Virgil, *Aen.* 6.551, who mentions the columns of solid "adamant" in the doorway of hell. There are similar passages in other ancient writers: See MacCulloch, *Harrowing of Hell,* pp. 221-22.

21. See Huidekoper, *Christ's Mission,* pp. 70-71. Cf. Hennecke, *Apocrypha* (The Gospel of Nicodemus), p. 472.

22. Isa. 45:3. See also the Nag Hammadi library, "The Paraphrase of Shem," where treasures like "the shining emerald," a "flourishing amaranth," and a "pure jacinth" seem to be produced from the hymen and vagina of the

underworld's darkness. This viewing of the underworld as giving the gift of matter and substance is connected with the viewing of the descent as being into the heart of the *earth* or, as the Gnostic vision had it, into matter itself. For example, Plotinus has this notion in *Ennead* 1.8.20ff.: "So it [the *psychē*] dies, as far as the soul can die, and its death, while it is still plunged in the body, is to sink in matter [*en hylē*] and be filled with it, and, when it has gone out of the body, to lie in matter till it raises itself and somehow manages to look away from the mud [*ek tou borborou*]: this is 'going to Hades.'" Cf. Jung, *CW,* 12.436, 439: "Death [in the Gnostic view] therefore represents the completion of the spirit's descent into matter. ... The purpose of the descent as universally exemplified in the myth of the hero is to show that only in the region of danger (watery abyss, cavern, forest, island, castle, etc.) can one find the 'treasure hard to attain' (jewel, virgin, life potion, victory over death). The dread and resistance which every natural human being experiences when it comes to delving too deeply into the self is, at bottom, the fear of the journey to Hades." But on the importance for the *psychē* of joining this journey into the "mud" and "matter," see Jung, *Letters,* ed. G. Adler, tr. R. F. C. Hull (Princeton: Princeton University Press, 1974), 2:556-58, where Jung writes: "I am weak and stupid enough to consider a certain amount of compassion, humility, love and feeling as indispensable for the understanding of the human soul and its woeful dough, i.e., the slime and mud at the bottom."
23. "The Paraphrase of Shem," 7.1.7-12.
24. Chrysostom, *Hom.* 40 in *Cor.* 15.29. Cf. Olivier Rousseau, "La descente aux enfers, fondement sotériologique du baptême chrétien," *Recherches science religieuse,* 40 (1952): 273-97.
25. See Leclercq and Cabrol, *"Descente du Christ,"* 696.
26. This theme of the *descensus* in relation to baptism has been addressed by Louis Beirnaert. See "The Mythical Dimension in Christian Baptism," *Eranos* 17—1949 (Zurich: Rhein-Verlag, 1950), and the reprint of the same essay in *Selection I,* ed. C. Hastings and D. Nichol (New York: Sheed and Ward, 1953), pp. 43-69. In ancient Fathers, see Cyril of Jerusalem, *Cat.* 12.15; 14-17; 2.11; and 3.6 and 9; Origen, *In*

lib. Jesu nave homilia, 4. See also, the modern work by P. Lundberg, *The Typology of Baptism in the Early Church* (Leipzig: A. Lorentz, 1942). James Hillman, from the psychological side, also has treated the theme of the descent into moisture in *Dream and the Underworld,* pp. 124-25, 135, 224; and in *The Myth of Analysis* (New York: Harper & Row, Publishers, 1972), p. 284, where he writes: "The descent is for the sake of moistening. Depression into these depths is experienced not as defeat ..., but as downwardness, darkening and becoming water. A major caution in alchemy was: Begin no operation until all has become water." In fact, the descent can be seen as a descent into any one of the four mythological elements, which suggests that the descent has the function of putting a person in touch with what is elemental, basic, and fundamental in its being. We have already touched upon the element *earth* (see n. 22, ch. 3, above) and now upon *water.* That hell is a place where one experiences *fire* ("the heat") is well known in popular myth and folk sayings. For the motif of "fire" in the descent, see Jung, *CW,* 12.440. Hillman notes the importance of *air* as a characteristic of the underworld in *Dream and the Underworld,* pp. 38, 124-25, 135, 149, and 186.

27. Morton Smith, Jesus *the Magician* (New York: Harper & Row, Publishers, 1978), pp. 114, 198, and note the spoof Smith cites from Lucian, where the descent is treated as the initiation of a magician (pp. 73-74).

28. Mircea Eliade, *Shamanism: Archaic Techniques of Ecstasy,* tr. W. Trask (New York: Pantheon Books, 1964), p. 5, but see also pp. 39, 51, 210-11, 234, and 311.

29. The connection between the *descensus* and the practice of magic has been well established in the critical literature. For example: Walter Burkert, "Goēs: Zum griechischen 'Schamanismus,'" *Rheinisches Museum für Philologie* (Frankfurt, 1962), n.s., 105, 36-55; MacCulloch, "Descent to Hades (Ethnic)," pp. 648ff.; and Josef Kroll, *Gott und Hölle,* who, after showing the connection between the *descensus* and magic in the Jewish tradition (p. 362), gives fifty-five pages of evidence for the connection of the motif with the antique magical tradition generally (pp. 467-522).

30. Vorgrimler, "Christ's Descent," 79.

31. See MacCulloch, *Harrowing of Hell,* p. 79.
32. The Nag Hammadi library, "The Teachings of Silvanus," 7.4.110. Cf. the same motif in The Teachings of Thaddeus, The Acts of Thomas, The Odes of Solomon, The Gospel of Nicodemus, The Gospel of Bartholomew, all of which have been noted and cited in MacCulloch's fine chapter, "The Breaking of the Gates of Hades," in *Harrowing of Hell* (ch. 13).
33. Origen, *De prin.,* 4.3.11; cf. 2.10.3-8, where Origen interprets "outer darkness" and other metaphors of the underworld in a figurative manner. See also the discussion of these matters in Origen by Patricia Cox, "In My Father's House Are Many Dwelling Places: *ktisma* in Origen's *De principiis,*" *Anglican Theological Review,* 62:322-37.
34. Origen, *De prin.,* 4.3.11.
35. Ibid., 4.3.4; cf. 4.1.6-7; 4.2.2; 4.3.4-5.
36. James Hillman, *Dream and the Underworld,* pp. 85ff.
37. See Tertullian, *De anima,* 55, and Irenaeus, *Adv. haer.,* 5.31.2.
38. See n. 25, ch. 3, above.
39. See MacCulloch, *Harrowing of Hell,* p. 195.
40. See ibid.
41. See ibid.

4. A DESCENT INTO THE MIDDLE: BETWEEN DEATH AND RESURRECTION

1. Quoted in Vogels, *Christi Abstieg,* p. 5.
2. Bousset, *Kyrios Christos,* p. 60.
3. J. Pohle, *Lehrbuch der Dogmatik* (1902, 1956), p. 280. This is cited by Vorgrimler, "Christ's Descent," 76-77, who says about it: "This is too glib to be true. Straightforward historical research shows that this teaching was certainly not inspired by modern curiosity as to where Christ's soul might have been during those three days" (ibid.). Whether Vorgrimler is historically and literally accurate, or whether he is not, the fact remains that there is a traditional theological fantasy of importance here, and it is especially important for the souls of people, as I am attempting to show.
4. J. Galot, *"Descente du Christ,"* 472 (my translation): "L'importance théologique de l'affirmation resulte déjà du seul fait qu'elle désigne l'événement comblant l'intervalle entre la mort et resurrection du Christ."

5. This formulation, save the comment about Saturn, is the one given in the Catholic encyclopedia, *Sacramentum Mundi* (New York: Herder, 1969), vol. 3, p. 9. Cf. Loofs, "Descent to Hades," 654: "The *dogma declaratum* ... is simply that Christ ... 'descendit ad inferos' in the interval between His burial and resurrection."

6. For further commentary on this "middle" and the "between," see Miller, *Christs,* ch. 25; and *Three Faces of God,* pt. 2, esp. pp. 65-80.

7. See Henry Corbin, *"Mundus imaginalis,* or the Imaginary and the Imaginal," *Spring 1972,* of which the French edition is *En Islam iranien: aspects spirituels et philosophiques,* tome 4, livre 7 (Paris: Gallimard, 1971). Cf. "Pour une charte de l'imaginal," *Corps spirituel et Terre céleste* (Paris: Editions Buchet/Chastel, 1979).

8. Cited by Gerhard Adler, "Remembering and Forgetting," *Panarion Conference,* 1976, tape (Los Angeles: Panarion Foundation, 1976).

9. I Cor. 15:30-31.

10. Cf. Jung, *CW,* 14.778: "The experience of the self is always a defeat for the ego."

11. Eugene O'Neill, *The Emperor Jones, Anna Christie, The Hairy Ape* (New York: Modern Library, 1937), p. 258.

5. A DESCENT INTO LAUGHTER:
THE ABOMINABLE FANCY

1. Denzinger-Bannwart, *Enchiridion, symbolorum,* no. 211; cf. D. P. Walker, *Decline of Hell,* p. 21. Throughout this section I am indebted to the work Walker has done in researching the theme "the abominable fancy."

2. See Walker, *Decline of Hell,* 22.

3. F. W. Farrar, *Eternal Hope* (five sermons preached in Westminster Abbey) (London, 1898), p. 66; cf. Walker, *Decline of Hell,* p. 31.

4. See Augustine, *City of God,* bk. 20, chs. 21, 22, and Aquinas, *Summa theologica,* suppl., quest. 94, art. 1.

5. Walker, *Decline of Hell,* chs. 1-2.

6. Bayle, *Œuvres div., vol.* 3, p. 863; quoted in Walker, *Decline of Hell,* p. 30.

7. See Tertullian, *De spectaculis,* col. 30; Migne, *Patr. lat.,* vol. 1, cols. 735-36.

8. Thomas Burnet, *De statu mortuorum et resurgentium tractatus* (London, 1733), p. 107; cf. Walker, *Decline of Hell,* p. 32.
9. G. Kittel, ed., *Theological Dictionary of the New Testament,* tr. G. W. Bromiley (Grand Rapids: Wm. B. Eerdmans Publishing Co., 1964), vol. 1, pp. 658ff.
10. Cited in John Dart, *The Laughing Savior* (New York: Harper & Row, Publishers, 1976), pp. 108-9; cf. Robert Grant, *Gnosticism and Early Christianity* (New York: Harper & Row, Publishers, 1966), pp. 192ff.
11. Cited in Dart, *Laughing Savior,* p. 108.
12. Cited in ibid., p. 107.
13. Aristotle, *Poetics,* 2, 5, in Paul Lauter, ed., *Theories of Comedy* (Garden City, N.Y.: Anchor Books, 1964), pp. 11, 13-14.
14. Cicero, *On the Character of the Orator,* 2.58, in Lauter, *Theories of Comedy,* pp. 24-25.
15. Donatus, *A Fragment on Comedy and Tragedy,* in ibid., pp. 28-29.
16. Francesco Robortello, *On Comedy,* in ibid., p. 52.
17. Vincenzo Maggi (Madius), *On the Ridiculous,* in ibid., pp. 65, 69-71.
18. Antonio Sebastiano Minturno, *The Art of Poetry,* in ibid., p. 74.
19. Lodovico Castelvetro, *Commentary on Aristotle's Poetics,* in ibid., p. 95, and note Castelvetro's saying: "Wickedness, insofar as it is ludicrous, may be imitated by Comedy. ... Comedy ... is an imitation of men who are worse than the average. ... The ludicrous is a defect and deformity that does not give pain and does no harm" (ibid., p. 87).
20. *King Lear,* 5.3.316-19. Cf. James Cunningham, *Woe or Wonder* (Denver: University of Denver Press, 1951).
21. Carlo Goldoni, *The Comic Theatre,* in Lauter, *Theories of Comedy,* p. 171.
22. Jean Francois Cailhava d'Estendoux, *The Art of Comedy,* in ibid., p. 179.
23. See John Dryden, *An Evening's Love,* "Preface"; William Congreve, "Concerning Humour in Comedy" (a letter to John Dennis); John Dennis, "A Large Account of the Taste in Poetry, and the Causes of the Degeneracy of It" (a letter to George Granville); Oliver Goldsmith, "A Comparison Between Laughing and Sentimental Comedy"; and William Hazlitt, *Lectures on the Comic Writers of Great* Britain—all in Lauter,

Theories of Comedy, pp. 194ff., 206ff., 215ff., 259ff., and 263ff.

24. Hobbes, *Human Nature,* 9.13. W. Molesworth, ed., *The English Works of Thomas Hobbes* (London: J. Boun, 1840), 4.46. Cf. Marie Collins Swabey, *Comic Laughter, a Philosophical Essay* (New Haven: Yale University Press, 1961), p. 212.
25. Charles Baudelaire, "The Essence of Laughter," ed. Peter Quennell (New York: Meridian, 1956), pp. 110-11.
26. Ibid., p. 112.
27. Ibid., pp. 117, 130.
28. Ibid., p. 120.
29. George Meredith, "An Essay on Comedy," in Wylie Sypher, ed., *Comedy* (Garden City, N.Y.: Doubleday, 1956), p. 19.
30. Ibid., pp. 42-43.
31. Henri Bergson, "Laughter," in ibid., p. 75.
32. Cf. Nelvin Vos, *The Drama of Comedy: Victim and Victor* (Richmond: John Knox Press, 1966).
33. Enid Welsford, *The Fool* (Garden City, N.Y.: Doubleday, 1961), p. 291.
34. Ibid., pp. 292, 302, 304.

6. A DESCENT INTO PSYCHOPATHOLOGY: ARCHETYPAL SADOMASOCHISM

1. Augustine, *City of God,* 20.22.
2. On December 14, 1909, Jung wrote to Freud about an article by Ferenczi. In the letter, Jung said, concerning the "sadistic component of libido": "I must remark that I don't like the idea of sadism being constitutional. I think of it rather as a reactive phenomenon." Five days later Freud wrote to Jung: "In defense of sadism I should like to observe that its nature as an original component or instinct can hardly be questioned. ... Reactive phenomena are not at all of the same nature as sadism; on the contrary, they are purely passive. ... By concentrating on the ego, which I have not adequately studied, you run the risk of neglecting the libido, to which I have done full justice." Then on Christmas day Jung wrote: "I note that my difficulties regarding the question of libido and also of sadism are obviously due to the fact that I have not yet adjusted my attitude sufficiently to yours. I still

haven't understood properly what you wrote me." See *The Freud/Jung Letters,* ed. William McGuire, tr. R. Manheim and R. F. C. Hull (Princeton: Princeton University Press, 1974), pp. 275, 277-78, 280.

3. Sigmund Freud, *A General Selection from the Works,* "Instincts and Their Vicissitudes," ed. J. Rickman (Garden City, N.Y.: Doubleday, 1957), p. 78.

4. On the important change by Freud in the direction of "instinctual dualism," particularly as it relates to his views on sadomasochism, see Norman O. Brown, *Life Against Death* (New York: Modern Library, 1959), pp. 97-101; and Paul Ricoeur, *Freud and Philosophy,* tr. D. Savage (New Haven: Yale University Press, 1970), pp. 124-25, 295.

5. Hillman, *The Myth of Analysis.* See pp. 37, 92-93, 145 ff., 199-200. For Jung's writing on these matters, see *CW,* 11.345-46; 13.94, 439-49; 12.417.

6. Hillman, *Myth of Analysis,* pp. 92-93.

7. Ibid., p. 146.

8. Ibid., p. 200.

9. Ibid., p. 199.

10. Ibid., p. 37. The psychological perspective being developed here is paralleled in an important and innovative work on masochism, which appeared after this chapter was written. The author, Lyn Cowan, writes: "The source of pleasure [in painful experiences) is not pain, but humiliation. ... [It] makes for humility, a continual relativizing of ego" *(Masochism: A Jungian View* [Dallas: Spring Publications, 1982], pp. 49, 52).

11. Hillman, *Dream and the Underworld,* p. 196.

12. Jung, *CW,* 9.2.72; cf. David L. Miller, "In the Middle of a Dark Way: *Descensus ad inferos* in C. G. Jung and James Hillman," L. Martin and J. Goss, eds., *Essays on Jung and the Study of Religion* (Lanham, Md.: University Press of America, 1985), pp. 192-203.

13. Heraclitus' words are : *hodox anō katō mia kai outō* (DK #60). This fragment was preserved by Hippolytus, 9; cf. Tertullian, *Adv. Marc.,* 2.28: "Quid enim ait Heraclitus ille tenebrousus? Eadem via sursum et deorsum." This experience of the soul, which is apparently paradoxical, is often given witness in the words "as above, so below," especially in the traditions of Hellenistic astrology, Hermetica, alchemy,

and Renaissance neoplatonism. Something similar may be intended by the mythological testimony that Zeus and Hades are brothers, not to mention the scriptural and iconographic traditions in which angels are said to be and are pictured as, not going up a ladder and not going down a ladder, but rather ascending *and* descending, as if these were one motion and one event. On this last matter, see David L. Miller, "Theologia imaginalis," in C. Winquist, ed., *The Archaeology of the Imagination* (Chico, Calif.: Scholars Press, 1981). That these ups and downs go together and are reversible is indicated in an interesting manner by Jung. He is noting, in his "Commentary on Kundalini Yoga," that the Tibetan way of imagining the person places ordinary ego-consciousness at the base of the spine in the *muladhara chakra,* and the deeper dimensions of the self (sexuality, heart, etc.) above. Jung says: "With us it is apparently the other way round. We do not go up to the unconscious, we go down; it is a *katabasis.* ... In the East the unconscious is above. ... Going through Christian baptism is going up, but that does not hinder its being represented by going down into the water. Christ doesn't climb up into the Jordan" *(Spring 1975,* 12-13).

14. Olson, *Selected Writings,* p. 185.

7. A DESCENT INTO THE HELLS OF MODERN LITERATURE: THE DARK INFERENCE AND NEGATIVE THEOLOGY

1. Dylan Thomas, "Do Not Go Gentle into That Good Night," R. Aldington, ed., *The Viking Book of Poetry* (New York: Viking Press, 1959), vol. 2, p. 1247.
2. Martin Heidegger, *Poetry, Language, Thought,* tr. A. Hofstadter (New York: Harper & Row, Publishers, 1971), p. 191; and *Unterwegs zur Sprache* (Pfullingen: Neske, 1975), p. 13. Heidegger also speaks in a way similar to the next quotation of Baudelaire when he is commenting on a late poem by Stefan Georg (*Das Wort,* "The Word"). The particular lines in question read: "So lernt ich traurig den verzicht: / Kein ding sei wo das wort gebricht" ("So I renounced and sadly see: Where the word breaks off no thing may be"). Heidegger writes: "The renunciation

which the poet learns is of that special kind of fulfilled self-denial to which alone is promised what has long been concealed and is essentially vouchsafed already. The poet, then, ought to rejoice at such an experience, which brings to him the most joyful gift a poet can receive. ... Renunciation is not a loss. Nor does 'sadly' refer to the substance of the renunciation, but rather to the fact that he has learned it. That sadness, however, is neither mere dejection nor despondency. True sadness is in harmony with what is most joyful. ... The poet could never go through the experience he undergoes with the word if the experience were not attuned to sadness, to the mood of releasement [*die Stimmung der Gelassenheit*] into the nearness of what is withdrawn but at the same time held in reserve for an originary advent" *(On the Way to Language,* tr. D. Hertz [New York: Harper & Row, Publishers, 1971], p. 66, and *Unterwegs zur Sprache,* p. 169). Later in the same book, Heidegger again comments on Georg's lines, saying, "The more joyful the joy, the more pure sadness slumbering within it. The deeper the sadness, the more summoning the joy resting within it. Sadness and joy play into each other. The play itself which attunes the two by letting the remote be near and the near be remote is pain [*Das Spiel ... ist der Schmerz*]. This is why both, highest joy and deepest sadness, are painful each in its way. But pain so touches the spirit of mortals that the spirit receives its gravity from pain. That gravity keeps mortals with all their wavering at rest in their being. The spirit [*Gemüt*] which answers to pain, the spirit attuned by pain and to pain, is melancholy. It can depress the spirit, but it can also lose its burdensomeness and let its 'secret breath' [*heimlich Hauch*] nestle into the soul, bestow upon it the jewel which arrays it in the precious relation to the world, and with this raiment shelters it" *(On the Way to Language,* p. 153; *Unterwegs zur Sprache,* p. 235).

3. Baudelaire, *Essence of Laughter,* p. 167.
4. Cited by Karl Kerényi, *The Religion of the Greeks and Romans* (New York: E. P. Dutton, 1962), p. 55.
5. R. M. Rilke, *Selected Poems,* p. 21.
6. Donald Hall, *Seasons at Eagle Pond* (New York: Ticknor and Fields, 1987), pp. 3-4.

7. Makoto Ueda, "The Making of the Comic Art: Toraaki on the Art of Comedy," *Literary and Art Theories in Japan* (Cleveland: Press of Western Reserve University, 1967), p. 108.
8. Ibid.
9. Ibid., p. 102.
10. I am indebted to my colleague Richard B. Pilgrim for this analysis. See his essay: "The Artistic Way and the Religio-Aesthetic Tradition in Japan," *Philosophy East and West,* 27, no. 3 (July 1977): 291ff.
11. On this concept, see Jung, *CW,* 12.433 and 14.741.
12. Cited in Pilgrim, "The Artistic Way," p. 296.
13. Gadjin M. Nagao, "Ascent and Descent: Two-Directional Activity in Buddhist Thought," *The Journal of the International Association of Buddhist Studies,* 7, no. 1 (1984): 179.
14. Julia Kristeva, *Powers of Horror,* p. 207. I am grateful to Sarah Halford for calling this to my attention in connection with the argument of this book.
15. David F. Krell, "Descensional Reflection," pp. 4, 10.
16. Alphonso Lingis, *Excesses: Eros and Culture* (New York: SUNY Press, 1983), p. 13.
17. Charles E. Winquist, *Epiphanies of Darkness,* cf. David L. Miller, "Hades and Dionysos," pp. 331-35.
18. Theodore Roethke, *Collected Poems* (Garden City, N.Y.: Doubleday, 1975), pp. 84, 231.
19. Wallace Stevens, *Collected Poems* (New York: Knopf, 1975), pp. 528, 437.
20. Denise Levertov, *Collected Earlier Poems 1940—1960* (New York: New Directions, 1959), p. 48. Copyright © 1959 by Denise Levertov Goodman. Reprinted by permission of New Directions Pub. Corp.
21. Ibid., p. 16.
22. Nikolai Berdyaev, *The Beginning and the End* (New York: Harper & Bros., 1957), p. 107; cf. pp. 99-100.
23. Ibid., p. 108.
24. John of the Cross, *The Ascent of Mt. Cannel,* 2.3.5, in Kavanaugh and Rodriguez, eds., *The Collected Works of St. John of the Cross* (Garden City, N.Y.: Doubleday, 1964), p. 111.
25. *The Ascent,* 2.3.6, in ibid., p. 112.
26. Raymond Blakney, tr., *Meister Eckhart* (New York: Harper & Bros., 1941), p. 17.

27. Bonaventure, *The Mind's Road to God,* tr. G. Boas (Indianapolis: Library of Liberal Arts, 1953), p. 45. The quotation is from Dionysius the Areopagite, *Mystic Theology,* ch. 1.
28. John Updike, "Gradations of Black (Third Floor, Whitney Museum)," *The New Yorker* (August 13, 1984), p. 30.
29. Ibid.
30. Eric Voegelin, *Order and History, Vol. 3: Plato and Aristotle* (Baton Rouge: Louisiana University Press, 1957), p. 84.
31. Wallace Stevens, *Opus Posthumous,* ed. Samuel French Morse (New York: Knopf, 1977), p. 55.
32. Stevens, *Collected Poems,* p. 45.
33. Stevens, *Opus Posthumous,* p. 100.
34. Stanley R. Hopper, "The Philosophy of No," *Why Persimmons and Other Poems* (Atlanta: Scholars Press, 1987), p. 23.
35. Jung, *CW,* 13.335.
36. Ibid., 9.2.595.
37. Ibid., 13.335.
38. Norman O. Brown, *Love's Body* (New York: Random House, 1966), p. 241.
39. From *History of the Psychoanalytic Movement,* cited in ibid.
40. Ibid.
41. Octavio Paz, "A Draft of Shadows," *Monte Mora* 6 (1979): 90.

8. HISTORY AS HELL

1. On the *via crucis* motif, see Stanley R. Hopper, *The Crisis of Faith* (Nashville/New York: Abingdon-Cokesbury Press, 1944), pp. 285ff.
2. Cited by Karl Kerényi, *Eleusis: Archetypal Image of Mother and Daughter,* tr. R. Manheim (New York: Pantheon, 1967), pp. 38-39.
3. Kerényi, *The Gods of the Greeks* (London: Thames and Hudson, 1979), pp. 243-44.
4. Ibid.
5. Kerényi, *Eleusis,* p. 40.
6. Ibid., p. 65.
7. I have been greatly instructed on this "as" of "is" by Stanley R. Hopper. See his essay, "The Bucket as It Is," *Beyond Metaphor* (Syracuse: Alteracts/Department of Religion, 1979), pp. 5-47, where the formula is, "When as is as as, then as is as is."

9. THE DEATH OF GHOSTS

1. Aniela Jaffé, ed., C. G. *Jung: Word and Image,* tr. K. Winston (Princeton: Princeton University Press, 1979), pp. 184-85 (here, my translation).
2. Matthew Arnold, "Geist's Grave," *The Poems of Matthew Arnold,* ed. Allott (New York: Barnes and Noble, 1965), 2.41-42 (p. 548). Permission granted by Barnes & Noble Books, Totowa, New Jersey.
3. Friedrich Nietzsche, 'The Madman," *The Gay Science,* para. 125, in Walter Kaufmann, tr., *The Portable Nietzsche* (New York: Viking Press, 1954), pp. 95-96; Plutarch, "De oraculorum defectu," *Moralia,* 419A-E.
4. Arnold, *"Geist's Grave,"* 2.13-16 (p. 547). Arnold himself gives the reference to Virgil's *Aeneid* in a footnote to the poem.
5. See Stanley R. Hopper, "Dust on the Mirror: The Poetic Quality of Consciousness East and West," unpublished manuscript, p. 5; Joseph Campbell, *The Masks of God: Creative Mythology* (New York: Viking Press, 1968), p. 179; and *The Masks of God: Oriental Mythology* (New York: Viking Press, 1962), p. 490.
6. Plotinus, *Enneads,* 4.9.3 (1).
7. Arnold, *"Geist's Grave,"* 1.80 (p. 549).
8. Gilbert Ryle, *The Concept of Mind* (New York: Barnes and Noble, 1949); Arthur Koestler, *The Ghost in the Machine* (New York: Macmillan, 1967), p. 202 and passim.
9. Paul Tillich, *Systematic Theology* (Chicago: University of Chicago Press, 1963), vol. 3, p. 292.
10. For this phrase I am indebted to Patricia Cox, who has developed its significance in *Biography in Late Antiquity: The Quest for the Holy Man* (Berkeley: University of California Press, 1983), p. 147 and passim.

10. GHASTLY, GUEST, HOST: THE GHOSTS IN LANGUAGE

1. Robert Young, *Analytical Concordance to the Bible* (Grand Rapids: Wm. B. Eerdmans Publishing Co., 1955), p. 488: Matt. 1:18, 20; 3:11; 12:32; 28:19; Mark 1:8; 3:29; 12:36; 13:11; Luke 1:15, 35, 41, 67; 2:25,26; 3:16, 22; 4:1; 12:10, 12; John 1:33; 14:26; 20:22; Acts 1:2, 5, 8, 16; etc.

2. Ibid., p. 389: Job 11:20; Jer. 15:9; Matt. 27:50; John 19:30; Gen. 25:8; Job 3:1; Mark 15:37; Luke 23:46; Acts 5:5.
3. John Ellison, ed., *Nelson's Complete Concordance of the Revised Standard Version Bible* (New York: Thomas Nelson & Sons, 1957), p. 707.
4. Tillich, *Systematic Theology,* vol. 3, p. 21.
5. Ibid., p. 23.
6. I Cor. 2:13 (RSV, alt. reading).
7. *The Compact Edition of the Oxford English Dictionary* (OED) (New York: Oxford University Press, 1971), vol. 1, pp. 1138-39.
8. Ibid., p. 1138.
9. Ibid., pp. 1223-24.
10. J. Hillis Miller, "The Critic as Host," H. Bloom, et al., *Deconstruction and Criticism* (New York: Seabury Press, 1979), esp. pp. 220ff.; Sigmund Freud, "The Antithetical Sense of Primal Words" (1910), and, "The Uncanny" (1919), *On Creativity and the Unconscious* (New York: Harper & Bros., 1958), pp. 55-62, 122-61.
11. *OED,* vol. 1, p. 1336; cf. Miller, "The Critic," who explains the *pot*-syllable: "The 'pes' or 'pit' in the Latin words and in such modern English words as 'hospital' or 'hospitality' is from another root, *pot,* meaning 'master.' The compound or bifurcated root *ghos-pot* meant 'master of guests'" (p. 221).
12. Miller, "The Critic," p. 221.
13. Martin Heidegger, *What Is Called Thinking?* tr. Wieck and Gray (New York: Harper & Row, Publishers, 1968), pp. 118-19.
14. Paul Kugler, *The Alchemy of Discourse: An Archetypal Approach to Language* (Lewisburg, Pa.: Bucknell University Press, 1982).
15. Jung, *CW,* 2.882.
16. Jung's conclusion is cited by Kugler, *Alchemy of Discourse,* p. 17.
17. Kugler, *Alchemy of Discourse,* p. 17.
18. Ibid.
19. Ibid., p. 18.
20. Ibid., p. 22; cf. p. 26. In this regard two comments made by Northrop Frye in a book on the Bible are important. Frye writes: "The ear of the AV translators for the rhythm of the spoken word, though there are many lapses, was very acute, and it is a sobering thought that it is sensitivity to one's own language, not scholarly knowledge of the original, that makes a translation permanent. A translator with a tin ear, including a translator of the Bible, is

continually mistranslating, whatever that person's scholarly knowledge." Earlier Frye had written: "The sound-associations within a language ... are of immense importance in building up linguistic responses.... they make up a texture that enters into the mental processes of all native speakers of the language." In *The Great Code: The Bible and Literature* (New York: Harcourt Brace Jovanovich, 1982), pp. 208, 204.

21. Kugler, *Alchemy of Discourse,* p. 32 n. 33.

11. THE GHOST OF OLD MRS. LEAKEY: THE GHOSTS OF HISTORY

1. This apt phrase is used by Brown in her important work, *The Fate of the Dead: A Study in Folk-Eschatology in the West Country After the Reformation* (Totowa, N.J.: Rowman and Littlefield, 1979), ch. 1.
2. Ibid., p. 8.
3. *The Book of Common Prayer* (New York: Seabury Press, 1977), p. 872.
4. Brown, *Fate of the Dead,* pp. 19-20; and see the full account given by Brown in, "The Ghost of Old Mrs. Leakey," in Davidson and Russell, eds., *The Folklore of Ghosts* (Cambridge: D. S. Brewer, 1981), pp. 141-54. The "whistling" to produce storms is a universal motif, and the particular case of Mrs. Leakey's whistling ghost influenced the poetries of Sir Walter Scott, Samuel Taylor Coleridge, and William Wordsworth—each of whom knew the tale, as Brown has demonstrated (ibid., pp. 141, 150-51).
5. Brown, "The Ghost," p. 151.
6. Ibid., pp. 141-44.
7. Ibid., p. 146.
8. Ibid., p. 148.
9. Ibid., p. 149.
10. Ibid., p. 150.
11. For example, see Brown, *Fate of the Dead,* pp. 19ff., where she cites other famous (or infamous) instances—"The Drummer of Tedworth" (1661), "The Botathen Ghost" (1665), etc.
12. Linda-May Ballard, "Before Death and Beyond—A Preliminary Survey of Death and Ghost Traditions with Particular Reference to Ulster," in Davidson and Russell, eds., *Folklore of Ghosts,* p. 13.

13. E. R. Dodds, *The Greeks and the Irrational* (Boston: Beacon Press, 1957), and "Supernormal Phenomena in Classical Antiquity," *Proceedings of the Society for Psychical Research,* 55 (1971): 189-237; L. Collison-Morley, *Greek and Roman Ghost Stories* (Chicago: Argonaut, 1968); and W. M. S. Russell, "Greek and Roman Ghosts," in Davidson and Russell, eds., *Folklore of Ghosts,* pp. 193-213. For other secondary sources, as well as for the classical references, see the notes to ibid., pp. 261-66.
14. J. R. Porter, "Ghosts in the Old Testament and the Ancient Near East," in ibid., pp. 215-38.
15. Richard A. Boyer, "The Role of the Ghost Story in Mediaeval Christianity," in ibid., pp. 177-92.
16. Dodds, "Supernormal Phenomena," 191.
17. Russell, "Greek and Roman Ghosts," p. 206.
18. Porter, "Ghosts in the Old Testament," p. 215.
19. See ibid., passim.
20. Boyer, "Role of the Ghost Story," p. 177.
21. Ibid.
22. Patricia Berry, "Hamlet's Poisoned Ear," *Echo's Subtle Body* (Dallas: Spring Publications, 1982), p. 130 and passim.
23. Brown, *Fate of the Dead,* p. 2.
24. Cited in ibid., p. 17, from *The Table Talk of John Seldon* (1634-1654), 98.
25. Brown, *Fate of the Dead,* pp. 17-18.
26. Ibid., p. 19. Steven Simmer has pointed out to me that even John Wesley's Father, Samuel, had difficulties with a ghost named "Jeffrey." See the work by Andrew Lang, *The Book of Dreams and Ghosts* (Hollywood, Calif.: Newcastle, 1972), pp. 210-21.
27. Brown, *Fate of the Dead,* p. 8. Cf. the interesting research and theorizing by psychoanalyst Richard Sterba in "On Halloween," *The American Imago,* 5, no. 3 (November 1948): 213-24.
28. Brown, *Fate of the Dead,* pp. 15-16.
29. Ibid., p. 16.
30. For reference to this literature, see David L. Miller, *The New Polytheism* (1981), p. 102, nn. 21 and 22.

12. THE GRATEFUL DEAD: THE GHOSTS OF FOLKLORE

1. Boyer, *"Role of the Ghost Story,"* p. 190.
2. Ibid., p. 182. I should like to express gratitude to my research assistant Lee Bailey, who helped with this section.
3. Plotinus, On the Nature of the Soul *(Ennead 4),* tr. Stephen MacKenna (London: The Medici Society, 1924), p. 143.
4. See W. K. C. Guthrie, *The Greeks and Their Gods* (Boston: Beacon Press, 1950), pp. 274ff.; Theodor H. Gaster, *Myth, Legend, and Custom in the Old Testament* (New York: Harper & Row, Publishers, 1969), p. 69.
5. Gaster, *Myth, Legend, and Custom,* p. 69.
6. A. Aarne and S. Thompson, *The Types of the Folktale* (Helsinki: Academia Scientiarum Fennica, 1961).
7. S. Thompson, ed., *Motif-Index of Folk Literature* (Bloomington: Indiana University Press, 1955-58).
8. See ibid., E341.
9. See Dov Noy, ed., *Folktales of Israel,* tr. Baharav (Chicago: University of Chicago Press, 1963), pp. 126-30; Geneviève Massignon, *Folktales of France,* tr. Hyland (Chicago: University of Chicago Press, 1968), pp. 44-48; cf. John Tatlock, "Levenoth and the Grateful Dead," *Modern Philology,* 22 (August-May, 1924–25): 211-14; and J. Bolte and G. Polívka, *Anmerkungen zu den Kinder- und Haus-märchen der Brüder Grimm,* Band 3 (Hildesheim: Georg Olms Verlag, 1963), pp. 490-517 ("Der dankbare Tote und die auks der Sklaverei erlöste Königstochter").
10. Gordon Gerould, *The Grateful Dead: The History of a Folk Story* (London: Folklore Society, 1907), p. 1 and passim.
11. For a review of these sources, see ibid., pp. 1-6.
12. See ibid., pp. 7-25, for the particular tales and their sources.
13. Cicero, *De divinatione,* 1.27; and it is referred to again in 2.65 and 66; cf. Gerould *The Grateful Dead,* p. 8; and Boyer, "Role of the Ghost Story," pp. 199-200.
14. Cf. David L. Miller, "Fairy Tale or Myth?" *Spring 1976* (Dallas), 157-64.
15. Collison-Morley, *Ghost* Stories, pp. 60-61; Russell, *Folklore of Ghosts,* pp. 201-2.
16. See Pausanias, 5.1.2, 6-7; 5.13.4; Apollodorus, *Epitome,* 2.3-9; and cf. Robert Graves, *The Greek Myths* (Baltimore: Penguin Books, 1955), vol. 2, para. 109 (pp. 31-37).

13. THE PARACLETE: GHOSTS OF SCRIPTURE

1. For a brief, critical review of Form Criticism, see Alfred M. Perry, "The Growth of the Gospels," in *The Interpreter's Bible* (Nashville/New York: Abingdon-Cokesbury Press, 1951), vol. 7, pp. 69-70.
2. See Marshall McLuhan, *The Gutenberg Galaxy: The Making of Typographic Man* (Toronto: University of Toronto Press, 1962); and, with Quentin Fiore, *The Medium Is the Message* (New York: Bantam Books, 1967).
3. James Hillman, "The Fiction of Case History: A Round," in James Wiggins, ed., *Religion as Story* (New York: Harper & Row, Publishers, 1975), esp. pp. 140-46.
4. Rudolf Bultmann, *The History of the Synoptic Tradition,* tr. J. Marsh (New York: Harper & Row, Publishers, 1963), pp. 46-47, 182ff., and passim.
5. Rudolf Bultmann, *The Gospel of John: A Commentary,* tr. Beasley-Murray (Philadelphia: Westminster Press, 1971), pp. 302 n. 3, 328 n. 5, and 310 n. 1.
6. There has been considerable scholarly debate over whether or not the Paraclete and the Holy Ghost are one and the same. For a review of this literature, see J. Behm, "Parakletos," in Friedrich, ed., *Theological Dictionary of the New Testament,* tr. Bromiley (Grand Rapids: Wm. B. Eerdmans Publishing Co., 1967), vol. 5, pp. 803-14; and Raymond Brown, ed., *The Gospel According to John, Anchor Bible* (Garden City, N.Y.: Doubleday, 1970), vol. 29A, pp. 1135-44. For purposes of the present argument, it is sufficient to note, without taking sides in the historical debate, that the Christian tradition has imagined that the two were one and the same. This is the fantasy of tradition's meaning that we are here examining. As Bultmann has put it, "It is clear that the Evangelist has taken the figure of the Paraclete from his source and interpreted it, in the context of the Christian tradition, as the *hagion pneuma* (*Gospel of John,* p. 566).
7. Brown, ed., *Gospel According to John,* p. 1136.
8. Except for the unusual use of cognate forms in some manuscripts, and then only in one instance: Namely, Job 16:2. Cf. Behm, "Parakletos," pp. 803-14.
9. Heraclitus (the Stoic), *Homeri allegoriae,* 59e; cf. Behm, "Parakletos," pp. 803-14.
10. Diogenes Laertius, 4.50; cf. Behm, "Parakletos," pp. 803-14.

11. See ed., Brown, *Gospel According to John,* p. 1136.
12. Behm, "Paraklētos," pp. 803-14.
13. For a critical treatment of the term "gnostic," which serves to demonstrate the problems with Bultmann's use, see Morton Smith, "The History of the Term *Gnostikos,"* in Layton, ed., *The Rediscovery of Gnosticism: Vol. 2: Sethian Gnosticism* (Leiden: Brill, 1980), pp. 796-807.
14. Bultmann, *Gospel of John,* p. 571.
15. Ibid.
16. For a review of this discussion and for a full bibliography, see Brown, ed., *Gospel According to John,* pp. 1137-38.
17. See Behm, "Paraklētos," pp. 803-14; cf. Brown, *Gospel According to John,* pp. 1138-39.
18. The work of Henry Corbin on the figure of the *daēna, a fravarti-helper,* in Persian Sufism, is relevant at this point. See my discussion of this "angelology" of Corbin, in "Theologia imaginalis," Winquist, ed., *The Archaeology of the Imagination* (Chico, Calif.: Scholars Press, 1981), pp. 1-18.
19. Morton Smith, *Jesus the Magician* (New York: Harper & Row, Publishers, 1978).
20. Ibid., esp. pp. 34-35, 97-98, 191 n. 97.
21. Gerould, *The Grateful Dead,* p. 87.
22. See ibid., p. 48.
23. See ibid., p. 129.
24. See ibid., p. 115.
25. See Rudolf Bultmann, *History of the Synoptic Tradition,* passim.

14. PROPER BURIAL: GHOSTS OF DEPTH PSYCHOLOGY

1. See McGuire, ed., *The Freud/Jung Letters,* pp. 250ff., 255, 258, 326, 332, 438-39, and 441, which letters span the period between October 14, 1909, and September 1, 1911, the period in which Freud was writing *Totem and Taboo* and Jung was writing *Symbols of Transformation.* The letter of June 19, 1910, shows Freud saying to Jung: "Don't be surprised if you recognize certain of your own statements in a paper of mine" (ibid., p. 332); and, again, Freud writes on August 20, 1911: "I have been working in a field where you will be surprised to meet me" (ibid., p. 438).
2. Freud, *Totem and Taboo,* tr. James Strachey (New York: W. W. Norton & Co., 1950), p. 38.

3. Ibid., p. 58.
4. Ibid.
5. Ibid., p. 63.
6. Ibid., p. 62.
7. Ibid., p. 65 and passim.
8. Jung, *CW*, 12.437.
9. Ibid., 12.437 n. 43.
10. Ibid., 11.20-21. For other comments by Jung on "ghosts," see ibid., 20, entry "ghosts."
11. Ibid., 11.22. For additional explanations of "split-off complexes," see ibid., 3.59; 5.39; 6.923; 13.45; 16.13; 18.383.
12. Ibid., 11.23. For a description of how Jung himself gave the dead "proper burial," dealing with ghosts imaginally, see Jung, *Memories, Dreams, Reflections,* ed. Jaffé, (New York: Vintage, 1965), pp. 190-91.
13. Edgar Herzog, *Psyche and Death: Death-Demons in Folklore, Myths and Modern Dreams,* tr. Cox and Rolfe (Dallas: Spring Publications, 1983); Aniela Jaffé, *Apparitions: An Archetypal Approach to Death Dreams and Ghosts* (Dallas: Spring Publications, 1979); Marie-Louise von Franz, *A Psychological Interpretation of Apuleius' Golden Ass* (Dallas: Spring Publications, 1980), pp. 65-66; Erich Neumann, *Amor and Psyche,* tr. R. Manheim (New York: Harper & Row, Publishers, 1962), p. 114n.
14. Norman O. Brown, *Life Against Death* (New York: Vintage Books, 1959), p. 172 and passim. Brown is quoting Freud's *Moses and Monotheism,* tr. Jones (New York: Knopf, 1939), pp. 178-79. Cf. Brown's comment in *Love's Body,* pp. 90, 96: "Personality is *persona,* a mask ... the voices coming through the masks are always ancestral voices ... a *danse macabre,* a visit of ancestral spirits."
15. Patricia Berry, *"Hamlet's Poisoned Ear,"* p. 144.
16. Ibid., p. 145.
17. Ibid., p. 144.
18. Ibid., p. 145.
19. On this notion of "entertaining" the self, see James Hillman, *Inter Views* (New York: Harper & Row, Publishers, 1983), pp. 16, 24, 38.
20. The perspective is here reported by one who studied with Lacan: namely, Stuart Schneiderman, *Jacques Lacan: The Death of an Intellectual Hero* (Cambridge: Harvard University Press, 1983), p. 146.

21. Ibid., p. 57.
22. Ibid., p. 151.
23. Ibid., p. 152.
24. Ibid., passim.
25. James Hillman, *Archetypal Psychology: A Brief Account* (Dallas: Spring Publications, 1983), p. 46.
26. James Hillman, *Dream and the Underworld, pp.* 40, 42, 97, 105, 137, 145, 174; cf. other important references to "ghosts" in Hillman's works: *Inter Views,* pp. 17, 18, 68, 70, 80, 180, 183; *Archetypal Psychology, pp.* 28, 46; *The Myth of Analysis,* p. 132; "Silver and White Earth, II," *Spring 1980* (Dallas), 39.
27. James Hillman, *Archetypal Psychology,* chs. 2-5.
28. Actually, neither Lacan nor Hillman wrote this sentence. It is a report by Schneiderman of Lacan's perspective, but it applies equally to James Hillman, for which references see n. 26, above. Schneiderman, *Jacques Lacan,* p. 165.
29. Jung, *CW,* 11.277; cf. 18.1632, 1640, 1650, 1668.
30. Tillich, *Systematic Theology,* vol. 3, p. 22.
31. Ibid., p. 23.
32. Ibid., passim.
33. The same point about the words "ghost" and "spirit" is made by Martin Heidegger in a completely different context: namely, when this philosopher is interpreting the poetry of Georg Trakl with an eye to a philosophy of poetic language and to a poetic philosophy of language. "'Ghostly' means," Heidegger writes, "what is by way of the spirit, stems from it and follows its nature. 'Ghostly' means spiritual, but not in the narrow sense that ties the word to 'spirituality,' the priestly orders or their church. ... Trakl sees spirit in terms of that being which is indicated in the original meaning of the word 'ghost'—a being terrified, beside itself, *ek-static.* Spirit or ghost understood in this way has its being in the possibility of *both* gentleness *and* destructiveness" *(On the Way to Language,* pp. 178-79).

15. OUR DARK ALPHABET: GHOSTS OF MODERN LITERATURE

1. Charles Péguy, "Clio," *Péguy and Les Cahiers de la Quinzaine* (London: Longman, Green, and Co., n.d.), cited in Stanley R. Hopper, ed., *Spiritual Problems in Contemporary Literature* (New York: Harper & Row, Publishers, 1955), p. 171.

NOTES

2. Laura Hofrichter, *Heinrich Heine,* tr. Barker Fairley (Oxford: Clarendon Press, 1963), pp. 90-91.
3. Harold Pinter, *Old Times, Plays 4* (New York: Grove Press, 1976), pp. 30-31.
4. Harold Pinter, *No Man's Land,* in ibid., p. 137; cf. David L. Miller, *Three Faces of God* (Philadelphia: Fortress Press, 1986), p. 123 and part 3, generally.
5. Pinter, *No Man's Land,* p. 137.
6. Pinter, *The Dwarfs, Plays 2* (New York: Grove Press, 1977), p. 100.
7. Novalis, *Hymns to the Night,* tr. D. Higgins (New Paltz, N.Y.: McPherson and Co., 1984, pp. 39, 17. Translation © 1978, 1984, 1988 by Richard C. Higgins. Reprinted by permission of McPherson & Co., P. O. Box 1126, Kingston, New York 12401.
8. Ibid., p. 17. Some editions of this poem give the term as *Nachbegeisterung,* "after-inspiration," but the original Athenaum version has *Nachtbegeisterung* (see ibid., p. 17n).
9. Cited in Hofrichter, *Heinrich Heine,* p. 31 (I have modified the translation). See the last poem in Heine's *Traumbilder,* whose title is Das Erwachen.
10. Cited in Ibid., p. 35 (translation altered).
11. See ibid., p. 41.
12. From "Das Erwachen," the last poem of Heine's *Traumbilder.*
13. From "Psalm," cited in Francis M. Sharp, *The Poet's Madness: A Reading of Georg Trakl* (Ithaca, N.Y.: Cornell University Press, 1981).
14. See ibid., pp. 101ff.
15. Allen Hoey, tr., *Transfigured Autumn: Selections from the German of Georg Trakl* (Syracuse, N.Y.: Tamarack Editions, 1984), unnumbered.
16. Ibid.
17. Cited in Martin Heidegger, "Language in the Poem: A Discussion of Georg Trakl's Poetic Work," *On the Way to Language,* p. 169.
18. Cited in ibid., pp. 169, 164.
19. Ibid., p. 179.
20. Ibid., pp. 179, 185. Cf. Heidegger's earlier "ghostly" allusion: "Dasein possesses what is past as a property which is still present at hand ...: Dasein 'is' its past. ... Its own past ... is not something which follows along after Dasein, but something which already goes ahead of it" *(Being and Time,* tr. M. Macquarrie and

E. Robinson [London: SCM Press, Ltd., 1962], p. 41).

21. Cited in Heidegger, *On the Way to Language,* p. 188.
22. Explanation by Christopher Maurer, in Federico García Lorca, *Deep Song and Other Prose,* tr. C. Maurer (New York: New Directions, 1980), p. viii.
23. Lorca, "Play and Theory of the Duende," ibid., pp. 42-43.
24. Ibid., p. 43.
25. Ibid., p. 44.
26. Ibid.
27. Ibid.
28. See Rupert Allen, *The Symbolic World of Federico Garcia Lorca* (Albuquerque: University of New Mexico Press, 1972), p. viii; cf. pp. 25, 27, 166.
29. Lorca, "Play and Theory," pp. 49-50.
30. Ibid., p. 46.
31. Conrad Aiken, "Preludes for Memnon," *Collected Poems* (New York: Oxford University Press, 1970), pp. 522-23.
32. Aiken, "Hallowe'en," in ibid., p. 894.
33. Aiken, "Preludes for Memnon," in ibid., p. 503.
34. Aiken, "Time in the Rock," in ibid., p. 730.
35. See Lillian Feder, *Ancient Myth in Modern Poetry* (Princeton: Princeton University Press, 1971), p. 139.
36. W. H. Auden, "Family Ghosts," *W. H. Auden: Collected Poetry,* ed. Edward Mendelson (New York: Random House, 1976), p. 47.
37. Auden, "The Question," ibid., pp. 141-42.
38. Auden, "This Loved One," ibid., p. 44.
39. Auden, "This Lunar Beauty," ibid., p. 57.
40. Wallace Stevens, 'The Comedian as the Letter C," *Collected Poems,* p. 27.
41. Stevens, "Ghosts as Cocoons," in ibid., p. 119.
42. Stevens, "Examination of the Hero in a Time of War," in ibid., p. 279.
43. Stevens, "Idea of Order at Key West," ibid., p. 128.
44. Ibid.
45. Ibid., p. 129.
46. Ibid.
47. Ibid., p. 130.
48. Stevens, "Adagia," *Opus Posthumous,* p. 173.
49. Stevens, "Idea of Order," *Collected Poems,* p. 130. Cf. Thomas F. Lombardi, "Wallace Stevens and the Haunts of Unimportant Ghosts," *The Wallace Stevens Journal,* 7, nos. 1-2 (spring 1983): 46-53.

50. Robert Penn Warren, "Natural History," *Selected Poems: 1923—1975* (New York: Random House, 1976), p. 22.
51. Delmore Schwartz, *Selected Poems: 1938—1958 (Summer Knowledge)* (New York: New Directions, 1967), p. 40. Copyright © 1959 by Delmore Schwartz. Reprinted by permission of New Directions Pub. Corp.
52. Hayden Carruth, *The Mythology of Dark and Light* (Syracuse, N.Y.: Tamarack Editions, 1982), unnumbered. Copyright © 1982 Hayden Carruth. Reprinted by permission of the author.
53. George Oppen, *Primitive* (Santa Barbara: Black Sparrow Press, 1978), pp. 30-31. Copyright © 1978 by George Oppen.
54. Charles Olson, "As the Dead Prey Upon Us" *Archaeologist of Morning* (London: Cape Goliard Press, 1970), unnumbered. Reprinted with permission of the estate of Charles Olson.
55. William Pitt Root, *Striking the Dark Air for Music* (New York: Atheneum, 1973), p. 21. Excerpted from "I Lie," reprinted with permission of Atheneum Publishers, an imprint of Macmillan Publishing Co., from *Striking the Dark Air for Music* by William Pitt Root. Copyright © 1973 by William Pitt Root.
56. Jack Spicer, *The Collected Books,* ed. Robin Blaser (Los Angeles: Black Sparrow Press, 1975), p. 318.
57. Ibid., p. 281.
58. Ibid., p. 64.
59. Ibid., p. 136.
60. Ibid., p. 179.
61. Ibid., pp. 182-83.
62. Ibid., p. 208.
63. Alice Walker, "Be Nobody's Darling," *Revolutionary Petunias* (New York: Harcourt Brace Jovanovich, 1973), p. 32.
64. Alfred Bendixen, *Haunted Women* (New York: Ungar Publishing Co., 1985), pp. 1-3. I am grateful to Susan Thistlethwaite for bringing this valuable book to my attention. See also Margaret Atwood, *Cat's Eye* (Garden City, N.Y.: Doubleday and Co., 1989), p. 407.
65. Cited in Hofrichter, *Heinrich Heine,* p. 92.
66. Shoshana Felman, "Turning the Screw of Interpretation," in S. Felman, ed., *Literature and Psychoanalysis: The Question of Reading, Otherwise* (Baltimore: Johns Hopkins University Press, 1982), pp. 94ff.
67. Ibid., pp. 149, 154.
68. Ibid., p. 152.

69. Ibid., p. 166.
70. Jacques Derrida, "Living On: Border Lines," in Bloom, et al., *Deconstruction and Criticism,* p. 86.
71. Ibid., p. 87 and passim.
72. Maurice Blanchot, *The Space of Literature,* tr. Ann Smock (Lincoln: University of Nebraska Press, 1982), p. 171.
73. Ibid., p. 178.
74. Harold Bloom, *The Breaking of the Vessels* (Chicago: University of Chicago Press, 1982), p. 67.
75. J. Hillis Miller, "The Critic as Host," p. 221.
76. Geoffrey Hartman, "Words, Wish, Worth: Wordsworth," in Bloom, et al., *Deconstruction and Criticism,* p. 193.
77. Roland Barthes, *Camera Lucida,* tr. Richard Howard (New York: Hill and Wang, 1981), p. 31.
78. Ibid., pp. 32-33.
79. Heidegger, *On the Way to Language,* p. 191.
80. J. Hillis Miller, *Fiction and Repetition* (Cambridge: Harvard University Press, 1980), p. 189.
81. Ibid., p. 199.
82. Ibid., p. 202.
83. "Old Furniture," quoted in J. Hillis Miller, *The Linguistic Moment* (Princeton: Princeton University Press, 1985), p. 285; see also pp. 287, 299.
84. See ibid., p. 303.
85. Michel de Certeau, *Heterologies,* tr. B. Massumi (Minneapolis: University of Minnesota Press, 1986), p. 8.
86. Ibid., pp. 3, 8 (the last phrase is a quotation by de Certeau of Barthes quoting Michelet; see ibid., p. 237 n. 11.
87. Ibid., p. 21.
88. Ibid., p. 36.
89. Ibid., p. 58.
90. Ibid., p. 30.
91. Michel de Certeau, "What We Do When We Believe," in Marshall Blonsky, ed., *On Signs* (Baltimore: Johns Hopkins University Press, 1985), p. 197.
92. Umberto Eco, *The Name of the Rose,* tr. William Weaver (New York: Harcourt Brace Jovanovich, 1983), p. 491.

16. CONCLUSION: WIMSEY OR WHIMSY?

1. Emil Brunner, *The Misunderstanding of the Church,* tr. H. Knight (Philadelphia: Westminster Press, 1953), pp. 48-49; see also Heinz Westman, *The Structure of Biblical Myths* (Dallas: Spring Publications, 1983), p. 194.
2. Dorothy L. Sayers, *Unnatural Death* (New York: Avon Books, 1964), p. vi, the whole of which reads: *"Arms:* 3 mice courant, argent; crest, a domestic cat crouched as to spring, proper; motto: As my whimsey takes me."
3. William V. Spanos, "The Detective and the Boundary: Some Notes on the Postmodern Literary Imagination," *Boundary 2,* 1, no. 1 (fall 1972): 150, 154, 156, 158 passim; cf. David L. Miller, *Three Faces of God,* pp. 76-77.
4. Robert Penn Warren, "Natural History," p. 24.
5. See Frank MacShane, "The Fantasy World of Italo Calvino," *New York Times Magazine* (July 10, 1983), p. 49.
6. Gabriel Marcel, *The Mystery of Being, I: Reflection and Mystery* (Chicago: Gateway, 1960), pp. 260, 257.
7. Ibid.
8. Matt. 12:31-32 KJV; cf. Mark 3:28-29 and Luke 12:10 KJV.
9. Lafcadio Hern, *Japan, an Interpretation,* cited in Paul Elmer More, *Shelburne Essays,* 2nd series (New York: Houghton Mifflin Co., 1905), vol. 2, p. 47.
10. Hopper, *Why Persimmons,* p. 23.

Index of Personal Names
(Historical and Mythological)

INDEX OF PERSONAL NAMES

INDEX OF PERSONAL NAMES

INDEX OF PERSONAL NAMES

Z